The Art of the Impossible

The
Art of the
Impossible

Politics as Morality in Practice

SPEECHES AND WRITINGS, 1990–1996

by VÁCLAV HAVEL

Translated from the Czech
by Paul Wilson and others

FROMM INTERNATIONAL
NEW YORK

First Fromm International paperback, 1998

Copyright © 1994, 1997 by Václav Havel and Paul Wilson

All rights reserved under International and Pan-American Copyright
Conventions. Published in the United States by Fromm International
Publishing Corporation, New York.
Reprinted by arrangement with Alfred A. Knopf, Inc.

Many of the selections in this work were first published in the Czech Republic
as part of *Toward a Civil Society* by Lidové Noviny Publishing House, Ltd.,
Prague, in 1994.

Portions of this work were originally published in somewhat different form in
Foreign Affairs, Harper's, Harvard Magazine, The New York Review of Books,
and *The Spectator.*

Library of Congress Cataloging-in-Publication Data

Havel, Václav.
[Selections. English. 1998]
The art of the impossible : politics as morality in practice :
speeches and writings, 1990-1996 / by Václav Havel; translated from the Czech
by Paul Wilson and others. — 1st Fromm International pbk.
p. cm.
Collection of Havel's political speeches originally published in
Toward a civil society, 1994 and in various magazines.
Includes bibliographical references (p.   ) and index.
ISBN 0-88064-195-9
1. Czech Republic—Politics and government—Moral and ethical
aspects. 2. Political ethics. 3. Citizenship—Moral and ethical aspects.
4. Post-communism. 5. Truth. 6. Responsibility. 7. Civilization,
Modern—1950- —Moral and ethical aspects.
I. Title.
DB2238.H38213   1998   98-14903
943.7105'092—dc21   CIP

10 9 8 7 6 5 4 3 2

Manufactured in the United States of America

Contents

Contents / vi

Foreword

We must not be afraid of dreaming the seemingly impossible
if we want the seemingly impossible to become a reality.

—VÁCLAV HAVEL

Most of the writings in this book have been selected from a privately published collection put together by the author. This collection contains English versions of thirty-five of the hundreds of speeches and articles he has written and delivered during his three years as president of Czechoslovakia and, since 1993, his four years as president of the Czech Republic. It represents a completed chapter of his thinking about, as he says, "the fundamental questions of our civilization, questions I have tried to answer . . . more as an inhabitant of this planet than as a representative of my country."

Havel's book is in front of me now on my desk. It is a handbound volume of 256 single-sided pages printed on a laser printer in Helvetica 10-point type and bound in white handmade paper with the author's last name embossed on the front cover. The book comes encased in its own cardboard sleeve. It is both elegant and simple, and is clearly intended as a ceremonial gift for visiting dignitaries and friends. But it raises a question. Why would the president of a country with a thriving publishing industry choose to manufacture a homemade book of his own speeches?

The answer lies in the object itself: more than a conventional book, it most resembles—in its heft, its feel, in the atmosphere it radiates—those typewritten, handmade samizdat books published by dissidents in the not-so-distant past, when freedom of the press was only a dream and "living in truth" seemed the only way forward. The book is the physical symbol of a continuity with his own past that Havel has been at pains to maintain in everything he has done.

Havel's book begins with his speech to the United States Congress in February 1990, and ends with an address to a conference on "The Future of Hope" in Hiroshima in December 1995. In the version you now hold, *The Art of the Impossible,* we have left out a number of speeches that are of a more local, European significance, or that reiterate themes the author developed more fully in other writing, and we have added some that develop specific aspects of his political thought. Among these are two New Year's addresses to the nation, one of which now begins this book, and a recent talk delivered to the Academy of Performing Arts in Prague in October 1996, which ends it. We have retained Havel's strictly chronological order.

If you run your eye down the contents pages, you will see the itinerary of a remarkable global odyssey. It begins in Prague, but quickly takes the author to Washington, Strasbourg, Jerusalem, and the United Nations in New York. He is called upon to address the Academy of Humanities and Political Sciences in Paris, the National Press Club in Canberra, a conference of intellectuals in Tokyo. He stands before audiences in Athens, the cradle of democracy, and in Dublin, the home of writers who have shaped his own work. He speaks to the graduating class at Harvard, and to academic assemblies in Wrocław, Stanford, and Wellington. He opens a festival in Salzburg, a conference in Oslo, accepts prizes in Copenhagen, Los Angeles, New Delhi, Barcelona, and Philadelphia. He speaks to the world theater community, and to his fellow writers at a PEN International Congress in Prague.

The pages of this book trace another journey, even more remarkable: the inner, personal journey of an artist and intellectual whose ideas germinated under totalitarianism, grew in the post-Stalinist thaw of the 1960s, toughened in the hard years after the Soviet invasion, matured during his four years in prison, and finally bore fruit in the Velvet Revolution of 1989.

The early speeches reflect his sense of bewilderment and wonder at the quickened pace of history that swept the old order out and ushered him and his colleagues into office. They radiate his deep satisfaction that their impossible faith in the triumph of truth and tolerance over hatred and lies is at last vindicated. He begins to redefine his notion of politics as "the art of the impossible, that is, the art of improving ourselves and the world." Sometimes he confesses to feelings of inadequacy and depression as the poetry of revolution gives way to the prose of everyday life. He worries aloud about whether the ideals that had sustained the dissidents in their struggle against the old regime would survive the daily struggle to renew democracy. He reflects on the temptations of high office, the dilemmas of power, the dangers of impatience, the need to recognize individual responsibility for collective destiny. He pleads for an end to habits of mind formed in the Cold War, for a reconciliation with old enemies, for the inclusion in Europe of the new democracies that once lay on the other side of an impenetrable wall. And beneath it all a theme emerges with increasing insistence: the need for a new "postmodern" politics, and for a new kind of politician. "A politician," he tells an august gathering of statesmen and economists in Davos, "must become a person again, someone who trusts not only a scientific representation and analysis of the world, but also the world itself. He must not only believe in sociological statistics, but in real people. He must not only trust an objective interpretation of reality, but also its soul; not only an adopted ideology, but also his own thoughts; not only the summary reports he receives each morning, but also his own instincts."

As the horizon of his concerns widens, Havel's speeches begin to probe the scientific, religious, and philosophical roots that different cultures and civilizations have in common. He calls for a new world order based on the recognition of these "common minimums," of values that transcend the immediate, pragmatic needs of politics, of the metaphysical dimension—which he calls Being—that underpins all human experience. Yet the past is never far from his thoughts. In Hiroshima, he reaches back to his own dark days in prison to ask again the question that faced him then: does it make sense to go on living in the face of inevitable death? The answer he gives is both profoundly personal and profoundly political.

In the final speech in this volume, Havel draws together two main strands of his life: his experience as a dramatist and his experience as a politician. The dramatic aspects of his speeches may not always be obvious on the page, but they are there nonetheless. It is not just that Havel chooses his themes with a dramatic flair and a daring sense of occasion—talking about Godot and political patience to the French, about Gandhi and nonviolence to the Indians, about Kafka and self-doubt to the Israelis, about historical truth to an audience in Salzburg that includes Kurt Waldheim. His speeches also implicitly pose the same questions he once said all drama implicitly poses: Who are we? What is the true nature of this world? And how should we live in it?

Who are we, the Czechs, he asks? Are we complicit in the totalitarian system that enslaved us? Or are we what we have always wanted to believe: a nation of democrats who espouse liberal values, who treasure their connection with Western democracy and the heritage of Greece and Rome, who belong to the West, though forced to live with the East? Can we become what we most desire to be? Can we change the course of our history by changing ourselves?

What is Eastern Europe? Is it the economic and social ruin communism has made of it, forever incapable of rising above its past? Or is it part of the West, severed by history for a time, now poised to become part of the great unity of Europe? Can Eastern

Europe rise above its past defeats and begin to build societies based on respect for the rule of law and human rights, and thus take its place in the pantheon of democracies?

What of Europe itself? Is it a continent in decline, plagued by civil war, the exporter of conflict to the rest of the world, a cauldron of seething rivalries, condemned to be held in check only by fragile alliances and empty promises? Or will it be a new, inclusive multinational entity that can radiate into the world the best qualities of its collective heritage of two or three thousand years?

What is the world? Is it still what it once was, the plaything of vast competing empires on which the sun never sets, a battlefield of ideologies? Or is it a mosaic of civilizations struggling to find ways to live in harmony? Can we create a new way of governing the world that will allow us to move forward, to engage with politics at a deeper level, to engage our whole beings—our consciences, our beliefs, our best intentions—and so save civilization from its own destructive hubris?

And what, finally, is man? Is he a tribal being, the captive of a single identity, driven by superstition, prejudice, ethnic and religious loyalties, hatred, nationalism, fear? Or is he a multifaceted citizen of this new global civilization, capable of creating institutions that are democratic, pluralistic, tolerant, embodying values that everyone can espouse without denying or rejecting the more basic aspects of identity?

In the brief seven years covered by the writings in this book, Havel has been the very active president of two different countries. These writings contain only hints of his tireless attention to the affairs of state, of the meticulous care he has lavished on everything from the design of new uniforms for the Castle guard to the formulation of two new constitutions, of the frustrations he has sometimes felt at the apparent slowness with which his countrymen are learning the arts of democratic governance. But when foreign dignitaries come to visit—often accompanied by their own speechwriters—what astonishes and sometimes intimidates them most of all is not the hectic pace of his life, or his reputation, but the fact that he writes his own speeches. Why does he do it?

I think he does it because—unlike the generations of politicians who have ruled his country in the past—Havel has always insisted on speaking his own mind, in his own way, with his own voice. It is his way of staying in touch with his original calling, with a time when his calling card read simply: "Václav Havel, Writer."

Writing is Havel's way of continuing to live in truth.

A word about the translations: In my experience, the best translations draw on the energy and impulses, and often the techniques, that lie behind the original text. This was certainly the case here. Most of the translations were made—as the originals were no doubt written—under the looming threat of deadlines and during time stolen from other duties. For instance, I completed my translation of Havel's first address to the United States Congress in the Toronto offices of an émigré publishing house run by Josef and Zdena Škvorecký, surrounded by agents of the Royal Canadian Mounted Police and their bomb-sniffing German shepherds who were securing the premises in anticipation of President Havel's imminent visit. I handed the final version to an aide, who then rushed it off to Washington to be printed in time for Havel's speech the next day. The introduction of fax machines and e-mail, as convenient as they are, only exacerbated the frantic pace of work, and often made me nostalgic for the good old days when Havel's letters and texts had to be smuggled out of the country and then, by a roundabout system involving couriers and surface mail, delivered to me and others to be translated at leisure.

Inevitably, some of these translations are the work of several hands. Sometimes my hand was there only to polish a draft made by someone else. Sometimes the hand of an invisible adviser would intervene to feather an edge deemed too sharp or too blunt for diplomatic consumption. Sometimes the English versions of these speeches were later edited for publication, and so may differ slightly from the version actually delivered by Havel or conveyed through an interpreter. Finally, the text of this book was combed once more by myself and editors at Knopf to remove inconsistencies from Havel's voice in English. For any imperfections at any stage in these processes, I accept full blame.

My thanks to the many people who helped: colleagues who filled in for my absences from the alas now-defunct *Idler* magazine, and from the CBC radio programs "The Arts Tonight" and "Morningside"; Daša Obereignerová, who copyedited many of the speeches in this book; Havel's interpreter Alexandra Brabcová, who translated some of the later speeches, and her collaborators, Roger Falcon, Alistair Barclay, and Lise Stone; Havel's assistants, Anna Freimanová and Vladimír Hanzel, for facilitating my communications with the president; Barbara Epstein, who guided many of these speeches into print in *The New York Review of Books*; Ash Green, at Knopf, who started this book on its way, and Jennifer Bernstein, who patiently saw it through to completion; and to Patricia Grant, my assistant and companion, for her support and help. Finally, my deepest thanks to the author for the privilege of being entrusted with his voice.

Paul Wilson
Toronto, January 1997

Author's Preface

Writing speeches is my joy and my misfortune. It's a joy because it is really one of the more creative aspects of being president, unlike all those matters of protocol and other official duties, and also because it connects me with my past as a writer and with my literary nature. At the same time, it's my misfortune because I cannot write as I once used to, when I would become inspired by an idea, sit down to write, and keep on writing for as long as I wanted, as long as I got pleasure from it. Now, I must write in strictly limited blocks of time and to strict deadlines, regardless of whether I am inspired or not. So the joy of writing becomes something like a religious observance, and yet I can't imagine carrying out my duties without it. I would certainly not want to be the kind of president who merely holds office. It seems to me, given my character and my nature—but also given the traditions of the presidency in our country—that more is expected of me. If the president were called upon to be no more than a bureaucrat, I would have to resign.

I would like to thank Paul Wilson, my translator of many years, for his sensitive work in preparing this book. I hope that people in the English-speaking world will read it with interest, particularly the passages I devote to issues facing the world today, to our present civilization as a whole.

Prague,
February 1997

The Art of the Impossible

New Year's Address to the Nation

For forty years on this day you heard, from my predecessors, variations on the same theme: how our country flourished, how many million tons of steel we produced, how happy we all were, how we trusted our government, and what bright perspectives were unfolding before us.

I assume you did not propose me for this office so that I, too, would lie to you.

Our country is not flourishing. The enormous creative and spiritual potential of our nations is not being used sensibly. Entire branches of industry are producing goods that are of no interest to anyone, while we are lacking the things we need. A state that calls itself a workers' state humiliates and exploits workers. Our obsolete economy squanders what little energy we have available. A country once proud of its educational standards now spends so little on education that it ranks seventy-second in the world. We have contaminated the soil, rivers, and forests bequeathed to us by our ancestors, and today we have the most polluted environment in Europe. Adults in our country die earlier than in most other European countries.

Allow me a little personal observation: When I flew to Bratislava recently, I found time during various discussions to look out of the plane window. I saw the industrial complex of the Slovnaft chemical factory and the giant Petržalka housing estate right behind it. The view was enough to make me realize that for decades our statesmen and political leaders did not look or did not want to look out of the windows of their airplanes. No available statistics could have enabled me to understand faster and better the situation into which we had gotten ourselves.

But all this is still not the main problem. The worst thing is that we live in a contaminated moral environment. We fell morally ill because we got used to saying something different from what we thought. We learned not to believe in anything, to ignore each other, to care only for ourselves. Concepts such as love, friendship, compassion, humility, and forgiveness lost their depth and dimensions, and for many of us they came to represent only psychological pecularities, or to resemble long-lost greetings from ancient times, a little ridiculous in the era of computers and spaceships. Only a few of us were able to cry aloud that the powers that be ought not to be all-powerful, and that the special farms which produce ecologically pure and top-quality food just for them should at least send their produce to schools, children's homes, and hospitals if our agriculture is unable to offer them to everyone. The previous regime—armed with its arrogant and intolerant ideology—reduced man to a force of production and nature to a tool of production. In this it attacked both their very essence, and their mutual relationship. It reduced gifted and autonomous people to nuts and bolts of some monstrously huge, noisy, and stinking machine, whose real meaning is not clear to anyone. It could do no more than slowly but inexorably wear itself out, along with its nuts and bolts.

When I talk about contaminated moral atmosphere, I am not talking just about the gentlemen who eat organic vegetables and do not look out of the plane windows. I am talking about all of us. We had all become used to the totalitarian system and accepted it as an unalterable fact of life, and thus we helped to perpetuate it. In other words, we are all—though naturally to differing extents—responsible for the operation of totalitarian machinery. None of us is just its victim: we are all also its cocreators.

Why do I say this? It would be quite unreasonable to understand the sad legacy of the last forty years as something alien, something bequeathed to us by some distant relative. On the contrary, we must accept this legacy as a sin we committed against ourselves. If we accept it as such, we will understand that it is up to us all, and up to us alone, to do something about it. We cannot blame the previous rulers for everything, not only because it would be untrue but also because it could blunt the duty each of us faces today, that is, the obligation to act independently, freely, reasonably, and quickly. Let us make no mistake: the best government in the world, the best parliament and the best president in the world cannot achieve much on their own. And it would also be wrong to expect a general remedy to come from them alone. Freedom and democracy require participation and therefore responsible action from us all.

If we realize this, then all the horrors the new Czechoslovak democracy has inherited will cease to appear so terrible. If we realize this, hope will return to our hearts.

In the effort to rectify matters of common concern, we have some strengths to draw on. The recent period—in particular the last six weeks of our peaceful revolution—has shown the enormous human, moral, and spiritual potential and civic culture that slumbered in our society under the enforced mask of apathy. Whenever someone categorically claimed that we were this or that, I always objected that society is a very mysterious creature and that it is not wise to trust only the face it presents to you. I am happy that I was not mistaken. Everywhere in the world people wonder where those meek, humiliated, skeptical, and seemingly cynical citizens of Czechoslovakia found the marvelous strength to shake the totalitarian yoke from their shoulders in several weeks, and in a decent and peaceful way. And let us ask: where did the young people who never knew another system find their desire for truth, their love of free thought, their political ideas, their civic courage and civic prudence? How did their parents—the very generation that had been considered as lost—come to join them? How is it possible that so many people immediately knew what to do, without advice or instruction?

I think that there are two main reasons for this hopeful face of our present situation: first of all, people are never just a product of the external world, but are also always able to relate themselves to something superior, however systematically the external world tries to kill that ability in them; second, the humanistic and democratic traditions, about which there had been so much idle talk, did indeed slumber in the unconsciousness of our nations and ethnic minorities, and were inconspicuously passed from one generation to another so that each of us could discover them at the right time and transform them into deeds.

And yet we have to pay for our present freedom. Many citizens perished in jails in the fifties, many were executed, thousands of human lives were destroyed, hundreds of thousands of talented people were forced to leave the country. Those who defended the honor of our nations in the Second World War, those who rebelled against totalitarian rule, and those who simply managed to remain true to themselves and think freely, were all persecuted. We should not forget any of those who paid for our present freedom in one way or another. Independent courts should impartially consider the possible guilt of those who were responsible for the persecutions, so that the truth about our recent past may be fully revealed.

We must also bear in mind that other nations have paid even more dearly than we have for their present freedom and that indirectly they have also paid for ours. The rivers of blood that flowed in Hungary, Poland, Germany, and most recently in such a horrific manner in Romania, as well as the sea of blood shed by the nations of the Soviet Union, must not be forgotten. First of all because every instance of human suffering concerns every other human being; but more than this: they must also not be forgotten because it is those great sacrifices that form the tragic background of today's freedom, and of the gradual emancipation of the nations of the Soviet bloc. They also form the background of our own newfound freedom: without the changes in the Soviet Union, Poland, Hungary, and the German Democratic Republic, what has happened in our country could scarcely have happened. In any event, it would not have followed such a peaceful course.

The fact that we enjoyed optimal international conditions does not mean that anyone else has directly helped us during the recent weeks. In fact, after hundreds of years, both our nations have raised their heads high on their own, without relying on the help of stronger nations or powers. This, it seems to me, is the great moral asset of the present moment. This moment contains the hope that in the future we will no longer suffer from the complex of those who must always express their gratitude to someone else. It is now entirely up to us whether this hope will be realized, and whether our civic, national, and political self-confidence will be awakened in a historically new way.

Self-confidence is not arrogance. Quite the contrary: only a person or a nation that is self-confident in the best sense of the word is capable of listening to others, accepting them as equals, forgiving its enemies, and regretting its own guilt. Let us try to introduce this kind of self-confidence into the life of our community and, as nations, into our behavior on the international stage. Only thus can we restore our self-respect and our respect for one another as well as gain the respect of other nations.

Our state must never again be an appendage or a poor relation of anyone else. It is true we must accept and learn many things from others, but we must do this, again, as their equal partner who also has something to offer.

Our first president wrote: "Jesus, not Caesar." In this he followed our philosophers Chelčický and Comenius. I dare say that we may even have an opportunity to spread this idea further and introduce a new element into European and global politics. Our country, if that is what we want, can now permanently radiate love, understanding, the power of the intellect and ideas. This is precisely what we can offer as our specific contribution to international politics.

Masaryk based his politics on morality. Let us try, in a new time and in a new way, to restore this concept of politics. Let us teach ourselves and others that politics should be an expression of a desire to contribute to the happiness of the community rather than of a need to cheat or rape the community. Let us teach ourselves and others that politics can be not only the art of the possible, especially if "the possible" includes the art of speculation, calculation, intrigue, secret deals, and pragmatic maneuvering, but that it can also be the art of the impossible, namely, the art of improving ourselves and the world.

We are a small country, yet at one time we were the spiritual crossroads of Europe. Is there any reason why we could not become so again? Would not it be another asset with which to recompense others for the help we are going to need?

Our home-grown mafia, those who do not look out of airplane windows and who eat specially fed pigs, may still be around and at times may muddy the waters, but they are no longer our main enemy. Even less so is our main enemy, the international mafia. Our main enemy today is our own worst nature: our indifference to the common good; vanity; personal ambition; selfishness; and rivalry. The main struggle will have to be fought on this field.

We have free elections ahead of us. Let us not allow this election campaign to dirty the, so far, clean face of our gentle revolution. Let us not allow the sympathies of the world, so quickly won, to be lost through our becoming entangled in the jungle of skirmishes for power. Let us not allow the desire to serve oneself to blossom once again under the fair mask of the desire to serve the common good. It is not really important now which party, club, or group will prevail in the elections. The important thing is that the winners be the best among us, in the moral, civic, political, and professional sense, regardless of their political affiliations. The future policies and prestige of our state will depend on who we nominate and later elect to serve in our representative bodies.

In conclusion, I would like to say that I want to be a president who will speak less and work more. To be a president who will not only look out of the windows of his airplane but who, first and foremost, will always be present among his fellow citizens and listen to them well.

You may ask what kind of a republic I dream of. Let me reply: I dream of a republic independent, free, and democratic, of a republic economically prosperous and yet socially just; in short, of a humane republic which serves the individual and which therefore holds the hope that the individual will serve it in turn. Of a republic of well-rounded people, because without such it is impossible to solve any of our problems, human, economic, ecological, social, or political.

The most distinguished of my predecessors opened his first speech with a quotation from the great Czech educator Comenius. Allow me to close my first speech with my own paraphrase of the same statement:

People, your government has returned to you!

A Joint Session
of the U.S. Congress

My advisers have advised me, on this important occasion, to speak in Czech. I don't know why. Perhaps they wanted you to enjoy the sound of my mother tongue.

The last time I was arrested, on October 27 of last year, I didn't know whether I was in for two days or two years. Exactly one month later, when the rock musician Michael Kocáb told me that I would probably be proposed as a presidential candidate, I thought it was one of his usual jokes.

On the 10th of December, 1989, when my actor friend Jiří Bartoška, in the name of the Civic Forum, nominated me as a candidate for the office of the president of the republic, I thought it was out of the question that the Parliament we had inherited from the previous regime would elect me.

Twelve days later, when I was unanimously elected president of my country, I had no idea that in two months I would be speaking in front of this famous and powerful assembly, or that I would be heard by millions of people who have never heard of me, or that politicians and political scientists would study every word I say.

When I was arrested on October 27, I was living in a country ruled by the most conservative communist government in Europe, and our society slumbered beneath the pall of a totalitarian system. Today, less than four months later, I am speaking to you as the representative of a country that has complete freedom of speech, that is preparing for free elections, and that seeks to establish a prosperous market economy and its own foreign policy.

It is all very extraordinary.

But I have not come here to speak about myself or my feelings, or merely to talk about my own country. I have used this small example of something I know well to illustrate something general and important.

We are living in extraordinary times. The human face of the world is changing so rapidly that none of the familiar political indicators are adequate.

We playwrights, who have to cram a lifetime or an entire historical era into a two-hour play, can scarcely understand this rapidity ourselves. And if it gives us trouble, think of the trouble it must give to political scientists, who spend their whole lives studying the realm of the probable and have even less experience with the realm of the improbable than playwrights do.

Let me try to explain why I think the velocity of the changes in my country, in Central and Eastern Europe, and of course in the Soviet Union itself, has had such an impact on the world today, and why it concerns the fate of us all, including Americans. I would like to look at this, first from the political point of view and then from a point of view we might call philosophical.

Twice in this century, the world has been threatened by a catastrophe. Twice this catastrophe was born in Europe, and twice Americans, along with others, were called upon to save Europe, the whole world, and yourselves. The first rescue provided significant help to Czechs and Slovaks.

Thanks to the great support of your President Wilson, our first president, Tomáš Garrigue Masaryk, was able to create a modern independent state. He founded it, as you know, on the same principles on which the United States of America had been founded, as Masaryk's manuscripts held by the Library of Congress testify.

At the same time, the United States made enormous strides. It became the most powerful nation on earth, and it understood the responsibility that flowed from this. Proof lies in the hundreds of thousands of young Americans who gave their lives for the liberation of Europe, and in the graves of American airmen and soldiers on Czechoslovak soil.

But something else was happening as well. The Soviet Union appeared, grew, and transformed the enormous sacrifices of its people suffering under totalitarian rule into a strength that, after the Second World War, made it the second most powerful nation in the world. It was a country that rightly gave people nightmares, because no one knew what would cause the mood of its rulers to worsen, or what country it would decide to conquer next and drag into its "sphere of influence," as the concept is called in political language.

All of this taught us to see the world in bipolar terms, as two enormous forces: one a defender of freedom, the other a source of nightmares. Europe became the point of friction between these two forces, and thus it was turned into a single enormous arsenal divided into two parts. In this process, one half of the arsenal became part of that nightmarish power, while the other—the free part—bordering on the ocean and having no wish to be driven into it, was compelled, together with you, to build a complicated security system, to which we Europeans probably owe the fact that we still exist.

So you may have contributed to the salvation of Europe, of the world, and thus of yourselves for a third time: you have helped us to survive until today—without a hot war this time, merely a cold one.

And now the totalitarian system in the Soviet Union and most of its satellites is breaking down, and our nations are seeking a way forward, to democracy and independence. The first act in this remarkable drama began when Mr. Gorbachev and those around him, faced with the sad reality in their country, initiated the policy of "perestroika." Apparently they had no idea what they were setting in motion, or how rapidly events would unfold. We knew a great deal about the enormous number of growing problems that slumbered beneath the benign, unchanging mask of socialism. But I don't think any of us knew how little it would take before these problems would manifest themselves in all their enormity, and before the longings of these nations would emerge in all their strength. The mask fell away so rapidly that, in the rush of work, we have had literally no time even to be astonished.

What does all this mean for the world in the long run? Obviously a number of things. It is, I am firmly convinced, a historically irreversible process, and as a result Europe will begin again to seek its own identity without the need to serve any longer as a divided armory. Perhaps this will create the hope that sooner or later your young men will no longer have to stand on guard for freedom in Europe or come to our rescue, because Europe will at last be able to stand guard for itself.

But the most important thing, it seems to me, is that these revolutionary changes will enable us to escape from the antiquated straitjacket of this bipolar view of the world, and to enter at last into an era of multipolarity. That is, into an era in which all of us, large and small, former slaves and former masters, will be able to create what your great President Lincoln called "the family of man." Can you imagine what a relief this would be to the part of the globe that for some reason is called the Third World, even though it is the largest?

I don't think it's appropriate simply to generalize, so let me be specific:

1) As you certainly know, most of the major wars and other European conflagrations over the centuries have traditionally begun and ended on the territory of modern Czechoslovakia, or else they were somehow related to that area, the Second World War being the most recent example. This is understandable: whether we like it or not, we are located in the very heart of Europe, with no view of the sea, and no real navy. I mention this because political stability in our country has traditionally been important for the whole of Europe. This is still true today. Our government of national understanding, our present Federal Assembly, the other bodies of the state, and I myself will person-

ally guarantee this stability until we hold free elections, planned for June.

We understand the terribly complex reasons, domestic political reasons above all, why the Soviet Union cannot withdraw its troops from our territory as quickly as they arrived in 1968. We understand that the arsenals built there over the past twenty years cannot be dismantled and removed overnight. Nevertheless, in our bilateral negotiations with the Soviet Union, we would like to have as many Soviet units as possible moved out of our country before the elections, in the interests of political stability. The more successful our negotiations, the more those who are elected will be able to guarantee political stability in our country even after the elections.

2) I often hear the question: how can the United States of America help us today? My reply is as paradoxical as the whole of my life has been: you can help us most of all if you help the Soviet Union on its irreversible, but immensely complicated, road to democracy. It is far more complicated than the road open to its former satellites in Europe. You yourselves probably know best how to support, as rapidly as possible, the nonviolent evolution of this enormous, multinational body politic toward democracy and autonomy for all of its peoples, and thus it is not fitting that I offer you any advice. I can only say that, the sooner, the more quickly, and the more peacefully the Soviet Union begins to move along the road toward genuine political pluralism, toward respect for the rights of nations to their own integrity and to a working—that is, a market-based—economy, the better it will be, not just for Czechs and Slovaks, but for the whole world. And the sooner you yourselves are able to reduce the burden of the military budget borne by the American people. To put it metaphorically, the millions you give to the East today will soon return to you in the form of billions in savings.

3) It is not true that the Czech writer Václav Havel wishes to dissolve the Warsaw Pact tomorrow and then NATO the day after that, as some eager journalists have written. Václav Havel

merely thinks what he has already said here, that American soldiers shouldn't have to be separated from their mothers for another hundred years simply because Europe is incapable of guaranteeing world peace, which it ought to be able to do, to make at least some amends for having given the world two major wars.

Sooner or later Europe must recover and come into its own, and decide for itself how many of those soldiers it needs, so that its own security, and all the wider implications of that security, may radiate peace into the whole world. Václav Havel cannot make decisions about things it is not proper for him to decide. He is merely putting in a good word for genuine peace, and for achieving it quickly.

4) Czechoslovakia thinks that the planned summit of countries participating in the Helsinki process should take place soon, and that in addition to what they wish to accomplish, the so-called Helsinki II Conference should be held earlier than 1992, as originally planned. Above all, we feel it could be something far more important than has so far seemed possible. We think Helsinki II should become the equivalent of a European peace conference, which has not yet been held; one that would finally bring the Second World War and all its unhappy consequences to a formal conclusion. Such a conference would officially bring a future united democratic Germany into a new pan-European structure which could determine its own security system. This would naturally require some participation by that part of the globe we might label the "Helsinki" part, stretching westward from Vladivostok all the way to Alaska. The borders of the European states, which by the way should become gradually less important, should finally be legally guaranteed by a common, regular treaty. It should be more than obvious that the basis for such a treaty would have to be general respect for human rights, genuine political pluralism, and genuinely free elections.

5) Naturally, we welcome the initiative of President Bush—essentially accepted by Mr. Gorbachev as well—to radically reduce the number of American and Soviet troops in Europe. It is

a magnificent shot in the arm for the Vienna disarmament talks and creates favorable conditions not only for our own efforts to achieve the quickest possible departure of Soviet troops from Czechoslovakia, but also, indirectly, for our own intention to make considerable cutbacks to the Czechoslovak army, which is disproportionately large in relation to our population. If Czechoslovakia were forced to defend itself against anyone, which we hope will not happen, it should be capable of doing so with a considerably smaller army, because for the first time in not just decades but even centuries its defense would be supported by the common and indivisible will of both of its nations and its leadership. Our freedom, our independence, and our newborn democracy have been purchased at great cost, and we will not surrender them. For clarity, I should add that whatever steps we take are not intended to complicate the Vienna disarmament talks but, on the contrary, to facilitate them.

6) Czechoslovakia is returning to Europe. In the general interest and its own interest as well, it wants to coordinate this return—both political and economic—with the other returnees, which means, above all, with its neighbors the Poles and the Hungarians. We are doing what we can to coordinate these returns. And at the same time, we are doing what we can so that Europe will be capable of really accepting us, its wayward children, which means opening itself to us and beginning to transform its structures—which are formally European but *de facto* Western European—in that direction, but in a way that will not be to its detriment but, rather, to its advantage.

7) I have already said this in our Parliament, and I would like to repeat it here, in this Congress, which is architecturally far more attractive: For many years, Czechoslovakia—as someone's meaningless satellite—has refused to face up honestly to its coresponsibility for the world. It has a lot to make up for. If I dwell on this and so many other important things here, it is only because I feel—along with my fellow citizens—a sense of culpability for our former reprehensible passivity and a rather ordinary sense of indebtedness.

8) Last but not least, we are of course delighted that your country is so readily lending its support to our fresh efforts to renew democracy. Both our peoples were deeply moved by the generous offers made a few days ago in Prague at the Charles University, one of the oldest in Europe, by your secretary of state, Mr. James Baker. We are ready to sit down and talk about them.

I have been president for only two months, and I haven't attended any schools for presidents. My only school was life itself. Therefore, I don't wish to burden you any longer with my political thoughts, but instead will move on to an area that is more familiar to me, to what I would call the philosophical aspect of the changes that still concern everyone, although they are taking place in our corner of the world.

As long as people are people, democracy in the full sense of the word will always remain an ideal. One may approach democracy as one would a horizon, and do so in ways that may be better or worse, but it can never be fully attained. In this sense you also are merely approaching democracy. You have thousands of problems of all kinds, as other countries do. But you have one great advantage: you have been approaching democracy continuously for more than two hundred years, and your journey toward that horizon has never been disrupted by a totalitarian system. Czechs and Slovaks, despite humanistic traditions that go back to the first millennium, approached democracy for a mere twenty years, between the two world wars, and now for three and a half months, since the 17th of November of last year.

The advantage you have over us is obvious at once.

The communist type of totalitarian system has left both our nations, Czechs and Slovaks—as it has all the nations of the Soviet Union, and the other countries the Soviet Union subjugated in its time—a legacy of countless dead, an infinite spectrum of human suffering, profound economic decline, and above all enormous human humiliation. It has brought us horrors that, fortunately, you have never known.

At the same time—unintentionally, of course—it has given us something positive: a special capacity to look, from time to time, somewhat further than those who have not undergone this bitter experience. Someone who cannot move and live a normal life because he is pinned under a boulder has more time to think about his hopes than someone who is not trapped in this way.

What I am trying to say is this: we must all learn many things from you, from how to educate our offspring and how to elect our representatives, to how to organize our economic life so that it will lead to prosperity and not poverty. But this doesn't have to be merely assistance from the well-educated, the powerful, and the wealthy to those who have nothing to offer in return.

We, too, can offer something to you: our experience and the knowledge that has come from it.

This is a subject for books, many of which have already been written and many of which have yet to be written. I shall therefore limit myself to a single idea.

The specific experience I'm talking about has given me one great certainty: Consciousness precedes Being, and not the other way around, as Marxists claim.

For this reason, the salvation of this human world lies nowhere else than in the human heart, in the human power to reflect, in human modesty, and in human responsibility.

Without a global revolution in the sphere of human consciousness, nothing will change for the better in the sphere of our Being as humans, and the catastrophe toward which this world is headed, whether it be ecological, social, demographic, or a general breakdown of civilization, will be unavoidable. If we are no longer threatened by world war or by the danger that the absurd mountains of accumulated nuclear weapons might blow up the world, this does not mean that we have won. We are in fact far from definite victory.

We are still a long way from that "family of man"; in fact, we seem to be receding from the ideal rather than drawing closer to it. Interests of all kinds—personal, selfish, state, national, group, and, if you like, company interests—still considerably outweigh genuinely common and global interests. We are still under the sway of the destructive and thoroughly vain belief that man is the pinnacle of creation, and not just a part of it, and that therefore everything is permitted to him. There are still many who say they are concerned not for themselves but for the cause, while they act demonstrably in their own interests and not for the cause at all. We are still destroying the planet that was entrusted to us. We still close our eyes to the growing social, ethnic, and cultural conflicts in the world. From time to time we say that the anonymous megamachinery we have created for ourselves no longer serves us but, rather, has enslaved us, yet we fail to do anything about it.

In other words, we still don't know how to put morality ahead of politics, science, and economics. We are still incapable of understanding that the only genuine core of all our actions—if they are to be moral—is responsibility. Responsibility to something higher than my family, my country, my firm, my success. Responsibility to the order of Being, where all our actions are indelibly recorded and where, and only where, they will be properly judged.

The interpreter or mediator between us and this higher authority is what is traditionally referred to as human conscience.

If I subordinate my political behavior to this imperative, I can't go far wrong. If, on the contrary, I am not guided by this voice, not even ten presidential schools with two thousand of the best political scientists in the world could help me.

This is why I finally decided—after resisting for a long time—to accept the burden of political responsibility.

I'm not the first intellectual, nor will I be the last, to do this. On the contrary, my feeling is that there will be more and more of them all the time. If the hope of the world lies in human consciousness, then it is obvious that intellectuals cannot avoid forever assuming their share of responsibility for the world and hiding their distaste for politics beneath an alleged need for independence.

It is easy to have independence in your program and then

leave others to carry out that program. If everyone thought that way, soon no one would be independent.

I think that Americans should understand this way of thinking. Wasn't it the best minds of your country, people you could call intellectuals, who wrote your famous Declaration of Independence, your Bill of Rights, and your Constitution, and who—above all—took upon themselves the practical responsibility for putting them into practice? The worker from Braník in Prague, whom your president referred to in his State of the Union message this year, is far from being the only person in Czechoslovakia, let alone in the world, to be inspired by those great documents. They inspire us all. They inspire us even though they are over two hundred years old. They inspire us to be citizens.

When Thomas Jefferson wrote that "Governments are instituted among Men, deriving their just powers from the Consent of the Governed," it was a simple and important act of the human spirit.

What gave meaning to that act, however, was the fact that the author backed it up with his life. His statement was not just words, it was deeds as well.

I will end where I began. History has accelerated. I believe that, once again, it will be the human spirit that will notice this acceleration, give it a name, and transform those words into deeds.

The Visit of German President Richard von Weizsäcker

PRAGUE, MARCH 15, 1990

A madman in jackboots crushed our first attempt at a democratic state when, on March 15, 1939, he burst into this castle to announce to the world that violence had triumphed over freedom and human dignity.

A herald of war burst in here. A herald of crudeness. A herald of lies. A herald of pride and evil, lawlessness and cruelty. A mass murderer burst in here. A murderer of nations.

Who let this interloper in? Who allowed him to desecrate these venerable halls?

Above all, it was some of his fellow citizens, who had succumbed to his primitive appeal to the treacherous side of their feelings, to archetypical visions, and to their national and social aspirations.

Next, it was the infinite shortsightedness of the governments of France and England at the time, which thought they would preserve peace by opening the door to that herald of war.

And, finally, it was our own leaders' fear of standing up to a numerically superior force, their fear of risking great misunderstanding and great sacrifice. Their fear was perhaps even tinged with a vague sense of common responsibility for the belittling attitude our former state had taken toward the rights of its national minorities. This undoubtedly influenced the fact that so many Czechoslovak citizens of German origin conspired with that madman against their own state.

His war against the civilized world did not begin until September 2, 1939, but the proclamation of that war actually took place earlier that year, on March 15. And it happened here, in the Prague Castle.

Today, as we stand at the beginning of our second attempt at democracy and recall what happened here fifty-one years ago, we welcome a different guest to this castle.

This guest is a representative of German democracy. A herald of peace. A herald of decency. A herald of truth. A herald of humanity. A bearer of the news that violence may never again prevail over freedom, lies over truth, and evil over human life.

A man who has said that nothing may be forgotten, because memory is the source of belief in redemption.

Fifty-one years ago, an enemy broke in uninvited. Today, a friend is here at our invitation.

That former visit brought the death of our prewar democracy. Today's visit heralds our new democracy.

That former visit marked the beginning of all our recent misfortunes. Today's visit coincides with their end.

The interloper opened the way to subjugation. Today's guest is here to congratulate us on our newly acquired freedom.

I believe this is an important day in several respects.

Above all, it could be the beginning of a new act in the thousand-year-old Czech-German drama, in which the themes of tension, discord, and struggle have been constantly and indivisibly knit together with the themes of fertile coexistence and deep mutual influence. In this new act, the latter group of themes could finally—after the bitter experience of the recent past—predominate over the former.

The time is ripe for us to shake hands at last with a friendly smile, certain that we no longer have reason to fear each other, because we are connected by mutual respect for human life, human rights, civil liberties, and general peace, a respect we have paid for dearly.

This common starting point opens a great horizon of potential cooperation. We can strive jointly for a democratic Europe, for a Europe that represents unity in diversity, for a Europe that does not give the world wars but radiates tolerance, for a Europe that draws on its best cultural traditions, for a Europe that no one will contaminate any longer with toxic fumes and poisoned water.

We agree that the basic prerequisite for a genuine friendship between our nations is truth, a truth that is always expressed, no matter how hard.

Our guest has already spoken hard truths about the pain that the world in general, and we in particular, have suffered as a result of the Germans, or, more precisely, the forebears of present-day Germans.

Have we, too, managed to say everything that ought to be said, from our point of view? I am not sure.

Six years of Nazi rule was enough, for example, for us to have allowed ourselves to be infected with the germ of evil. We informed on one another, both during and after the war; we accepted—in just, as well as exaggerated, indignation—the principle of collective guilt. Instead of giving all those who betrayed this state a proper trial, we drove them out of the country and punished them with the kind of retribution that went beyond the rule of law. This was not punishment. It was revenge.

Moreover, we did not expel these people on the basis of demonstrable individual guilt, but simply because they belonged to a certain nation. And thus, on the assumption that we were clearing the way for historical justice, we hurt many innocent people, most of all women and children. And, as is usually the case in history, we hurt ourselves even more: we settled accounts with totalitarianism in a way that allowed the spirit of totalitarianism to penetrate our own activities and thus our own souls. Shortly afterward, it returned to us cruelly in the form of our inability to resist a new totalitarianism imported from elsewhere. And what is more, many of us actively helped that other totalitarianism into the world.

But in other respects as well, the decisions of those days after the war did not serve us well. We devastated large tracts of our land, and let the weed of devastation into our whole country.

Sacrifices that will be demanded for redress will therefore also be taxes for the errors and sins of our fathers.

We cannot reverse history, and so, besides freely investigating the truth, we can do only one thing. We can extend a friendly welcome to those who come with peace in their hearts to bow before the graves of their ancestors or to see what is left of the villages where they were born.

The relationship of Germany to the family of European nations, and of this family to Germany—if only because of its size, strength, and central position—have traditionally been the most important element of European stability.

This still holds true today. The whole of Europe must be grateful to the Germans for beginning to tear down the wall that divided them, because with that they also began tearing down the wall that divides Europe. Nevertheless, many Europeans still fear a united Germany.

As a consequence Germans, I believe, have a great historical opportunity. It is largely up to them to dispel the fears of other Europeans. If, for instance, they unambiguously confirm the final validity of all existing borders, including those with Poland—if they stand up to all those who still have the audacity to flirt with Nazi ideology—they will do much to allay Europe's fears and encourage its speedy unification.

It is also incumbent upon the Germans to determine whether their own unification becomes the engine of a pan-European unification, or whether, on the contrary, it slows the process down. In their own interest, they ought to harness that famous love of order. If they work in haste or confusion, especially if this is merely the product of electoral politics, it will not increase Germany's trustworthiness.

If, on the other hand, the process unfolds rationally, it will be possible to look forward to the day all of Europe has been yearning to see for a long time: the day when the Second World War and all its unfortunate consequences will finally be put behind us—including the division of Europe in two, and the two gigantic arsenals it became. If the process unfolds rationally and in an atmosphere of mutual understanding, this could even happen next year, and it will certainly be better than the former settlement at Versailles. Europe will then, at last, be set to realize its old dream: to be an amicable union of free nations and democratic states, founded on mutual respect for all human rights. The forty-five years since the end of the war are a sufficiently long interval to make possible a genuinely wise agreement, one no longer made in anger, regardless of how understandable that anger may once have been.

Clearly, the future fate of us all once more depends primarily on German developments.

Is it any wonder that the newly born democratic Czechoslovakia is so interested in events in both German states?

Is it any wonder that, on the third day after my election as president, I visited both German states?

Is it any wonder that we are so delighted to welcome a guest at the Prague Castle who embodies the best spiritual traditions of Germany?

Is it any wonder that we place such great importance on this day when two nations who lived for so long in mutual distrust symbolically shake hands?

I was speaking about the historic tasks facing Germany today. I must also, therefore, say what we ourselves must do.

Even after everything positive that has happened, there is still much fear of Germans and a greater Germany. There are people still living who experienced the war, lost their loved ones, suffered in concentration camps, hid from the Gestapo. Their distrust is understandable, and it is completely natural that it has spread to others.

It follows that our task is to overcome this fear. We have to understand that it was not the German nation that caused our agony, but particular human individuals. Spite, blind obedience, indifference to our fellow man—all these are characteristics of people, not of nations. Were there not more than a few bad Czechs and Slovaks? Were there not many among us who informed to the Gestapo and, later, to the secret police? Was there not in us a large degree of indifference and selfishness in allowing our country to be devastated over years and decades while remaining silent so as not to lose our bonuses and our peace and quiet by the television set, even when there was no longer the threat—at least in recent times—of death, or often even of prison! And when all is said and done, were we not actually the very ones who performed this baneful work?

It was, in fact, the Nazis who treacherously identified their affairs with the affairs of Germany. We cannot follow in their footsteps! If we were to accept their lie as our own, we would only be passing the torch of their destructive errors on to others.

People who speak a different language are occasionally detestable to other nations, especially if it is the language spoken by a tyrant. But a language cannot be blamed for the tyrant who speaks it. To judge someone on the basis of his language, the color of his skin, his origin, or the shape of his nose is to be, consciously or unconsciously, a racist. To speak abusively about Germans in general, about Vietnamese, or about members of any other nation is to condemn them merely for their nationality. To fear them only for that reason is the same as being anti-Semitic.

In other words, to accept the idea of collective guilt and collective responsibility means directly or unwittingly to weaken the guilt or the responsibility of individuals. And that is very dangerous. Just remember how many of us evaded our individual responsibility by saying that we Czechs are simply this way or that way and will probably never change. This type of thinking is the subtle embryo of nihilism.

Obviously, there are things that differentiate Czechs or Slovaks from others, as well as from one another. We have different preferences, different tastes, different dreams, different memories, and different experiences. Simply being Czech or Slovak or German or Vietnamese or Jewish does not make us good or bad.

To impose the guilt of some Germans upon the entire German nation is to absolve those particular individuals of their guilt and, with a pessimistic fatalism, to submerge them in an irresponsible anonymity, and to take any kind of hope away from ourselves. It would be the same if someone were to call us Stalinists, as a nation. Suffering obliges one to practice justice, not injustice. Those who have really suffered usually know that.

The gift of forgiveness, and thus freedom from one's own anger, can flourish only on the terrain of justice.

This day strikes me as important for one more reason. I do not know whether, in a future multipolar world, a unified Germany will still be called a great power. In one sense it has long been a potential great power: as one of the possible pillars of European spirituality, which—if it wishes to—can help us all withstand the destructive pressure of technological civilization, with its stupefying dictatorship of consumerism and its omnipresent commercialism, a pressure that leads precisely to the alienation that German philosophers have so often analyzed.

If Germany definitively builds and confirms its statehood, for which it has traditionally exerted its systematic, hierarchy-making spirit, and with which it has occupied itself for so long, then it will be able, without inhibition, to devote its creative potential to the renewal of global human responsibility, the only possible salvation of the contemporary world, and thus to a task to which the spirit of the German intellectual tradition is so well suited.

If today is another small step toward understanding in the center of Europe, then at the same time it can be a small step toward awakening us all from the drugged sleep that unscrupulous materialism throws us into daily, the consequence of which is a feeling of indifference to what comes after us.

I see today's visit of President Richard von Weizsäcker to Prague as the polar opposite of that painful, long-ago visitation we recall today.

Whereas that earlier visitation portended approaching horror and intensifying hopelessness, today's visit represents a great hope for us all. Hope for a world whose center will be the individual human being who fixes his searching gaze on the heavens to draw that mysterious strength which alone is capable of bringing moral order to our souls.

This is the very thing that can be the main guarantee of a meaningful, human future.

The Hebrew University

First, I would like to thank you for the great honor of being awarded an honorary doctorate from your university today. This is by no means the first honorary doctorate I have received, but I accept it with the same sensation that I always do: with deep shame. Because of my rather sporadic education, I suffer from feelings of unworthiness, and so I accept this degree as a strange gift, a continuing source of bewilderment. I can easily imagine a familiar-looking gentleman appearing at any moment, snatching the newly acquired diploma from my hands, taking me by the scruff of my neck, and throwing me out of the hall, because it has all been a mistake, compounded by my own audacity.

I'm sure you can see where this odd expression of my gratitude is leading: I want to take this opportunity to confess my long and intimate affinity with one of the great sons of the Jewish people, the Prague writer Franz Kafka. I'm not an expert on Kafka, and I'm not eager to read the secondary literature on him. I can't even say that I've read everything Kafka has written. I do, however, have a rather special reason for my indifference to Kafka studies: I sometimes feel that I'm the only one who really understands Kafka, and that no one else has any business trying to make his work more accessible to me. And my somewhat desultory attitude to studying his works comes from my vague feeling that I don't need to read and reread everything Kafka has written because I already know what's there. I'm even secretly persuaded that, if Kafka did not exist, and if I were a better writer than I am, I would have written his works myself.

What I've just said may sound odd, but I'm sure you understand what I mean. All I'm really saying is that in Kafka I have found a large portion of my own experience of the world, of myself, and of my way of being in the world. I will try, briefly and in broad terms, to name some of the more easily defined forms of this experience.

One of them is a profound, banal, and therefore utterly vague sensation of culpability, as though my very existence were a kind of sin. Then there is a powerful feeling of general alienation, both my own and one that relates to everything around me that helps to create such feelings; an experience of unbearable oppressiveness, a need constantly to explain myself to someone, to defend myself, a longing for an unattainable order of things, a longing that increases as the terrain I walk through becomes more muddled and confusing. I sometimes feel the need to confirm my identity by sounding off at others and demanding my rights. Such outbursts are, of course, quite unnecessary, and any response fails to reach the right ears and vanishes into the black hole that surrounds me. Everything I encounter displays to me its absurd aspect first. I feel as though I am constantly lagging behind powerful, self-confident men whom I can never overtake, let alone emulate. I find myself essentially hateful, deserving only mockery.

I can already hear your objections—that I style myself in these Kafkaesque outlines only because in reality I'm entirely different: someone who quietly and persistently fights for something, someone whose idealism has carried him to the head of his nation.

Yes, I admit that superficially I may appear to be the precise opposite of all those Ks—Josef K., the surveyor K., and Franz K.— although I stand behind everything I've said about myself. I would only add that, in my opinion, the hidden motor driving all my dogged efforts is precisely this innermost feeling of being excluded, of belonging nowhere, a state of disinheritance, of fundamental nonbelonging. Moreover, I would say that it's precisely my desperate longing for order that keeps plunging me into the most improbable ventures. I would even venture to say that everything worthwhile I've ever accomplished has been done to conceal my almost metaphysical feeling of guilt. The real reason I am always creating something, organizing something, it would seem, is to defend my permanently questionable right to exist.

You may well ask how someone who thinks of himself this way can be the president of a country. It's a paradox, but I must admit that, if I am a better president than many others would be in my place, it is precisely because somewhere in the deepest substratum of my work lies this constant doubt about myself and my right to hold office. I am the kind of person who would not be in the least surprised if, in the very middle of my presidency, I were summoned and led off to stand trial before some shadowy tribunal, or taken straight to a quarry to break rocks. Nor would I be surprised if I were suddenly to hear the reveille and wake up in my prison cell, and then, with great bemusement, proceed to tell my fellow prisoners everything that I had dreamed had happened to me in the past six months.

The lower I am, the more proper my place seems; and the higher I am, the stronger my suspicion is that there has been some mistake. And every step of the way, I feel what a great advantage it is for doing a good job as president to know that I do not belong in the position and that I can at any moment, and justifiably, be removed from it.

This is not intended to be a lecture or an essay, merely a brief comment on the subject of Franz Kafka and my presidency. I think it is appropriate that these things be expressed here in Jerusalem, at the Hebrew University, and by a Czech. Perhaps I have put more of my cards on the table than I wanted to, and perhaps my advisers will reprimand me for it. But I won't mind, because I expect it and deserve it. My readiness for the anticipated reprimand is just another example of what an advantage it is, in my job, of being prepared at all times for the worst.

Once more, I thank you for the honor, and after what I've said here, I'm ashamed to repeat that I accept it with a sense of shame.

The Council of Europe

The twelve stars in the emblem of the Council of Europe are a symbol of—among other things—the rhythmical passage of time, with its twelve hours of the day and night and twelve months of the year. The emblem of the institution in which I now have the honor of speaking strengthens my conviction that I am speaking to people who have a sensitive perception of the acceleration of European time we are witnessing today—to people with an understanding of someone like me, who not only desires but actually has the duty to project this acceleration into political action.

If you will bear with me, I shall once again attempt to think aloud on this subject, in a place that is perhaps the most suitable environment of all for such reflections.

Let me start with a personal experience.

Throughout my life, whenever I have thought aloud about public affairs, about civic, political, and moral matters, some reasonable person has inevitably pointed out, in the name of reason, that I, too, should be reasonable, should put aside my wild ideas, and accept once and for all that nothing can change for the better because the world is divided forever into two parts. Both these half-worlds are content with this division, and neither wants to change. It is pointless to behave according to one's conscience, because no one can change anything, and those who do not want war should just keep quiet. I often had to listen to this "voice of reason" following Brezhnev's invasion of Czechoslovakia, after which such so-called reasonable people felt revivified, because they had been given a new argument for their indifference to public affairs. They could say: "There you are, that's the way it goes, they've written us off, nobody cares, there is nothing we can do, everything's in vain, you'd better learn your lesson and keep silent! Unless, of course, you want to go to jail."

I was far from the only one to disregard such wisdom. There were many of us in my country who continued to do what we thought right. We were not afraid of being considered fools. We went on thinking about how to make the world a better place, and we made no secret of our ideas. Our efforts eventually merged into a single, coordinated initiative which we called Charter 77. All of us in the Charter, together and individually, thought about freedom and injustice, about human rights, about democracy and political pluralism, about a market economy, and about many other things. We thought, and hence we also dreamed. We dreamed, both in and out of prison, of a Europe without barbed wire, high walls, artificially separated nations, or gigantic stockpiles of weapons, of a Europe that had done away with "blocs," of a European policy based on respect for man and human rights, of a politics not subordinated to transient and particular interests. Yes, we dreamed of a Europe that would be an amicable community of independent nations and democratic states. When I had the chance to snatch a quarter of an hour's conversation with my friend Jiří Dienstbier (now deputy prime minister and minister of foreign affairs) as we changed machines at the end of a shift in the Heřmanice prison, we sometimes dreamed of these things aloud. Later, when he was working as a stocker, Jiří Dienstbier wrote a book called *Dreaming of Europe*. "What's the point of a stoker's writing utopian visions of the future when he can't exert the slightest influence on this future and can only bring more harassment upon himself?" asked the friends of reason, shaking their wise heads uncomprehendingly.

And then a strange thing happened. Time suddenly accelerated, and what would otherwise have taken a year suddenly happened in an hour. Everything started to change at a surprising speed, the impossible suddenly became possible, and the dream became reality. The stoker's dream became the daily routine of the minister of foreign affairs. And the advocates of reason have now split into three groups. The first are quietly waiting for things to go wrong that will give them yet another argument for their nihilistic ideology; the second are looking for ways to push the dreamers out of government and replace them again with "reasonable" pragmatists; and the third are loudly proclaiming that, at last, what they have always known would happen has come to pass.

I am telling you of this not to ridicule my allegedly reasonable fellow citizens, but for a very different reason: to show that it is never pointless to think about alternatives that may at the moment seem improbable, impossible, or simply fantastic.

We don't dream, of course, just because our dreams might one day prove useful. We dream, as it were, on principle. Yet it would now appear that there can be moments in history when having "dreamed on principle" may in fact prove useful.

Time flies. And flying here in this hall as well. I can therefore detain you no longer with these literary reflections and must come to the point.

First a few words about my country.

Following the police attack against the students last November 17, our patience finally gave out, and we quickly overthrew the totalitarian system that had dominated our country for forty-two years. We have set out on the road toward democracy, political pluralism, and a market economy. The press in our country is free, and in a month's time we shall hold our first free elections in forty-two years, with a broad range of political forces taking part. I am firmly convinced that these elections will stand the test both at home, and in the eyes of all foreign observers as well. In our country there is spiritual and intellectual freedom; once again, for the first time since the Second World War, all the Catholic dioceses have bishops, and the religious orders are functioning again.

Our state has no ideology. The only idea it wants to instill in its domestic and foreign policy is a respect for human rights in the broadest sense of the word, and respect for the uniqueness of every human being. Our Parliament has passed some important economic legislation to enact the transition to a market economy and put meaning back into human labor. We are preparing democratic constitutions for our federation and for both national republics. We want at last to give full legal expression to the identity of our two nations and ensure the collective rights of our national minorities. We are a sovereign state, we want to live in friendship with all nations, but if need be, we are determined to defend that sovereignty.

I believe we have a right to the status of observer at your Assembly, and I thank you on behalf of our people for having granted us this status three days ago. I am firmly convinced that the Council of Europe will understand and accept our application for full membership.

What I have told you about my country does not mean that Czechoslovakia today is an oasis of harmony. Quite the opposite. We are now going through an extremely difficult period, because we are awash in a vast array of enormous problems that were latent and have only now surfaced with our newly won freedom. From the former regime we have inherited a devastated landscape, a disrupted economy, and, above all, a mutilated moral sensibility.

The overthrow of totalitarian power was an important first step, but it was just the beginning of our journey. We will make rapid progress, but there are many pitfalls ahead.

We are finding that we are not good at much of anything, and there is much we have yet to learn. We must learn how to create a political culture; we must learn independent thinking and responsible civic behavior.

We are well aware of all this, perhaps more so than many who watch us from afar with concern and exasperation at our clumsiness.

I am not saying all this to gain an undeserved advantage, or even to elicit your compassion, but because I am used to speaking the truth, even when it might seem more advantageous to lie, or at least to keep silent. It is my opinion that the advantage of a clear conscience is always paramount.

Now that I have briefly acquainted you with my country, I can begin thinking aloud about the Europe of today and tomorrow. These thoughts will not be simply a recapitulation of some far-off dissident dreams. They also will reflect what I have learned in office and from many conversations with the foreign statesmen I have had the good fortune to meet.

It would be pointless to repeat what everybody knows, that today unprecedented prospects are opening up for Europe: the possibility of becoming a continent of peaceful and amicable cooperation among all its nations.

I will therefore move directly to some specific measures in the sphere of structures, institutions, and treaties that must be created and implemented, either at once or in some agreed-upon sequence, if the newly emerging hope is to become a reality. I shall start by assuming that the structures born of the old system should either be transformed or merged with new structures, or abolished and left to wither. Entirely new structures should be created in parallel as starting points of a future order. For the sake of clarity, let us divide this sphere into four categories: security measures, and political, economic, and civic structures, institutions, or mechanisms.

In the realm of security and the military, as the outward expression of the postwar division of Europe, there are two existing pacts—the North Atlantic Treaty Organization and the Warsaw Pact. These are military groupings of a rather different nature and history, and they have different missions. Whereas NATO was born as an instrument for the defense of Western European democracies against the danger of expansion by a Stalinist Soviet Union, the Warsaw Pact was conceived as an offshoot of the Soviet army and as an instrument of Soviet policy. The aim was to confirm the satellite status of the European countries over which Stalin had gained control after the Second World War. If we then consider the geopolitical context—namely, that the Western European democracies adjoin the ocean in the West, and the former Soviet satellites border upon the Soviet Union in the East—we can easily grasp the asymmetry of the whole situation.

In spite of this, I believe that in this radically new situation both groupings should gradually move toward the ideal of an entirely new security system, one that would be the forerunner of a future united Europe and would provide some sort of security or security guarantees. It could be a security community involving a large part of the Northern Hemisphere. Hence the guarantors of the process of unification in Europe would have to include not only the United States and Canada in the West, but also the Soviet Union in the East. When I say Soviet Union, I mean the community of nations that country is in the process of becoming today.

What are the implications of this for NATO and the Warsaw Pact in light of the asymmetry to which I have referred?

For both pacts, it means considerably strengthening a role they are already playing to some extent, the role of political players in joint disarmament negotiations. It also means a diminution of their former role as instruments for defending one half of Europe against a possible attack from the other half. In brief, both pacts should function more clearly as instruments of disarmament rather than instruments of armament.

It seems that NATO, as a more meaningful, more democratic, and more effective structure, could become the germ of a new European security system with less trouble than could the Warsaw Pact. But NATO, too, must change. Above all it should—in the face of today's reality—alter its military doctrine. And it should soon—in view of its changing role—change its name as well. This should happen because of the victory of historical reason over historical absurdity, and not because of any victory of the West over the East. The present name is so closely linked to the Cold War that it would signal a lack of understanding of present-day developments if Europe were to unite under the NATO flag. If the present structure of Western Europe's security alliance becomes the precursor or seed bed of a future pan-

European alliance, it will certainly not have been because the West will have won the Cold War but because historical justice has triumphed. A further reason for changing the name is its obvious geographical inappropriateness. In a future security system, only a minority of members would border on the Atlantic Ocean.

As for the Warsaw Pact, it seems that, when it ends its role as a political instrument of European disarmament, and as the escort of some countries in their return to Europe, it will lose its purpose and can be dissolved. What originally came into being as a symbol of Stalinist expansion will, in time, lose its entire raison d'être.

The great "Northern" security zone, as is obvious at first sight, may essentially be called the "Helsinki" zone: the countries that could, and should, belong to it are in fact participants in the Helsinki process. And what this implies is obvious enough. The new structures, which would emerge in parallel with the transformation or gradual dissolution of the old, could grow out of the Helsinki process. The Czechoslovak proposal to establish a European Security Commission as a starting point for a united "Helsinki" security system and a guarantee of a united Europe stems from this idea. The participating states in the Conference on Security and Cooperation in Europe have been informed of this initiative, and I don't need to explain it here again. As the Warsaw Pact gradually dissolves or loses its purpose, and as NATO gradually transforms itself, the significance of this commission would grow, along with any new structures around it.

Let me try to summarize these considerations. If the Helsinki security process were to start expanding beyond making recommendations to participating states, to include joint treaty commitments, a broad framework of guarantees could be created for the emerging political unity of Europe.

The accelerated course of history compels us to project every political consideration immediately into some comprehensive timetable. I shall attempt to do this for the question at hand.

It is possible—and let us hope it will happen—that a summit

of the states participating in the Conference on Security and Cooperation in Europe will be convened sometime this year. I would like to assure those states proposing to hold it in Prague that Czechoslovakia would consider this a great honor and would do its utmost to ensure the conference's success. However, more important than the venue of this summit are its substance and its purpose. We have already suggested that it could do more than the present agenda calls for.

In the first place, the summit could—if all the participating states agreed—establish the proposed European Commission for Security, which would begin working as of January 1, 1991. Czechoslovakia proposes Prague as its headquarters. The Secretariat, or its representative part, could have its headquarters in one of the beautiful palaces near the Prague Castle.

This year's summit, should it be convened, could also decide that the conference known under the working name of Helsinki II and planned for 1992 would be held in the autumn of next year.

The third and most important decision that could be made at this year's summit would be on the substance and purpose of Helsinki II and on the immediate start of its preparations, for which purpose the proposed commission could also serve. Its task would be to draft and perhaps sign a new generation of Helsinki Accords. The novelty of these accords would be that they would consist not merely of an extensive set of recommendations to governments and states, but of a set of treaties on cooperation and assistance in the sphere of security. In other words, there would be some sort of obligation to provide mutual assistance in the case of an attack from the outside and to submit local conflicts within the zone to arbitration. Clearly, such negotiations and accords would finally fix the existing European borders and, through a system of treaties and guarantees, could close the chapter on the Second World War and all its nefarious consequences, the chief of which is the prolonged and artificial division of Europe.

In conclusion, by the end of next year the foundations of a

new and united "Helsinki" security system could be laid, providing all European states with the certainty that they no longer have to fear one another because they are all part of the same system of mutual guarantees, based on the principle of the equality of all participants and their obligation to protect the independence of each participating country.

Allow me one more remark, concerning nuclear weapons in Europe. In the postwar period these weapons—produced never to be used—became part of a security model that, paradoxically, ensured peace through a balance of fear. The nations of Central and Eastern Europe, however, paid a heavy price for the efficiency of this nuclear model by remaining in the grip of a totalitarian straitjacket.

An excessive quantity of any type of weapon, particularly of the nuclear variety, inevitably has a distorting effect on any territory on which it is deployed. This applies particularly to weapons that can only reach beyond their backyards and that we call "tactical."

We therefore welcome President Bush's proposal to abandon the planned modernization of these weapons. Should the summer NATO conference decide on the gradual elimination of the less modern missiles now deployed in Central Europe, we would welcome this move with a great sense of satisfaction. What justification is there for the existence of weapons that can only strike Czechoslovakia, the eastern part of Germany (now in the process of unification), and possibly Poland? Whom will they deter? The new governments elected in the first free elections after several decades? The new, democratically elected parliaments?

I said in my address to the Polish Parliament [in January] that our society sometimes reminds me of freshly amnestied prisoners who have problems adapting to freedom. People are full of prejudices, stereotypes, and notions shaped by long years of totalitarianism. Can they be expected to understand the purpose of weapons targeted at them? The supporters of the former regimes in our country and elsewhere are still lying in wait for their chance. It would be a historical irony if this chance were to be provided by those who helped us in the past in our struggle against totalitarian regimes.

In my opinion, the main disaster of our modern world has been its bipolarity, the fact that the tension between the two main powers and their allies was transferred in one way or another to the whole world. This situation persists to this day. The world is constantly being torn apart by this tension and stifled by the existing superpowers. The chief victims of this unfortunate state of affairs are the one hundred or so states inaccurately called the Third World, the developing world, or the nonaligned world. The anxiety of this "world" over the possibility that the emergence of a united "Helsinki" security zone could only widen the gap between the North and the South is understandable but groundless. The very opposite is true. Such a zone would be an important step from bipolarity to multipolarity. It would establish a large, European connecting link between the powerful North American continent and the rapidly changing and liberating community of nations of today's Soviet Union. These three entities, living in peace and mutual cooperation, would indirectly open up new opportunities for a full-fledged existence to other countries, other communities of countries. The entire international community would start shifting from an arena of mutual competition, of direct or indirect expansion of the two superpowers, into an arena of peaceful cooperation among equal partners. The North would cease to threaten the South through the export of its interests and its supremacy. Instead it would radiate toward the South the idea of equal cooperation for all.

Against the massive background of this broad "Northern" or "Helsinki" security zone, or simultaneously with its emergence, Europe could relatively swiftly, and without the obstacles that until recently seemed insurmountable, become politically integrated as a democratic community of democratic states. This process would no doubt go through several stages and be accomplished through several different mechanisms. It may be that in the first stage—say, within five years—a community could be established on European soil that we might call the Organization of European States and, with the beginning of the third millennium, God willing, we could start to build the European Confederation proposed by President Mitterrand. With the gradual consolidation and stabilization and growing competence of the future confederation, the whole "Helsinki" security system would ultimately be able to ensure its own security, at which point the last American soldier could leave Europe.

Every move leading to this goal should be encouraged. The more varied and simultaneous the attempts undertaken, the better, because the greater the chance will be that one of them will succeed. Hence Czechoslovakia supports very different initiatives, from such smaller, working regional communities as Initiative Four (the Danubian-Adriatic Community) to [Polish] Prime Minister Mazowiecki's idea for setting up a permanent political body of the foreign ministers of all European states.

You will certainly understand why I have spoken so extensively about these ideas here in this Assembly, before the representatives of the oldest and largest political organization in Europe, one that has such solid foundations and has already done so much useful work. Yes, the spiritual and moral values on which the Council of Europe is based, which are the common heritage of all European nations, are the best possible foundations for a future integrated Europe. I can see no reason why your Parliamentary Assembly and your executive bodies could not be the core around which a future European Confederation would crystallize. Czechoslovakia considers all the criteria for the admission of new states to the Council of Europe to be excellent: it accepts them without reservation and rejoices that the Council of Europe is opening up to the emerging democracies of the former Soviet satellites, which are now establishing their relations with the Soviet Union on the principles of equality and full respect for the sovereignty of individual states. I am firmly convinced that the day will come when all European states will fulfill your criteria and will become full members of the council. The Council of Europe was, after all, founded as a pan-European institution, and it was only the sad course of history that turned it for so long into a merely Western European institution.

Obviously, the states that have been ruled by a totalitarian system and are now overcoming its consequences and want, as we say, to return to Europe, can do so most rapidly and efficiently not by competing and contending against one another but by helping one another in solidarity. If these countries want to open up to the new Europe, they must first open to one another. The new democratic government in Czechoslovakia, therefore, wants to do everything in its power to contribute to the coordination of efforts by the Central European countries to enter various European institutions. That is why we so often appeal to different institutions that are theoretically European, but in fact are so far only Western European, to open more flexibly to those who for long years were segregated and who logically belong in them.

The highest level of integration has no doubt been achieved by the twelve countries of the European Economic Community. The countries of Central and Eastern Europe, working on the transition from a centralized "noneconomy" to a normal market economy and trying to enter the world of normal economic relations and achieve the convertibility of their currencies, now look upon the EC as a distant and almost unattainable horizon. In seeking to get closer to it, they should coordinate their efforts. On the other hand, the EC should create some flexible transitional ground, on which the economies of these states could more easily recover. This would serve not only the interest of these countries, but of the EC itself, and would further the ideal of an integrated democratic Europe.

The harsh lesson of living under a totalitarian system has taught us to respect human and civic rights, and it is no accident that the emerging democracies in our countries have mostly sprung from independent civic movements like the Czecho-slovak Charter 77. We cannot forget the soil out of which we have grown and the principles that have governed our struggle for freedom. We therefore realize how indispensable it is for the efforts to integrate states, governments, and parliaments to be accompanied, or even inspired, by parallel civic efforts. For this reason, I have recently supported, along with Lech Wałesa, a proposal for a European Civic Assembly. I trust that the Western European governments will also demonstrate an understanding for this plan.

Before I conclude, I should mention two topics that are of interest to practically the whole world and are closely related to the future of Europe.

The first is Germany. We have already formulated the Czechoslovak viewpoint, but I will repeat it. It was always clear to us that the artificially divided German nation would one day reunite in a single state. There were times when such a view—publicly proclaimed—sounded deliberately provocative, and was considered as such by many Germans. We are glad, not only because we are not in favor of the artificial division of any nation, but also because we perceive the fall of the Berlin Wall as the fall of the whole Iron Curtain and thus as a liberating phenomenon for us all. As we have said time and again, the unification of Germany into a single democratic state is no obstacle to the European unification process but should in fact be understood as its motivating force. Our thoughts and actions toward the construction of a new European order should keep step with the unification of Germany. Hence we welcome the so-called Four-Plus-Two plan. At the same time, we fully understand our Polish brothers' concern over the western border of their state. We consider this border final and support Poland's full participation in all negotiations related to its borders. Such negotiations could, in our view, be concluded at the Helsinki II Conference, which should not only formally confirm existing borders, as did the first Helsinki Conference, but provide legal guarantees for them as well.

The second urgent theme is the future of the Soviet Union. Czechoslovakia unreservedly recognizes every nation's right to its own identity and to the free choice of its state and political system. I am convinced that the present process of democratization we are witnessing in the Soviet Union is irreversible. I am convinced that all the nations of the Soviet Union will peacefully move to the type of political sovereignty they desire, and that the Soviet leadership will prefer the free transition to sovereignty over the threat of a violent confrontation. The time is not too distant when some republics will become completely independent and others will establish a new type of community, whether a confederative association or a looser type. In my view, there is no reason why, against the background of an extensive "Helsinki" security system, some or all of the European nations within the present Soviet Union could not at the same time be members of a European confederation and of some eventual "post-Soviet" confederation. The present Soviet leadership, which proclaims a scientific understanding of historical processes, undoubtedly understands that all nations naturally aspire to their own identity and that the present structure of the Soviet state—inherited from czarist, and later Stalinist, hegemony—is artificial. For all these reasons, we believe that the West should at last free itself from its traditional terror of the Soviet Union. One can hardly admire Mr. Gorbachev and fear him at the same time. We cannot scare one another endlessly with the specter of hawkish, conservative forces poised to overthrow Mr. Gorbachev and return the Soviet Union to the nineteen-fifties. And in no way can one cultivate this specter simply to provide the military industry with work orders. There is no way back, and the future of the world today no longer stands or falls with one person. Nor is it any longer within anyone's power to stop this new and strikingly forward-looking course of history.

In conclusion, allow me to mention an anxiety we frequently meet with nowadays: the fear of national, ethnic, and social conflicts in the Central European arena, which might be fostered by the growth of long-unresolved problems. This fear leads to the question of whether our part of Europe will soon become a powder keg of the Balkan type.

It is our common task to exclude the possibility of such a threat and render such fears immaterial. This is chiefly the responsibility of our own countries, which must proceed with speed, coordination, and complete mutual understanding to solve the problems we have inherited. But it is also the responsibility of the Western European countries, which could help us a great deal by supporting us in this complicated process.

In 1464, the Czech King George of Poděbrady sent a momentous message to the French King Louis XI, proposing that he preside over a league of peace and invite Christian rulers to a convention that, on the basis of binding international law, would prevent war among members of the union and ensure their common defense. It seems to me that it was no accident that one of the first serious attempts to achieve a peaceful unification of Europe emerged from Central Europe. As the traditional crossroads of all European conflicts, this region has a particular interest in European peace and security. I am happy to have been able to speak about these matters here in Strasbourg, a place that was once the symbol of traditional conflicts and is now a symbol of European unity.

Honored by this opportunity to speak here at the most important European political forum, I naturally devoted my attention to political structures, systems, institutions, and mechanisms, but this doesn't mean I am unaware of the obvious—that no truly new structures can be set up, or existing structures daringly altered, without radical changes in human thinking and behavior and in social consciousness. Without courageous people, courageous structural changes are unthinkable.

With this remark I come back to where I started—that is, to dreams. Everything seems to indicate that we must not be afraid of dreaming the seemingly impossible if we want the seemingly impossible to become a reality. We shall never build a better Europe if we cannot dream of a better Europe.

I understand the twelve stars in your emblem not as the proud conviction that the Council of Europe will build a heaven on this earth. There will never be a heaven on earth. But I perceive these twelve stars as a reminder that the world can become a better place if we sometimes have the courage to look up at the stars.

The Salzburg Festival

This June, our country held its first free elections in many long decades. Demanding days of putting together a new coalition government followed. On July 5, a freely elected Parliament re-elected me president of Czechoslovakia, and shortly thereafter approved the new Cabinet. These events marked the culmination of one of the most dramatic periods of our modern history: the shattering of the totalitarian system. It was a time of excitement, swift decision, and countless improvisations—an utterly thrilling, even adventurous time. It was a little like a mildly bewildering but essentially wonderful dream. It was, in a way, a fairy tale. There were so many things that could have gone wrong. We were traveling on totally unknown terrain, and none of us had any reason to believe that it wouldn't collapse under our feet.

But it didn't. And now the time has come when there is indeed reason to rejoice. The revolution, with all its perils, is behind us, and the prospect of building a democratic state, in peace, lies before us. Could there be a happier moment in the life of a land that has suffered so long under totalitarianism?

And yet, precisely as that splendid historical moment dawned, a peculiar thing happened to me. When I arrived at work for the first time after my re-election, I found I was depressed. I was in some sort of profoundly subdued state. I felt strangely paralyzed, empty inside. I seemed to have suddenly lost all my ideas and goals, my skills, hope, and resolve. I felt deflated, spent, lacking in imagination. Even though just a few days earlier I had been terribly busy, I suddenly had no idea what I was supposed to be doing.

The pressure of exhilarating events, which until then had

aroused in me a surprising level of energy, abruptly vanished, and I found myself standing bewildered, lacking the inner motivation for anything at all, feeling exhausted, almost irrelevant. It was an extremely odd sensation, comparable to a bad hangover after some wild binge, to awakening from a pleasant dream to the ugly reality of cold daylight, to the shock of a man in love discovering his sweetheart's treachery.

I wasn't the only one with these strange feelings; many of my colleagues at Prague Castle felt the very same way. We realized that the poetry was over and the prose was beginning; that the county fair had ended and everyday reality was back. It was only then that we realized how challenging, and in many ways unrewarding, was the work that lay ahead of us, how heavy a burden we had shouldered. It was as if up to that moment the wild torrent of events had not allowed us to step back and consider whether we were up to the tasks we had undertaken. We had simply been tossed into the current and forced to swim.

It seemed to us that only now could we begin to appreciate fully the weight of the destiny we had chosen. That realization brought with it a sudden, and under the circumstances seemingly illogical and groundless, sense of hopelessness.

Somewhere in the depths of this feeling lay fear: fear that we had taken on too much, fear that we wouldn't be up to the job, fear of our own inadequacy—in short, fear of our very selves.

At the deepest core of this feeling there was, ultimately, a sensation of the absurd: what Sisyphus might have felt if one fine day his boulder stopped, rested on the hilltop, and failed to roll back down. It was the sensation of a Sisyphus mentally unprepared for the possibility that his efforts might succeed, a Sisyphus whose life had lost its old purpose and hadn't yet developed a new one.

About a year ago, when I was asked to launch this august festival with a brief lecture, I never considered that I might be able to attend in person. Still, I was pleased to accept the offer and planned to submit my contribution in writing. During the tranquil Christmas season, I would calmly compose a little essay on the theme of fear and the sense of danger in Central European literature. But history got in my way, robbing me of both time and concentration. So I decided to complete the task after the elections; in fact, I was truly looking forward to it, because it would allow me to enjoy a brief return to my original profession as a writer, and because I planned to use the occasion as a dividing mark between the first, revolutionary, stage of my political commitment and the second stage, a calmer one, which involved building up rather than tearing down.

I did, in fact, find the time to write. But the time I found was the period of my peculiar political hangover. First history got in my way; now I was getting in my own way. I was simply unable to write anything; I was depleted, paralyzed, powerless.

What a paradox: I had wanted to write about fear, and here it was fear that was incapacitating me in my writing. Fear of my subject matter, fear of the act of writing itself, fear of my own inadequacy, fear of myself.

All I could do about this paradox was to try to approach the topic paradoxically: by describing the situation that had led to my inability to approach it. There is nothing new in that. In fact, part of why most writers write is to divert their despair into their work and thus overcome it. Perhaps this explains why I am talking so much about myself here. It isn't out of any complacent egocentrism but because, simply, I have no other options.

No inventory of the characteristics specific to Central European culture and literature would be complete without one particularly important one: an increased perception of danger, a heightened sensitivity to the phenomenon of fear. It makes perfect sense. In a place where history has always been so intricately tangled, in a place with such complex cultural, ethnic, social, and political structures, in a place that saw the origins of the most varied of European catastrophes, fear and danger are the very dimensions of human experience that must be felt and analyzed most intensely.

The heterogeneity of Central Europe explains clearly enough, I think, the two characteristic poles of its life, and thus of its literature as well. On the one hand, history is miniaturized; it becomes idyll, anecdote, an almost folkloric cult of locality. On the other hand, there are obsessive and often quite terrifyingly prescient fears of the dangers presented by the so-called great movements of history. The jovial neighborliness typical of this region has its inevitable counterpart, deriving precisely from the heightened fear of history, in varieties of fanaticism and nationalism. The nations and ethnic groups living under this constant sensation of threat seek to defend themselves by national or nationalistic self-affirmation. Ethnic groups that could never develop politically in freedom wage a constant struggle to affirm their identity, and one of the ways they do this is by dwelling on their own differences and being hypersensitive to the danger they feel from the differences of others.

I believe that even the kind of fear I experienced is typical of the Central European spiritual and intellectual world, or at least is understandable against its background. Certainly it would be hard to imagine that in England, France, or the United States a person could be depressed by his political victory. In Central Europe, it seems perfectly natural.

For that matter, the experience of the hangoverlike void is certainly not unique to me, nor is that odd sense of fear. I have observed variations of that fear and emptiness quite often, not only in Czechoslovakia but also in the other countries of Central and Eastern Europe that have shaken off totalitarianism.

It was with a great deal of effort that people in these lands attained the freedom they yearned for. The moment they gained that freedom, however, it was as if they had been ambushed by it. Unaccustomed to freedom, they now, suddenly, don't know what to do with it; they are afraid of it; they don't know what to fill it with. Their Sisyphean struggle for freedom has left a vacuum; life seems to have lost its purpose.

Similarly, in this part of the world we observe symptoms of a new fear of the future. Unlike in totalitarian times, when the future, though wretched, was certain, today it is very unclear. The single (if ubiquitous) familiar danger represented by totalitarian oppression seems to have been replaced by an entire spectrum of new and unfamiliar—or long-forgotten—dangers: from the danger of national conflicts to the danger of losing social-welfare protection to the danger of the new totalitarianism of consumption, commerce, and money.

We were very good at being persecuted and at losing. That may be why we are so flustered by our victories and so disconcerted that no one is persecuting us. Now and then I even encounter indications of nostalgia for the time when life flowed between banks that, as narrow as they were, were unchanging and apparent to everyone. Today we don't know where the riverbanks lie and we find this unsettling.

We are like prisoners who have grown used to their prisons and, suddenly given their longed-for freedom, do not know what to do with it, and are deranged by the constant need to think for themselves.

I repeat that the existential situation I illustrated for you from my own experience, and which I have also observed in various forms in my fellow citizens, is, in my opinion, a particularly Central European one. Our literature contains innumerable examples of it in the recent past, in the atmosphere following both the First and the Second World Wars.

In short, it seems that fate has ordained that we, more frequently than others, and often in unexpected situations, shall know fear.

For us, fear of history is not just fear of the future but also fear of the past. I would even say that these two fears are conditional, one on the other: a person who is afraid of what is yet to come is generally also reluctant to look in the face of what has been; and a person afraid to look at his own past must fear what is to come.

All too often in this part of the world, fear of one lie gives birth to another lie, in the foolish hope that by protecting ourselves from the first lie we will be protected from lies in general. But a lie can never protect us from a lie. Just as nothing protected us in Czechoslovakia, from the Stalinist lie about the socialist paradise on earth, we will not be protected by the lie about Hitler's racist allies as alleged inheritors of an ancient princely throne. Those who falsify history do not protect the freedom of a nation but, rather, constitute a threat to it.

The idea that a person can rewrite his autobiography is one of the traditional self-deceptions of Central Europe. Trying to do that is to hurt oneself and one's fellow countrymen. When a truth is not given complete freedom, freedom is not complete.

One way or another, many of us are guilty. But we cannot be forgiven, nor can there be peace in our souls, until we at least confess our guilt.

Confession is liberating. I know how it once liberated me when I found the strength to admit my own mistake. I have many reasons for believing that truth purges one of fear. Many of us who, in recent years, strove to speak the truth in spite of everything, were able to maintain an inner perspective, a willingness to endure, a sense of proportion, an ability to understand and forgive others, and a light heart only because we were speaking the truth. Otherwise, we might have perished from despair.

Our specifically Central European fear has led to many a misfortune. It could be shown that in it lies the primal origin of not only countless local conflicts but also some global ones. Here, the fear that possesses petty souls has often led to violence, brutality, and fanatical hatred.

But fear is not only a destructive condition. Fear of our own incompetence can evoke new competency; fear of God or of our own conscience can evoke courage; fear of defeat can make us prevail. Fear of freedom could be the very thing that ultimately teaches us to create a freedom of real value. And fear of the future could be exactly what we need to bring about a better future.

The more sensitive a person is to all the dangers that threaten him, the better able he is to defend against them. For that matter, I have always thought that feeling empty and losing touch with the meaning of life are in essence only a challenge to seek new things to fill one's life, a new meaning for one's existence and one's work. Isn't it the moment of most profound doubt that gives birth to new certainties? Perhaps hopelessness is the very soil that nourishes human hope; perhaps one could never find sense in life without first experiencing its absurdity.

In spite of having spoken in such an unstatesmanlike manner about my moments of hopelessness, I will conclude on a constructive note, that is, with an appeal to all of us Central Europeans. Let us endeavor to confront our traditional fears by systematically eliminating every possible reason we might have for harboring them. Let us try, quickly and together, to build the kind of system of mutual political, cultural, and economic ties that will gradually, once and for all, eliminate all the potential dangers that lurk in our common future. Only thus will we eliminate the reasons for our fears.

Let us finally endeavor, in this sorely tried place, to get rid of not only our fear of lies but also our fear of truth. Let us finally take a direct, calm, and unwavering look into our own countenances: our past, our present, and our future. We will only be able to escape their ambiguity when we understand them.

Let us try to delve into the core of our doubts, our fears, and our despair, to come up with the seeds of a new European self-confidence—the self-confidence of those who are not afraid to look beyond the horizon of their personal and community interests, beyond the horizon of this moment.

The Oslo Conference on "The Anatomy of Hate"

As I look over this assembly, I don't imagine there are many of us who could contemplate our theme—hate—from the inside, as a kind of autopsy, as a state of the soul that we have personally experienced. We are, rather, uneasy observers of this phenomenon, and thus we try to reflect on it only from the outside. This applies to me as well. Among my bad qualities—and there are certainly enough of them—there is not, oddly enough, the capacity to hate. So I, too, relate to hatred only as an observer, whose understanding of it is not profound, but whose concern about it is.

When I think about the people who have hated me personally, or still do, I realize that they share several characteristics which, when you put them together and analyze them, suggest a certain general interpretation of the origin of their hatred.

They are never hollow, empty, passive, indifferent, apathetic people. Their hatred always seems to me the expression of a large and unquenchable longing, a permanently unfulfilled and unfulfillable desire, a kind of desperate ambition. In other words, it is an active inner capacity that always leads the person to fixate on something, always pushes him in a certain direction, and is in a sense stronger than he is. I certainly don't think hatred is the mere absence of love or humanity, a mere vacuum in the human spirit. On the contrary, it has a lot in common with love, chiefly with that self-transcending aspect of love, the fixation on others, the dependence on them, and, in fact, the delegation of a piece of one's own identity to them. Just as a lover longs for the loved one and cannot get along without him, the hater longs for the object of his hatred. And, like love, hatred is ultimately an expression of longing for the absolute, albeit an expression that has become tragically inverted.

People who hate, at least those I have known, harbor a permanent, ineradicable feeling of injury, a feeling that is, of course, out of all proportion to reality. It is as though these people wanted to be endlessly honored, loved, and respected, as though they suffered from the chronic and painful awareness that others are ungrateful and unforgivably unjust toward them, not only because they don't honor and love them boundlessly, as they ought, but because they even—or so it seems—ignore them.

In the subconscious of haters there slumbers a perverse feeling that they alone possess the truth, that they are some kind of superhuman or even god, and thus deserve the world's complete recognition, even its complete submissiveness and loyalty, if not its blind obedience. They want to be the center of the world and are constantly frustrated and irritated because the world does not accept and recognize them as such; indeed, it may not pay any attention to them, and perhaps it even ridicules them.

They are like spoiled or badly brought-up children who think their mother exists only to worship them, and who think ill of her because she occasionally does something else, like spend time with her other children, her husband, a book, or her work. They feel all this as an injustice, an injury, a personal slight, a questioning of their own self-worth. The inner charge of energy, which might have been love, is perverted into hatred toward the imputed source of injury.

In hatred—just as in unhappy love—there is a desperate kind of transcendentalism. People who hate wish to attain the unattainable and are consumed by the impossibility of attaining it. They see the cause of this in the shameful world that prevents them from attaining their object. Hatred is a diabolical attribute of the fallen angel. It is a state of the spirit that aspires to be God, that may even think it is God, and is tormented by evidence that it is not and cannot be. It is the attribute of a creature who is jealous of God and eats his heart out because the road to the throne of God, where he thinks he should be sitting, is blocked by an unjust world conspiring against him.

The person who hates is never able to see the cause of his metaphysical failure in himself and the way he so completely overestimates his own worth. In his eyes, it is the surrounding world that is to blame. The trouble is that this is too abstract, vague, and incomprehensible. It has to be personified, because hatred—as a very particular kind of tumescence of the soul—requires a particular object. And so the person who hates seeks out a particular offender. Of course this offender is merely a stand-in, arbitrarily chosen and therefore easily replaceable. I have observed that, for the hater, hatred is more important than its object; he can rapidly change objects without changing anything essential in the relationship. This is understandable. He does not harbor hatred toward a particular person, but toward what that person represents: a complex of obstacles to the absolute, to absolute recognition, absolute power, total identification with God, truth, and the order of the world. Hatred for one's neighbor, therefore, would seem to be only a physiological embodiment of hatred for the universe that is perceived to be the cause of one's own universal failure.

It is said that those who hate suffer from an inferiority complex. This may not be the most precise way to put it. I would, rather, say that they are people with a complex based on the fatal perception that the world does not appreciate their true worth.

Another observation seems worth making here. The man who hates does not smile, he merely smirks; he is incapable of making a joke, only of bitter ridicule; he can't be genuinely ironic because he can't be ironic about himself. Only those who can laugh at themselves can laugh authentically. A serious face, quickness to take offense, strong language, shouting, the inability to step outside himself and see his own foolishness—these are typical of one who hates.

Such qualities reveal something very significant. The hater utterly lacks a sense of belonging, of taste, of shame, of objectivity. He lacks the capacity to doubt and ask questions, the awareness of his own transience and the transience of all things; he lacks the experience of genuine absurdity, that is, the absurdity of his own existence, the feeling of his own alienation, his awkwardness, his failure, his limitations, or his guilt. The common denominator of all this is clearly a tragic, almost metaphysical lack of a sense of proportion. The hateful person has not grasped the measure of things, the measure of his own possibilities, the measure of his rights, the measure of his own existence, and the measure of recognition and love that he can expect. He wants the world to belong to him with no strings attached; that is, he wants the world's recognition to be limitless. He does not understand that the right to the miracle of his own existence and the recognition of that miracle are things he must earn through his actions. He sees them, on the contrary, as a right granted to him once and for all, unlimited and never called into question. In short, he believes that he has something like an unconditional free pass to anywhere, even to heaven. Anyone who dares to scrutinize his pass is an enemy who does him wrong. If this is how he understands his right to existence and recognition, then he must be constantly angry at someone for not drawing the proper conclusions.

I have noticed that all haters accuse their neighbors—and through them the whole world—of being evil. The motive force behind this wrath is the feeling that these evil people and the evil world are denying them what is naturally theirs. In other words, haters project their own anger onto others. Here, too, they are like spoiled children. They don't see that they must sometimes show themselves worthy of something and that, if they don't automatically have everything they think they should, this is not because someone is being nasty to them.

In hatred there is great egocentrism and great self-love. Because they long for absolute self-confirmation and do not encounter it, hating people feel that they are the victims of an insidious evil, an omnipresent injustice that has to be eliminated to give justice its due. But in their minds, justice is turned on its head. They see it as the duty of justice to grant them something that cannot be granted: the whole world.

The person who hates is unhappy because, whatever he does to achieve full recognition and to destroy those he thinks are responsible for his lack of recognition, he can never attain the success he longs for—that is, the success of the absolute. The full horror of his powerlessness, or, rather, his incapacity to be God, will always burst through from somewhere—perhaps from the happy, conciliatory, and forgiving smile of his victim.

There is only one hatred; there is no difference between individual hatred and group hatred. Anyone who hates an individual is almost always capable of succumbing to group hatred or even of spreading it. I would even say that group hatred—be it religious, ideological, or doctrinal, social, national, or of any other kind—is a sort of funnel that ultimately draws into itself everyone disposed toward hatred. In other words, the most proper background of all group hatred is a collection of people who are capable of hating individuals.

But more than that, collective hatred shared, spread, and deepened by people capable of hatred has a special magnetic attraction and therefore has the power to draw countless other people into its vortex, people who did not initially seem endowed with the ability to hate. They are merely small and morally weak, selfish people with lazy intellects, incapable of thinking for themselves, and therefore susceptible to the suggestive influence of those who hate.

The attraction of collective hatred—infinitely more dangerous than the hatred of individuals for other individuals—derives from several apparent advantages.

1) Collective hatred eliminates loneliness, weakness, powerlessness, a sense of being ignored or abandoned. This, of course, helps people deal with lack of recognition, lack of success, because it offers them a sense of togetherness. It creates a strange brotherhood, founded on a simple form of mutual understanding that makes no demands whatsoever. The conditions of membership are easily met, and no one need fear that he will not pass

muster. What could be simpler than sharing a common object of aversion and accepting a common "ideology of injury" that justifies the aversion expressed to that object? To say, for instance, that Germans, Arabs, blacks, Vietnamese, Hungarians, Czechs, Gypsies, or Jews are responsible for all the misery of the world, and above all for the despair in every wronged soul, is so easy and so understandable! You can always find enough Vietnamese, Hungarians, Czechs, Gypsies, or Jews whose behavior can be made to illustrate the notion that they are responsible for everything.

2) The community of those who hate offers another great advantage to its members. They can endlessly reassure one another of their own worth, either through exaggerated expressions of hatred for the chosen group of offenders, or through a cult of symbols and rituals that affirm the worth of the hating community. Uniforms, common dress, insignia, flags, and favorite songs bring the participants closer together, confirm their identity, increase, strengthen, and multiply their own value in their eyes.

3) Whereas individual aggressiveness is always risky because it raises the specter of individual responsibility, a society of hating individuals in a sense legitimizes aggressiveness. Expressing it as a group creates the illusion of legitimacy, or at least the sense of a "common cover." Hidden within a group, a pack, or a mob, every potentially violent person can dare to do more; each one eggs the other on, and all of them—precisely because there are more of them—justify one another.

4) Ultimately, the principle of group hatred considerably simplifies the lives of all those who hate and all those who are incapable of independent thinking, because it offers them a very simple and immediately recognizable object of hatred. The process of focusing the general injustice of the world onto a particular person who therefore must be hated is made wonderfully easier if the "offender" is identifiable by the color of his skin, his name, his language, his religion, or where he lives.

Collective hatred has yet another insidious advantage: the modest circumstances of its birth. There are many apparently innocent and common states of mind that create the almost unnoticeable antecedents for hatred, a wide and fertile field on which the seeds of hatred will quickly germinate and take root.

Let me at least give you three examples.

Where can this particularizing feeling of universal injustice flourish better than where genuine injustice has been done? Feelings of not being appreciated, logically enough, grow best in a situation where someone really has been humiliated, insulted, or cheated. The best environment for a chronic feeling of injury is one of genuine injury. In short, collective hatred gains veracity and allure most easily wherever a group of people lives in genuine want, in an environment of human misery.

A second example: The miracle of human thought and human reason is bound up with the capacity to generalize. It is hard to imagine the history of the human spirit without this great power. In a sense, anyone who thinks generalizes. On the other hand, the ability to generalize is a fragile gift that has to be handled with great care. It is all too easy to overlook the hidden seeds of injustice that may lie in the act of generalization. We have all made observations or expressed opinions of one kind or another about various peoples. We may say that the French, the English, or the Russians are like this or that. We don't mean ill by it; we are only trying, through our generalizations, to see reality better. But there is a grave danger hidden in this kind of generalization. A group of people defined in a certain way—in this case ethnically—is, in a sense, subtly deprived of its individual spirits and individual responsibilities and endowed with an abstract, collective sense of responsibility. Clearly, this is a wonderful starting point for collective hatred. Individuals become *a priori* bad or evil simply because of their origin. The evil of racism, one of the worst evils in the world today, depends among other things directly on this type of careless generalization.

Finally, the third antecedent of collective hatred I want to mention here is something I would call collective "otherness." One aspect of the immense and wonderful color and mystery of life is not only that each person is different and that no one can perfectly understand anyone else, but also that groups of people differ from one another as groups: in the customs, their traditions, their temperaments, their ways of life and thinking, their hierarchies of values, and of course in their faiths, the colors of their skin, their ways of dressing, and so on. This "otherness" is truly collective. And it is quite understandable that the "otherness" of one group can make it seem, to the group we belong to, surprising, alien, and even ridiculous. And just as we are surprised at how different others are, so others are surprised by how different we are from them.

This "otherness" of different communities can of course be accepted with understanding and tolerance as something that enriches life; it can be honored and respected, even enjoyed. But by the same token, it can be a source of misunderstanding and aversion toward others. And therefore—once again—it is fertile ground for future hatred.

Few of those who move on the thin, ambiguous, and dangerous terrain created by the knowledge of a genuine wrong, the ability to generalize, and that negative awareness of "otherness" can from the outset detect the presence of the cuckoo's eggs of collective hatred that can be laid in this terrain, or that have already been laid there.

Some observers describe Central and Eastern Europe today as a powder keg, an area of growing nationalism, ethnic intolerance, and expressions of collective hatred. This area is often described even as a possible source of future European instability and as a serious threat to peace. In the subtext of such pessimistic reflections, one can sense, here and there, a kind of nostalgia for the good old days of the Cold War, when the two halves of Europe kept each other in check and produced a kind of peace.

I don't share the pessimism of such observers. Even so, I admit that the corner of the world I come from could become—if we do not maintain vigilance and common sense—fertile soil in which collective hatred could grow. This is so for many more or less understandable reasons.

In the first place, you have to realize that living in Central and Eastern Europe are many nations and ethnic groups that have blended together in various ways. It is almost impossible to imagine ideal borders that could separate these nations and ethnic groups into territories of their own. Thus, there are many minorities, and minorities within minorities, within existing borders that are sometimes rather artificial, so that in fact the area is a kind of international melting pot. At the same time, these nations have had very few historic opportunities to seek their own political identity and their own statehood. For centuries they lived under the shelter of the Austro-Hungarian monarchy, and after a brief pause between the wars they were, in one way or another, subjugated by Hitler and then immediately, or shortly thereafter, by Stalin. The nations of Western Europe have had decades and centuries to develop to where they are now; the nations of Central Europe have had only a few years between the two world wars.

Understandably, then, they carry within their collective subconscious a feeling that history has done them wrong. An exaggerated feeling of injustice—a condition for hatred—could quite logically find fertile ground for its birth and growth here.

The totalitarian system that held sway for so long in most of these countries was outstanding, among other things, for its tendency to make everything the same, to control and coordinate things, to make them uniform. For decades it harshly suppressed whatever authenticity—or, if you like, "otherness"—the subjected nations had. From the structure of the state administrations to the red stars on the rooftops, everything was the same—that is, imported from the Soviet Union. Is it any wonder, then, that, the moment these countries rid themselves of the totalitarian system, they suddenly perceived, with unusual clarity, their mutual and suddenly liberated "otherness"? And would it be any wonder if this long-invisible, and therefore necessarily untested and intellectually undigested, "otherness" did not cause surprise? Rid of the uniforms and the masks that were imposed on us, we are looking for the first time into one another's real faces. Something has come about that might be called the "shock of otherness." And this has given rise to another favorable condition for collective aversion, which in the proper circumstances could grow into collective hatred.

The simple fact is not only that the nations of this area have not had enough time to mature as states, but also that they have not had enough time to get used to one another's politically defining otherness.

Here we may once more invoke a comparison with children. In many regards, these nations have simply not had enough time to become political adults.

After all they have gone through, they feel a natural need to make their existence quickly visible and to achieve swift recognition and acknowledgment. They simply wish to be known, to be consulted along with the rest of the world. They want their special "otherness" to be acknowledged. And at the same time, still full of inner uncertainty about themselves and the degree of recognition they enjoy, they look at one another somewhat nervously and ask whether those other nations—which, moreover, have suddenly become as different as themselves—are not stealing some of the attention that is rightfully theirs.

For years the totalitarian system in this part of Europe suppressed civic autonomy and the rights of individuals, whom it tried to turn into pliant cogs in its machine. The lack of civic culture, which the system destroyed, and the general demoralizing pressure may ultimately have encouraged the careless generalizing that always goes along with national intolerance. Respect for human rights, which rejects the principle of collective responsibility, is always the result of a minimal level of civic culture.

It may be clear, from this rather brief and thus necessarily simplified account, that in our part of Europe conditions are relatively favorable for the rise of national intolerance or even hatred.

There is one more important factor here. After the initial joy about our own liberation comes the inevitable phase of disillusionment and depression. It is only now, when we can describe and name everything truthfully, that we see the full extent of the awful legacy left to us by the totalitarian system, and realize how long and difficult will be the task of repairing all the damage.

This state of general frustration may provoke some to vent their anger on substitute victims, who will stand as proxies for the main and now liquidated offender, the totalitarian system. Helpless rage seeks its lightning rod.

I repeat that, if I speak of the nationalistic hatred in Central and Eastern Europe, I'm talking about it not as our certain future but as a potential threat.

We must understand this threat in order to confront it effectively. It is a task that faces all of us who live in the former Soviet bloc.

We must struggle energetically against all the incipient forms of collective hatred, not only on principle, because evil must always be confronted, but in our own interests.

The Hindus have a legend concerning a mythical bird called Bherunda. The bird had a single body but two necks, two heads, and two separate consciousnesses. After an eternity together, these two heads began to hate each other and decided to harm each other. Both of them swallowed pebbles and poison, and the result was predictable: the whole Bherunda bird went into spasms and died, with loud cries of pain. It was brought back to life by the infinite mercy of Krishna, to remind people forever how all hatred ends up.

We who live in the newly created democracies of Europe should remind ourselves of this legend each day. As soon as one of us succumbs to the temptation to hate another, we will all end up like the Bherunda bird.

With this difference: there will be no earthly Krishna around to liberate us from our new misfortune.

The United Nations World Summit for Children

A thousand times over the past decades I have seen backs bent in my country allegedly in the interest of children. A thousand times I have heard people defend their servitude to a hated regime by arguing that they were only doing it for their children: so they could feed them, make it possible for them to study, afford seaside vacations for them. A thousand times both acquaintances and strangers have confided to me that they were heart, mind, and soul totally on our side—that is, on the side of the so-called dissidents—but that they had signed various petitions aimed against us, and organized by the totalitarian government, only because they had children and thus could not afford the luxury of resistance. Immorality was committed in the name of children, and evil was served for their alleged good.

But I have seen even greater perversities, if only in the movies or on television. I saw Hitler waving in a friendly way to fanaticized little girls of Hitlerjugend; I saw the mass murderer Stalin kissing a child wearing the red communist youth-organization scarf, a child whose parents ended up like so many others in gulags; I saw Gottwald, the Stalin of Czechoslovakia, joking with young miners, the builders of socialism who were later to become cripples; I saw the Iraqi President Hussein patting the children of his hostages on the head, hostages whom he now says he is ready to have shot.

I know and have experienced how in Czechoslovakia thousands of people suffered in communist concentration camps, how hundreds of them were executed or tortured to death, and all this for the false happiness of generations yet unborn in some false paradise. How much evil has already been committed in the name of children!

I have also experienced something very different, even as recently as several months ago, a year ago, two years ago. I have experienced a beautiful revolt of children against the lie that their parents had served, allegedly in the interest of those very children. Our antitotalitarian revolution was—at least in its beginnings—a children's revolution. It was high-school students and apprentices, adolescents, who marched in the streets. They marched when their parents were still afraid, afraid for their children and for themselves. They locked their children in at home, took them away from the cities on weekends. Then they began marching with them in the streets. First out of fear for their children, later because they became infected by their enthusiasm. The children evoked from their parents their better selves. They convinced them that they were lying and forced them to take a stand on the side of truth.

And what about the children of dissidents? Although they could not study and had to endure the arrests and persecutions of their parents, they did not blame them but instead respected them. They were drawn more to the moral example than to advantages stemming from a bent back.

Children in our country have demonstrated that the ideology of sacrificing truth in the alleged interest of children is false. They revolted against parents who advocated this ideology; they joined the few who had been convinced from the very beginning that they would serve their children best if they did not look for excuses and did not lie but, rather, lived in truth and thus gave an example to their children.

The international community has achieved something unprecedented. Most of the countries of the world have, within months, joined in an exceptionally good, precise, and exhaustive international agreement for the protection of children. I rejoice, as we all do, in this achievement and am proud that I had the honor of signing the agreement on behalf of my country this morning.

At the same time, however, I do not believe that this agreement—or any other conceivable international document—can protect children from pseudo-protection, that is, from their parents' commission of more evil in the name and in the interest of children—whether they do so in good faith, in self-delusion, or by deliberate lies—nor can it prevent parents from hurting themselves even more than they hurt the children.

As with any law, this one, too, can only acquire real meaning and significance if it is accompanied by real moral awareness, by which I mean the moral awareness of parents.

You cannot put that into a law. However, if it were possible, I would add another paragraph to the agreement I signed this morning. This paragraph would say that it is forbidden for parents and adults in general, in the name and allegedly in the interest of children, to lie, serve dictatorships, inform, bend their backs, be afraid of tyrants, or betray their friends and ideals. And that it is forbidden for all murderers and dictators to pat children on the head.

The Sonning Prize

The prize I've been honored with today is usually given to intellectuals, not to politicians. I am obviously what can be called an intellectual, but at the same time, fate has determined that I find myself—literally overnight—in what is called the world of high politics.

With your permission, I would like to take advantage of my unusual experience and try to cast the critical eye of an intellectual on the phenomenon of power as I have been able to observe it so far from the inside, and especially on the nature of the temptation that power represents.

Why is it that people long for political power, and why, when they have achieved it, are they so reluctant to give it up?

I think the essential reasons for this longing can be divided into three categories.

In the first place, people are driven into politics by ideas about a better way to organize society, by faith in certain values or ideals, be they impeccable or dubious, and the irresistible desire to fight for those ideas and turn them into reality.

In the second place, they are probably motivated by the natural longing every human being has for self-affirmation. Is it possible to imagine a more attractive way to affirm your own existence and its importance than that offered by political power? In essence, it gives you a tremendous opportunity to leave your mark, in the broadest sense, on your surroundings, to shape the world around you in your own image, to enjoy the respect that every political office almost automatically bestows upon the one who holds it.

In the third place, many people long for political power and are so reluctant to part with it because of the wide range of perks that are a necessary part of political life—even under the most democratic of conditions.

These three categories are always, I have observed, intertwined in complicated ways, and at times it is almost impossible to determine which of them predominates. The second and third categories, for instance, are usually subsumed under the first category. I have never met a politician who could admit to the world, or even to himself, that he was running for office only because he wanted to affirm his own importance, or because he wanted to enjoy the perks that come with political power. On the contrary, we all repeat over and over that we care not about power as such but about certain general values. We say it is only our sense of responsibility to the community that compels us to take upon ourselves the burden of public office. At times, only God Himself knows whether that is true, or simply a more palatable way of justifying to the world and ourselves our longing for power, and our need to affirm, through that power and its reach, that we exist in a truly valid and respectable way.

The situation is made more complicated because the need for self-affirmation is not essentially reprehensible. It is intrinsically human, and I can hardly imagine a human being who does not long for recognition, affirmation, and a visible manifestation of his own being.

I am one of those people who consider their term in political office as an expression of responsibility and duty toward the whole community, and even as a sort of sacrifice. But, observing other politicians whom I know very well and who make the same claim, I feel compelled again and again to examine my own motives and ask whether I am not beginning to deceive myself. Might I not be more concerned with satisfying an unacknowledged longing for self-affirmation—a desire to prove that I mean something and that therefore I exist—than I am with pure public service? In short, I am beginning to have suspicions about myself. More precisely, my experience so far with politics and politicians compels me to have these suspicions. In fact, every new prize I receive compels me to be a degree more suspicious.

The third category of reasons for desiring political power— longing for the advantages power brings, or simply getting used to those advantages—deserves special attention. It is interesting to observe how diabolical the temptations of power are, precisely in this sphere. This is best observed among those of us who had never held power of any kind before. Bravely, we used to condemn the powerful for enjoying advantages that deepened the gulf between them and the rest. Now we ourselves are in power.

We are beginning, inadvertently but dangerously, to resemble in some ways our contemptible precursors. It bothers us, it upsets us, but we are discovering that we simply can't, or don't know how to, put a stop to it.

I will give you several examples.

It would make no sense whatever for a government minister to miss an important cabinet discussion of a law that will influence the country for decades to come simply because he has a toothache and has to wait all afternoon at the dentist's until his turn comes. So—in the interests of his country—he arranges to be treated by a special dentist, someone he doesn't have to wait for.

It would certainly not make sense for a politician to miss an important state meeting with a foreign colleague simply because he has been held up by the vagaries of public transport. So—he has a government car and a chauffeur.

It would certainly not make sense for a president or a prime minister to miss such a meeting simply because his car is caught in a traffic jam, so he has the special right to pass cars that are ahead of him or to go through red lights, and in his case the traffic police tolerate it.

It would certainly make no sense for a politician to waste valuable time sweating over a stove and cooking an official meal for a counterpart from abroad. So he has a personal cook and waiters to do it for him.

It would certainly make no sense for the president's cook to go from butcher shop to butcher shop like a normal homemaker in a postsocialist country in search of meat good enough to offer without shame to an important guest. So special deliveries of supplies are arranged for prominent people and their cooks.

It would certainly make no sense if a president or a premier had to look up numbers in the telephone book himself and then keep trying again and again until he reached the person or until the line became free. Quite logically, then, this is done by an assistant.

To sum up: I go to a special doctor, I don't have to drive a car, and my driver need not lose his temper going through Prague at a snail's pace. I needn't cook or shop for myself, and I needn't even dial my own telephone when I want to talk to someone.

In other words, I find myself in the world of privileges, exceptions, perks; in the world of VIPs who gradually lose track of how much butter or a streetcar ticket costs, how to make a cup of coffee, how to drive a car, and how to place a telephone call. I find myself on the very threshold of the world of the communist fat cats whom I have criticized all my life.

And worst of all, everything has its own unassailable logic. It would be laughable and contemptible for me to miss a meeting that served the interests of my country because I had spent my presidential time in a dentist's waiting room, or lining up for meat, or nervously battling the decrepit Prague telephone system, or engaging in the hopeless task of finding a taxi in Prague when I am obviously not from the West and therefore not in possession of dollars.

But where do logic and objective necessity stop and excuses begin? Where does the interest of the country stop and the love of privileges begin? Do we know, and are we at all capable of recognizing, the moment when we cease to be concerned with the interests of the country for whose sake we tolerate these privileges, and start to be concerned with the advantages themselves, which we excuse by appealing to the interests of the country?

Regardless of how pure his intentions may originally have been, it takes a high degree of self-awareness and critical distance for someone in power—however well meaning at the start—to recognize that moment. I myself wage a constant and rather unsuccessful struggle with the advantages I enjoy, and I would not dare say that I can always identify that moment clearly. You get used to things, and gradually, without being aware of it, you may lose your sense of judgment.

Again, being in power makes me permanently suspicious of myself. What is more, I suddenly have a greater understanding of those who are starting to lose their battle with the temptations of power. In attempting to persuade themselves that they are still merely serving their country, they increasingly persuade themselves of nothing more than their own excellence, and begin to take their privileges for granted.

There is something treacherous, delusive, and ambiguous in the temptation of power. On the one hand, political power gives you the wonderful opportunity to confirm, day in and day out, that you really exist, that you have your own undeniable identity, that with every word and deed you are leaving a highly visible mark on the world around you. Yet within that same political power and in everything that logically belongs to it lies a terrible danger: that, while pretending to confirm our existence and our identity, political power will in fact rob us of them.

Someone who forgets how to drive a car, do the shopping, make himself coffee, and place a telephone call is not the same person who had known how to do those things all his life. A person who has never before had to look into the lens of a television camera and now has to submit his every movement to its watchful eye is not the same person he once was.

He becomes a captive of his position, his perks, his office. What apparently confirms his identity and thus his existence in fact subtly takes that identity and existence away from him. He is no longer in control of himself, because he is controlled by something else: by his position and its exigencies, its consequences, its aspects, and its privileges.

There is something deadening about this temptation. Under the mantle of existential self-affirmation, existence is confiscated, alienated, deadened. A person is transformed into a stone bust of himself. The bust may accentuate his undying importance and fame, but at the same time it is no more than a piece of dead stone.

Kierkegaard wrote *Sickness unto Death*. Allow me to paraphrase your excellent countryman and coin the phrase "power unto death."

What may we conclude from this?

Certainly not that it is improper to devote oneself to politics because politics is, in principle, immoral.

What follows is something else. Politics is an area of human endeavor that places greater stress on moral sensitivity, on the ability to reflect critically on oneself, on genuine responsibility, on taste and tact, on the capacity to empathize with others, on a sense of moderation, on humility. It is a job for modest people, for people who cannot be deceived.

Those who claim that politics is a dirty business are lying to us. Politics is work of a kind that requires especially pure people, because it is especially easy to become morally tainted.

So easy, in fact, that a less vigilant spirit may not notice it happening at all.

Politics, therefore, ought to be carried on by people who are vigilant, sensitive to the ambiguous promise of existential self-affirmation that comes with it.

I have no idea whether I am such a person. I only know that I ought to be, because I have accepted this office.

A Concert in Memory of Czechoslovak Holocaust Victims

PRAGUE, OCTOBER 19, 1991

Whenever I am faced with documents on the Holocaust, the concentration camps, the mass extermination of Jews by Hitler, the racial laws, and the endless suffering of the Jewish people during the Second World War, I feel strangely paralyzed: I know that I should say something, do something, draw conclusions, yet I feel that any words would be false, inadequate, inept, or deficient. I can only stand in silence and incomprehension. I know that one must not remain silent, yet I am utterly speechless. That state of paralysis proceeds from a deep—perhaps even a metaphysical—feeling of shame. I am ashamed, if I may put it this way, of the human race. I feel that this is man's crime and man's disgrace, and therefore it is my crime and my disgrace, too. That paralysis allows me to perceive human guilt, and my own co-responsibility for human actions and the condition of our world, from the bottom up. As a human being, I feel responsible for humanity as such and, staring uncomprehendingly at this cruelty, I cease to understand myself—for I, too, am human.

I have been thinking about what it means when we say that the Jews are the Chosen People. One of the things it may mean is that humanity chose them as its scapegoat, as a substitute sacrifice. Aware of their own narrow-mindedness, mediocrity, and inadequacy, tormented by a hopeless lack of self-affirmation, permanently disappointed by the world and by themselves, haunted by the demon of their complexes and unable to cope with their existential grief, people looked for someone to blame for their misfortune, for their wretchedness, for their failure. Such feelings were the breeding ground for anti-Semitism, and subsequently for the Holocaust. Thus, they were a breeding ground for something that compels us to perceive the true weight of our responsibility for this world. And, because of that, we suddenly see that the Jews were chosen in another sense of the word as well: they were chosen by fate for the horrible task of confronting modern man, through their suffering and sacrifice, with his global responsibility, of casting him down to the depth of his true metaphysical self-awareness. A look at the atrocities he is capable of committing awakens him—through shame—to an increased sense of responsibility for the conduct of the whole human community. The senseless suffering of the Jews in the Second World War has thus acquired an additional tragic meaning, and become a lasting challenge to each and every member of the human race to uphold his or her humanity.

It was the hand of a Czech official of the Protectorate that once penned an order, in Czech, containing the following sentence: "Seats may be occupied by Jews only when they are not required for Aryans." It was the hand of a Slovak journalist that once committed to paper, in Slovak, this boastful headline: "The strictest racial laws concerning Jews are Slovak laws."

I believe that orders and newspaper headlines of this kind, written by nonhomicidal murderers, should be forever recorded, as a warning, in all Czech and Slovak history textbooks. I believe that the appeal to our sense of responsibility for this world which speaks to us from the Holocaust era, when thousands of anonymous, nonhomicidal anti-Semites helped send their fellow citizens to the gas chambers, must never again be silenced, suppressed, or pushed out of sight. It must be heard by all future generations.

When I was a little boy I envied some other children the

yellow six-pointed stars they wore on their breasts. I thought it was a badge of honor.

If children are never again to be forced to wear brands on their clothes designed to warn others, to indicate inferiority, we need to remind ourselves over and over again of the horrors that befell the Jewish people, who were chosen to arouse the conscience of humanity through their suffering.

People tend instinctively to avoid what shocks them. Yet we all need to be repeatedly exposed, in our own interest, to a certain kind of shock—one that tells us we cannot evade the universal nature of our responsibility.

We need to talk about the suffering of the Jewish people even though it is so difficult.

University of California, Los Angeles

I have come to beautiful, sunny California from a country where forests are dying, where rivers resemble open sewers, where people are sometimes advised not to open their windows, and where television advertises gas masks for children to wear on their way to and from school. I have come to the West Coast of the United States of America from a small country in the middle of Europe where the borders between fields have been destroyed, the land is eroding, the soil is disintegrating and poisoned by chemical fertilizers that in turn contaminate the groundwater, where birds that used to live in the fields have lost their nesting places and are dying out, where agronomists are forced to combat pests with even more chemicals. I have come from a country that supplies the whole of Europe with a strange export: sulfur dioxide.

For years I was one of those who criticized all this; now I am one of those who are criticized for it.

When I think about what has brought about this terrible state of affairs and encounter on a daily basis obstacles that keep us from taking quick action to change it, I cannot help concluding that its root causes are less technical or economic in nature than philosophical. For what I see in Marxist ideology and the communist pattern of rule is an extreme and cautionary instance of the arrogance of modern man, who styles himself the master of nature and the world, the only one who understands them, the one whom everything must serve, the one for whom our planet exists. Intoxicated by the achievements of his mind, by modern science and technology, he forgets that his knowledge has limits and that beyond these limits lies a great mystery, something higher and infinitely more sophisticated than his own intellect.

I am increasingly inclined to believe that even the term "environment," which is inscribed on the banners of many commendable civic movements, is in its own way misguided, because it is unwittingly the product of the very anthropocentrism that has caused extensive devastation of our earth. The word "environment" tacitly implies that whatever is not human merely envelops us and is therefore inferior to us, something we need care for only if it is in our interest to do so. I do not believe this to be the case. The world is not divided into two types of being, one superior and the other merely surrounding it. Being, nature, the universe—they are all one infinitely complex and mysterious metaorganism of which we are but a part, though a unique one.

Every one of us is a crossroads of thousands of relations, links, influences, and communications—physical, chemical, biological, and others of which we know nothing. Though without humans there would have been no Challenger space shuttle, there would have been no humans without air, water, earth, without thousands of events that could not have been fortuitous and thanks to which there can be a planet on which there can be life. And though each of us is a very special and complex network of space, time, matter, and energy, we are nothing more than their network; we are unthinkable without them, and without the order of the universe, whose dimensions they are.

None of us knows how the quiver of a shrub in California affects the mental state of a coal miner in North Bohemia, or how his mental state affects the quivering of the shrub. I believe that we have little chance of averting an environmental catastrophe unless we recognize that we are not the masters of Being, but only a part of Being, and it makes little difference that we are the only part of Being known so far that is not only conscious of its own being but is even conscious of the fact that it will one day come to an end.

Yet anyone who has said "A" must also say "B." Having recognized that we are no more than tiny particles in the grand physical structure of things, we must eventually recognize that we are also no more than specks in the grand metaphysical structure of things. We must recognize that we are related to more than the present moment and the present place, that we are related to the world as a whole and to eternity. We must recognize that, by failing to reflect universal, supraindividual and supratemporal interests, we do a disservice to our specific, local, and immediate interests. Only people with a sense of responsibility for the world and to the world are truly responsible to and for themselves.

The communist rulers of Czechoslovakia acted according to the principle of *"après nous le déluge."* Hoping that no one would notice, they secured absolute power for themselves by bribing the entire population with money stolen from future generations. Miners extracting low-quality brown coal from open-face mines—coal that was then burned without filters or scrubbers—were satisfied because they could easily buy VCRs and then, tired from work, sit down to watch a video, not noticing that the children watching with them had runny eyes.

Their wives noticed. Glad as they were that their husbands were earning relatively decent wages, they began to suspect what those wages represented; they began to realize that, had the wages been lower and the difference invested in cleaner, more efficient means of generating power, their children would not have chronic conjunctivitis. *"Après nous le déluge"* is the principle of a man who is related to no order but that of his own benefit. It is the nihilistic principle of a man who has forgotten that he is only a part of the world, not its owner, of a man who feels no relation to eternity and styles himself master of space and time.

I believe that the devastation of the environment brought about by the communist regimes is a warning to all of contemporary civilization. I believe that you should read the message coming to you from our part of the world as an appeal to protect the world against all those who despise the mystery of Being, whether they be cynical businessmen with only the interests of their corporations at heart, or left-wing saviors high on cheap ideological utopias. Both lack what I would call a metaphysical anchor, that is, a humble respect for the whole of creation, and a consciousness of our obligation to it.

It is not my intention to lecture anyone, least of all teachers and students of this esteemed university. But I have felt it necessary to share with you the philosophical experience that I, like so many of my fellow citizens, have gained in the environment I come from. I would say that this experience is the principal article that we can and should export from my country at this time.

Were I to encapsulate that experience in one sentence, I would probably phrase it as follows: if parents believe in God, their children will not have to go to school wearing gas masks, and their eyes will be free of pus.

New York University

Imagine the following somewhat absurd situation. A literary critic famous for his merciless judgments and his capacity to expose the minutest dishonesty in a novel or a story is suddenly required to write a novel himself. Naturally, everyone awaits the result with curiosity, and even, perhaps, with a certain malicious delight. How well will he meet the high standards he set before knowing that one day he would have to measure up to them himself?

The situation I have just described is rather like my own. For years I criticized practical politics as no more than a technique in the struggle for power, as a purely pragmatic activity whose aim was not to serve people selflessly and responsibly in harmony with one's conscience, but merely to win their favor through a variety of techniques, with a view to staying in power or gaining more.

As an independent intellectual and on principle a lifelong opponent of the ruling regime, I continually expounded on *my* notion of politics—politics as selfless service to one's fellow human beings, as morality in practice, based on conscience and truth. I tentatively termed this kind of politics "nonpolitical politics." I wrote about it because I felt the need and the obligation, as a writer, to take a stand on the immoral nature of the totalitarian system I lived in and the policies pursued by those who embodied that system. I would have betrayed my mission as a writer had I remained silent in the face of all that. I did not pursue this inquiry because I wanted to engage in practical politics myself, or because I believed I would make a better politician than others.

And then the revolution broke out, and I suddenly found

myself, almost overnight, at the head of my country. I had neither aspired to this position nor striven to attain it. Destiny had indeed played a strange joke on me, as if it were telling me, through all those who persuaded me to accept the office: Since you think you're so smart, now is your chance to show everyone you have ever criticized the right way to do things.

In short, I was not unlike the literary critic who must now write a novel that measures up to the standards he once applied to other novelists.

And so, not surprisingly, I am now in a rather unenviable position. All my political activities, and perhaps all the domestic and foreign policies pursued by Czechoslovakia as well, are being examined under a microscope I once constructed myself without knowing where it would lead.

Nor is it surprising that the question most frequently put to me by reporters, and by foreign journalists in particular, is how the notion of "life in truth" or "nonpolitical politics" stands up in practice. Now that I hold a high public office myself, have I had to reconsider the views I once advocated as an independent critic of politics and politicians?

Recently I answered that question in the following words:

"There may be some who won't believe me, but after a year and a half of being president in a land full of problems that presidents in stable democracies never even dream of, I can safely say that I have not been compelled to recant anything of what I wrote earlier, or to change my mind about anything. It may seem incredible, but it is so. Not only have I not had to change my mind, but my opinions have even been confirmed.

"Despite the political distress I face every day, I am still deeply convinced that politics is not an essentially disreputable business; and to the extent that it is, it is only disreputable people who make it so. I would concede that it can, more than other spheres of human activity, tempt one to disreputable practices, and that it therefore places higher demands on people. But it is simply not true that a politician must lie or intrigue. That is an utter nonsense, put about by people who—for whatever reasons—

want to discourage others from taking an interest in public affairs.

"Of course, in politics, as anywhere else in life, it is impossible and pointless to say everything, all at once, to just anyone. But that does not mean having to lie. All you need is tact, the proper instincts, and good taste. One surprising experience from 'high politics' is this: I have discovered that good taste is more useful here than a degree in political science. It is largely a matter of form: knowing how long to speak, when to begin, and when to finish; how to say something politely that your opposite number may not want to hear; how to say, always, what is most significant at a given moment, and not to speak of what is not important or relevant; how to insist on your own position without offending; how to create the kind of friendly atmosphere that makes complex negotiations easier; how to keep a conversation going without prying or being aloof; how to balance serious political themes with lighter, more relaxing topics; how to plan your official journeys judiciously and know when it is more appropriate not to go somewhere; when to be open and when reticent, and to what degree.

"But more than that, it means having a certain instinct for the time, the atmosphere of the time, the mood of the people, the nature of their worries, their frame of mind—that, too, can perhaps be more useful than sociological surveys. An education in political science, law, economics, history, and culture is an invaluable asset to any politician, but I have been persuaded, again and again, that it is not the most important asset. Qualities like fellow feeling, the ability to talk to others, insight, the capacity to grasp quickly not only problems but also human character, the ability to make contact, and a sense of moderation: all these are immensely more important in politics. I am not saying, heaven forbid, that I myself an endowed with these qualities; not at all! These are merely my observations.

"To sum up: If your heart is in the right place and you have good taste, not only will you pass muster in politics, you are destined for it. If you are modest and do not lust after power, not only are you suited to politics, you absolutely belong there. The *sine qua non* of a politician is not the ability to lie; he need only be sensitive and know when, to whom, and how to say what he has to say. It is not true that a person of principle does not belong in politics; it is enough for his principles to be leavened with patience, deliberation, a sense of proportion, and an understanding of others. It is not true that only the unfeeling cynic, the vain, the brash, and the vulgar can succeed in politics; such people, it is true, are drawn to politics, but in the end, decorum and good taste will always count for more.

"I think my experience and observations confirm that politics as the practice of morality is possible. I do not deny, however, that it is not always easy to go that route, nor have I ever claimed that it was."

I wrote that several weeks ago, while reviewing my experience of the presidency. I had no way of knowing then that, soon afterward, I would again discover that there are occasions when it is indeed difficult to go that route. Again, fate played a joke on me. It punished me for my self-assurance by exposing me to an immensely difficult dilemma. A democratically elected Parliament passed a bill that I considered to be morally flawed, yet our constitution required me to sign it. What was I to do?

The bill aimed at preventing those who had violated human rights in the past from working in the civil service. The citizens of my country find it hard to accept that, when they have dealings with the public administration, they often encounter the same people who were working there under the totalitarian regime. Their anger at this is justified, and Parliament's desire to purge the public service is entirely legitimate. The problem is that the legislation is based on the principle of collective responsibility; it prohibits certain persons from holding certain positions solely because they belonged to groups defined by their external characteristics. It does not allow their cases to be heard individually. This runs counter to the basic principles of democratic law. The files kept by the now abolished secret police are made the final and sole arbiter of eligibility to work. It is a necessary law, an extraordinary law, a rigorous law. Yet, from the viewpoint of fundamental human rights, it is fraught with problems.

What was I to do?

Essentially, I had two choices. The first was to do my duty, sign the bill, thus confirming its validity, and learn to live with the fact that my signature was on a paper whose contents I could not fully support. The second choice was simply to refuse to sign the bill. In that case, it would have gone into effect even without my signature, and I would have found myself in open conflict with Parliament, creating a political crisis and further destabilizing the country. It would have been a morally upright yet immensely risky act of civil disobedience, one typical of a dissident. My friends fell into two camps; some recommended that I sign it, others that I refuse.

I finally decided on a third alternative: I signed the bill and then proposed that Parliament amend it. Under the constitution, Parliament is obliged to consider my proposal, though not to act upon it. It may thus easily come to pass that the bill with my name on it, having become law, will remain valid in its present wording, and that a number of people will be treated unfairly as a result.

I do not know whether my resolution of the dilemma was a good one or not. I do not know whether I have helped or harmed my fellow citizens. I do not know whether my signature on the bill, combined with the proposal for its amendment, is a novel that would meet the literary critic's standards I once applied to novelists. History can probably be the only judge of that.

Even after this experience, I still do not think that politics, by its very nature, requires one to behave immorally.

My latest experience, however, makes me want to underline five times a sentence that, until a few weeks ago, I thought unnecessary to underline even once: that the way of a truly moral politics is neither simple nor easy.

World Economic Forum

For many years, decades in fact, the West was defined against the background of the communist world. As a common enemy and a common threat, it was this communist world that kept the West united, both politically and in terms of security arrangements. Against its will, it also helped the West strengthen, cultivate, and develop its time-tested principles and values, such as civil society, parliamentary democracy, market economy, and human and civil rights. Confronted by the gloomy, dangerous, and expansionist world of communist totalitarianism, the West was continually proving its commitment to freedom, truth, democracy, broader cooperation, and growing prosperity. In other words, the communist world was instrumental in the West's own self-affirmation.

Yet, in a way, it was a rather equivocal self-affirmation. There was something soothing about it. While stimulating many good things, it also led Western politics to embrace unwittingly certain stereotypes that grew from a feeling that its own status was beyond question. The "nontime" and "nonhistory" of the totalitarian regimes infected the West as well. The West became too used to the bipolar division of the world into blocs based on power and ideology. It became too used to the status quo of the Cold War, to nuclear peace, and to things' staying pretty much the way they were.

As the eighties became the nineties, the whole Second World, as it used to be known, exploded and, in a rather frenzied fashion, caved in on itself. In its place, a crater has suddenly opened up before the eyes of an astonished world, one that is now spewing forth a lava of postcommunist surprises. Mixed up in this lava is a long-forgotten history coming back to haunt us, a history full of thousands of economic, social, ethnic, territorial, cultural, and political problems that remained latent and unnoticed under the surface of totalitarian tedium.

As far as I can tell, this explosion astonished the West as much as it did the East. In a way, it has put Western policy-making into a state of shock. Every day we see evidence of how difficult it is for the West to respond and adjust to the new reality, to break itself of established habits. The West feels that everything has changed, but it does not know exactly what to do about it. We have even begun to hear expressions of nostalgia for the days when the world was easier to understand. How can we deal with all these new states that have broken away from the older systems of order forged in Helsinki, Yalta, and Versailles? How are we to respond to the demise of centralized economies and the threat of economic and social crises that go along with it? What are we to do about regional conflicts, actual or potential, about eruptions of ethnic passions and hatreds? How will we cope with the geopolitical changes—so difficult to foresee—that will result from these developments?

It seems that the West is not only somewhat confused by these tremors in the East, it is beginning to shake a little itself as the structure of its former certainties is beginning to come loose. A broad range of geopolitical interests, rivalries, and ambitions, dormant until recently, are now coming back to life. Alliances unquestioned until recently are now being called into question, because the pressures that once made them necessary are disappearing. Particular interests buried by history are suddenly emerging and clashing. There are even signs here and there of the temptation to exploit the demise of the divided world to create new divisions.

In short, the end of communism took us all by surprise. But we all know and understand it by now, at least to a certain extent. With your permission, I would like to talk about another aspect of these developments, one that is less visible, yet more profound and substantial. It is an aspect of the matter that, to my knowledge, has not yet made the front pages.

The end of communism is, first and foremost, a message to the human race. It is a message we have not yet fully deciphered and comprehended.

In its deepest sense, the end of communism has, I believe, brought a major era in human history to a close. It has brought a close not just to the nineteenth and twentieth centuries, but to the modern age as a whole.

The modern era has been dominated by the culminating belief, expressed in different forms, that the world—and Being as such—is a wholly knowable system governed by a finite number of universal laws that man can grasp and rationally direct for his own benefit. This era, beginning in the Renaissance and developing from the Enlightenment to socialism, from positivism to scientism, from the Industrial Revolution to the information revolution, was characterized by rapid advances in rational, cognitive thinking. This, in turn, gave rise to the proud belief that man, as the pinnacle of everything that exists, was capable of objectively describing, explaining, and controlling everything that exists, and of possessing the one and only truth about the world. It was an era in which there was a cult of depersonalized objectivity, an era in which objective knowledge was accumulated and technologically exploited, an era of belief in automatic progress brokered by the scientific method. It was an era of systems, institutions, mechanisms, and statistical averages. It was an era of freely transferable, existentially ungrounded information. It was an era of ideologies, doctrines, absolute interpretations of reality, an era when the goal was to find a universal theory of the world, and thus a universal key to unlock its prosperity.

Communism was the perverse extreme of this trend. It was an attempt, on the basis of a few propositions masquerading as the only scientific truth, to organize all of life according to a single model, and to subject it to central planning and control regardless of whether or not that was what life wanted.

The fall of communism can be regarded as a sign that modern thought—based on the premise that the world is objectively knowable, and that the knowledge so obtained can be absolutely generalized—has come to a final crisis. This era has created the first global, or planetary, technical civilization, but it has reached the limit of its potential, the point beyond which the abyss begins. I think the end of communism is a serious warning to all mankind. It is a signal that the era of arrogant, absolutist reason is drawing to a close, and that it is high time to draw conclusions from that fact.

Communism was not defeated by military force, but by life, by the human spirit, by conscience, by the resistance of Being and man to manipulation. It was defeated by a revolt of color, authenticity, history in all its variety, and human individuality against imprisonment within a uniform ideology.

This powerful signal, this important message to the human race, is coming at the eleventh hour.

We all know that our civilization is in danger. The population explosion and the greenhouse effect, holes in the ozone layer, AIDS, the threat of nuclear terrorism, the dramatically widening gap between the rich North and the poor South, the danger of famine, the depletion of the biosphere and the mineral resources of the planet, the expansion of commercial-television culture, and the growing threat of regional wars—all this combined with thousands of other things represents a general threat to mankind.

The large paradox at the moment is that man—a great collector of information—is well aware of all this, yet is absolutely incapable of dealing with the danger to himself. Traditional science, with its usual coolness, can describe the different ways we might destroy ourselves, but it cannot offer us truly effective and practicable instructions on how to avert them. There is too much to know; the information is muddled or poorly organized; these processes can no longer be fully grasped and understood, let alone contained or halted. Modern man, proud of having used impersonal reason to release a giant genie from its bottle, is now impersonally distressed to find he can't drive it back into the bottle again.

We cannot do it because we cannot step beyond our own shadow. We are trying to deal with what we have unleashed by employing the same means we used to unleash it in the first place. We are looking for new scientific recipes, new ideologies, new control systems, new institutions, new instruments to eliminate the dreadful consequences of our previous recipes, ideologies, control systems, institutions, and instruments. We treat the fatal consequences of technology as though they were a technical defect that could be remedied by technology alone. We are looking for an objective way out of the crisis of objectivism.

Everything would seem to suggest that this is not the way to go. We cannot devise, within the traditional modern attitude to reality, a system that will eliminate all the disastrous consequences of previous systems. We cannot discover a law or theory whose technical application will eliminate all the disastrous consequences of the technical application of earlier laws and theories.

What is needed is something different, something larger. Man's attitude toward the world must be radically changed. We have to abandon the arrogant belief that the world is merely a puzzle to be solved, a machine with instructions for use waiting to be discovered, a body of information to be fed into a computer in the hope that sooner or later it will spit out a universal solution.

It is my profound conviction that we have to release from the sphere of private whim and rejuvenate such forces as a natural, unique, and unrepeatable experience of the world, an elementary sense of justice, the ability to see things as others do, a sense of transcendental responsibility, archetypal wisdom, good taste, courage, compassion, and faith in the importance of particular measures that do not aspire to be a universal, thus an objective or technical, key to salvation. Things must once more be given a chance to present themselves as they are, to be perceived in their individuality. We must see the pluralism of the world, and not bind it by seeking common denominators or reducing everything to a single common equation. We must try harder to understand rather than to explain. The way forward is not in the mere construction of universal systemic solutions, to be applied to reality from the outside; it is also in seeking to get to the heart of reality through personal experience. Such an approach promotes an atmosphere of tolerant solidarity and unity in diversity based on mutual respect, genuine pluralism, and parallelism. In short, human uniqueness, human action, and the human spirit must be rehabilitated.

The world, too, has something like a spirit or soul. That, however, is something more than a mere body of information that can be externally grasped and objectified and mechanically assembled. Yet this does not mean we have no access to it. Figuratively speaking, the human spirit is made from the same material as the spirit of the world. Man is not just an observer, a spectator, an analyst, or a manager of the world. Man is a part of the world, and his spirit is part of the spirit of the world. We are merely a peculiar node of Being, a living atom within it, or, rather, a cell that, if sufficiently open to itself and its own mystery, can also experience the mystery, the will, the pain, and the hope of the world.

The world today is a world in which generality, objectivity, and universality are in crisis. This world presents a great challenge to the practice of politics, which, it seems to me, still has a technocratic, utilitarian approach to Being, and therefore to political power as well. After they have gone through the mill of objective analysis and prognosis, original ideas and actions, unique and therefore always risky, often lose their human ethos and therefore, *de facto*, their spirit. Many of the traditional mechanisms of democracy created and developed and conserved in the modern era are so linked to the cult of objectivity and statistical average that they can annul human individuality. We can see this in political language, where cliché often squeezes out personal tone. And when personal tone does crop up, it is usually calculated, not an outburst of individual authenticity.

It is my impression that sooner or later politics will be faced with the task of finding a new, postmodern face. A politician must become a person again, someone who trusts not only a scientific representation and analysis of the world, but also the world itself. He must believe not only in sociological statistics, but in real people. He must trust not only an objective interpretation of reality, but also its soul; not only an adopted ideology, but also his own thoughts; not only the summary reports he receives each morning, but also his own instincts.

Soul, individual spirituality, firsthand personal insight into things, the courage to be oneself and go the way one's conscience points, humility in the face of the mysterious order of Being, confidence in its natural direction, and, above all, trust in one's own subjectivity as the principal link with the subjectivity of the world—these, in my view, are the qualities that politicians of the future should cultivate.

Looking at politics "from the inside," as it were, has if anything confirmed my belief that the world of today—with the dramatic changes it is going through, and in its determination not to destroy itself—presents a great challenge to politicians.

It is not that we should simply seek new and better ways of managing society, the economy, and the world as such. The point is that we should fundamentally change how we behave. And who but politicians should lead the way? Their changed attitude toward the world, toward themselves, and toward their responsibility can in turn give rise to truly effective systemic and institutional changes.

You have certainly heard of the "butterfly effect." It is a belief that everything in the world is so mysteriously and completely interconnected that a slight, seemingly insignificant wave of a butterfly's wings in a single spot on this planet can unleash a typhoon thousands of miles away.

I think we must believe in this effect for politics. We cannot assume that our microscopic yet truly unique everyday actions are of no consequence simply because they apparently cannot resolve the immense problems of today. That would be an *a priori* nihilistic assertion, and an expression of the arrogant, modern rationality that believes it knows how the world works.

But what do we really know about it?

Can we say that a casual conversation between two bankers and the Prince of Wales over dinner in Davos tonight will not sow a seed from which a wonderful flower will one day grow for the whole world to admire?

In a world of global civilization, only those who are looking for a technical trick to save that civilization need feel despair. But those who believe, in all modesty, in the mysterious power of their own human Being, which mediates between them and the mysterious power of the world's Being, have no reason to despair at all.

Asahi Hall

This is my first visit to Japan, and my first day of that visit. But at every step I have encountered something I have always found fascinating about Japan, though my knowledge of it is rudimentary and mostly theoretical: the way in which life in this country—a great economic power at the pinnacle of contemporary technological civilization—is imbued with a profound spiritual and intellectual tradition, with esteem for its own history as well as for the order of nature, and with respect for the human virtues cultivated here over centuries. This experience has prompted me to use the opportunity to reflect on a question that is very current in the part of the world I come from, and which also happens to be one of my main personal concerns as well. The question relates to the presence and activity of the intellectual—who should be the guardian and the bearer of spiritual qualities—in the realm of practical politics.

The totalitarian system of the communist type, as established in the former Soviet Union and subsequently imposed on all countries in the Soviet sphere of influence, not only destroyed political pluralism and the prospects of real political opposition, but annihilated politics itself as a field of practical human activity. All power ultimately became concentrated in the hands of a strictly centralized bureaucracy. Consequently, politicians were gradually replaced by mere administrators who obediently carried out the will of the power center.

If there was something that could be called an opposition, it appeared mostly in the intellectual milieu. The riskier expressions of public protest against the communist system most frequently came, for entirely understandable reasons, from rebellious writers, artists, scholars, and scientists.

Occasionally, they came from those who had originally belonged to the power apparatus but later broke with it or, having manifested dissenting views, were expelled from it. Broader circles of the population sometimes revolted as well, but such revolts—so often suppressed—were frequently headed or masterminded by intellectuals.

Thus, when the totalitarian system began to break down in the Soviet bloc in 1989, and especially when it was crumbling— as if swept away by an avalanche—in the countries of Central and Eastern Europe, it was quite natural that many of the leaders of the popular revolts were intellectuals well known for their earlier criticisms of the ruling regime. It was natural, too, that the revolutionary movements elevated a number of them to the highest public offices. Because our countries had no professional democratic politicians to call upon, there was no other solution. And so—in the initial phase at least—many so-called dissidents, most of whom were and had always been somewhat rebellious, liberal-minded, independent intellectuals, came to power.

Poets, philosophers, singers became members of Parliament, government ministers, or even presidents. The president of Bulgaria is a philosopher, and the vice-president of that country is a poet. In Hungary the president is a writer and the prime minister a historian. The president of Lithuania is a pianist. Poland has a leader of the workers' revolt as head of state, but around him, both in government and in Parliament, there are intellectuals who belonged to the former opposition and were for many years leading figures in the protest against communist power. The president of Czechoslovakia is a playwright, and in our Parliament and government, as well as in the leadership of the newly emerging political parties, you will find philosophers, journalists, economic theorists and forecasters. The situation is similar in other postcommunist countries.

The leaders of stable and prosperous democracies, on the other hand, tend to be experienced politicians who have received a proper education, engaged in politics since their youth, dedicated their lives to it, and held many public offices in succession. When such people deal with the postcommunist countries, their counterparts are often people whom one might call, with a touch of malice, political amateurs or beginners. This is one of the great paradoxes of the moment.

A British friend of mine has said that one of the biggest problems of the postcommunist states lies in the leaders' inability to make up their minds about who they are: are they independent intellectuals or practicing politicians? In his opinion, they have to confront this dilemma and draw the necessary conclusions. They could relinquish their posts to those who have chosen to become career politicians and once again become independent intellectuals, taking advantage of the new freedom to fulfill their essential mission, which is to hold up a critical mirror to their surroundings. Or they could turn professional themselves—that is, become real politicians, give up their intellectual habits, and submit to the strict rules that have traditionally applied to those who wish to practice politics successfully in functioning democracies.

I completely understand this kind of thinking, because I know well, from my own experience and that of many of my colleagues, how difficult it is for an independent intellectual to adjust overnight to the world of practical politics when he has spent his whole life critically analyzing the world and defending certain chemically pure tenets. Where a quick and unequivocal decision has to be made between two alternatives, neither of which is ideal, an intellectual will tend to resort to philosophical mediation, which in most cases makes things worse than they would have been even had he opted for the worse alternative.

Where he should make a clear, simple, comprehensible appeal, he may feel inclined to launch into complex reflections that voters find difficult to follow. When he should say in clear and unambiguous terms that he is running for office because he is the best person for the job, and then campaign to get elected, he is beset by doubts about his qualifications; he hesitates, refuses to fight, questions his own motives, and constantly reassures people of something they do not want to hear, which is that he is not lusting after power and will only accept the office out of necessity, as an act of self-sacrifice.

People do not want leaders who understand their mission as sacrifice and suffering. Where he should be pragmatic and open to workable compromises, he invokes his commitment to a principle and becomes incapable of communication. Where, on the contrary, he should stand up for a principle and risk a clash, he invokes the notion of tolerance and tries, with excessive and even masochistic fervor, to see things the way his opponent does. When life, necessity, political realities, and the responsibility of public office require him to defend something he would strongly condemn were he still a free intellectual, he feels embarrassed, and his evasions are worse than a decisive word by someone who has always known that politics is the art of the possible.

Besides, a politician must also be a good executive officer, surrounding himself with efficient people and delegating responsibility. An intellectual has never supervised or employed anyone; consequently, he will tend to do everything himself and work to the point of exhaustion, though the output of his office is often rather meager and almost imperceptible. Because he is likely to be a sensitive soul, he takes this—as he does everything else—very much to heart. It distresses him and often drives him to despair and depression. I could go on for some time describing all the handicaps of an intellectual in politics.

So I understand very well what my British friend has in mind. I know he means well, because for years he supported opposition intellectuals in our part of the world and is now concerned that their impractical and inept presence on the political scene may ultimately jeopardize the fruits born of the struggle they waged for so many years.

And yet I must admit that something in me is reluctant to accept that there are only two courses of action to choose from.

What if this is not the case at all?

What if the strange situation in which many independent

intellectuals in the postcommunist countries have found themselves is not a dilemma, but a historic challenge? What if in fact it
were to challenge them to introduce a new tone, a new element,
a new dimension into politics? It may well be that destiny, by
thrusting us so unexpectedly into this position, actually meant to
entrust us with a special mission.

I have said more than once that the decades we spent under
totalitarianism were not entirely wasted. They gave us a specific
intellectual and spiritual experience that can be drawn upon
and put to good use and can help increase our knowledge of
ourselves. I do not believe that we can do no more than turn to
the developed world with repeated requests for assistance. I believe that we, too, have something special to offer to the rest of
the world.

What if that something were a new wind, a new spirit, a new
spirituality that might be injected into the established stereotypes
of present-day politics?

I do not know if this is what will happen. But why should we
automatically rule out such a possibility?

When I look around the world today I feel strongly that contemporary politics needs a new impulse, one that would add a
badly needed spiritual dimension. Perhaps this impulse will come
from some place other than the postcommunist countries. Yet it
seems to me that come it must.

Civilization today is at a crucial juncture. On the one hand, it
has fantastic achievements to its credit; on the other hand, it is
largely civilization's fault that the human race as a whole is now
endangered, perhaps for the very first time. A population explosion, combined with a rapidly widening gap between rich and
poor, the resulting danger of major ethnic and social unrest, the
acute threat to the environment, the inexorable depletion of the
mineral resources of the earth, the existence of nuclear arsenals
capable of annihilating life which some states are so reluctant and
slow to give up—all these and many other things create a huge,
dangerous cloud that hangs over us and could well burst unless
something happens.

And where else could that something happen but in the sphere of the spirit, of human consciousness and self-knowledge, of man's relationship to himself and to the world? What else must be changed but the way modern man looks at himself? Where but in politics should such a change begin if it is to bear fruit? And how else should it begin but by changing the very spirit and ethos of politics?

It is, of course, improper for a politician to give in to depression and despair. It is even less proper to show this in public. On the other hand, I believe it would be a good thing if politicians were more emotionally committed, not only to their own political fate but also to the fate of the world. Rather than merely seeking to satisfy the many special interests and pressures they must accommodate if they wish to stay in power, they should listen more to the voice of their unique, individual conscience—the way poets do.

That is why I wonder whether genuine intellectuals, philosophers, and poets are not virtually duty-bound to stop fearing and loathing politics and to take upon themselves all the risks and requirements that go with it, even though they find them rather strange. Is it not time for intellectuals to try to give politics a new and, as it were, postmodern face?

Who, for that matter, is better equipped to perceive the global context in which political actions take place, to assume a share of the responsibility for the state of the world, and to restore to political prominence values such as conscience, love for one's fellow humans, and respect for nature, for the order of Being, and for the pluralism of cultures? Who else should give politics that much-needed spiritual and transcendental dimension and bring to it that dwindling supply of human perception and sensitivity? Who else is equipped to combat the growing notion that politicians are power-grabbing machines run by public-relations experts and tuned solely to the public opinion of the moment?

Of course, I do not consider it right to entrust people who are poor managers with the management of public offices. Someone who cannot speak to voters in clear and understandable terms is not the right person to seek their favor. Nor do I think it right to replace decision-making with philosophizing and dreaming.

It merely seems to me that the world of politics should be widely humanized and its intellectual and spiritual dimension cultivated. Politics, in my view, should be more than just the art of the possible, and power should not be an end in itself. I believe that even the least significant politician in the least significant country should feel responsible not only to his party, his constituency, and his state, but also for the fate of at least a fraction of the miracle of creation, the one represented by the human race and life on this planet. Obviously, he cannot feel that way if he has no experience of transcendence.

Philosophers and poets in ministerial chairs will not, of course, single-handedly save the world. But they could—under certain circumstances—contribute to its salvation.

We live in a world of specialists and specializations. Politics, too, is becoming far too much the domain of specialists—people who have received special schooling and have special interests. In my view, however, politics should be principally the domain of people with a heightened sense of responsibility and a heightened understanding of the mysterious complexity of Being. If intellectuals claim to be such people, they would virtually be denying the truth of that claim by refusing to take upon themselves the burden of public office on the grounds that it would mean dirtying their hands. Those who say that politics is disreputable in fact help make it so.

As I said before, I do not know whether history will not ultimately prove my British friend right, with his concern that poets catapulted into high politics by the fall of communism will do nothing but harm unless they surrender their previous identity, or at least a greater part of it. But I do believe that their presence in politics could contribute something that politics badly needs. That, of course, can happen only if they learn to move in politics in a way that develops rather than denies their identity.

Thus, I think of what has happened to certain independent intellectuals in the postcommunist countries as a task, or a challenge—a challenge to take a great risk and launch a great adventure. It is up to us, and us alone, to demonstrate that we are able to meet this challenge and fulfill this task. It is up to those of us whom fate has put in this position to demonstrate whether my British friend has shown foresight, or has simply been too influenced by the banal idea that everyone should stick to his own trade.

The Academy of Humanities and Political Sciences

PARIS, OCTOBER 27, 1992

The honor you have bestowed upon me by electing me to the famous French Academy of Humanities and Political Sciences is a great source of encouragement to me in the present and of commitment for the future. If I am to be one of you until the end of my days, I must be worthy of it until the end of my days. I promise you I will try.

It is my pleasant duty—in the spirit of the wonderful tradition of this academy—to recall with deep respect my predecessor, the Italian economist Giuseppe Ugo Papi, whose life's work was concerned, among other things, with creating and developing international structures for economic cooperation, and who was important far beyond the borders of his native country.

I come to you from a country that waited many long years for its freedom. Allow me to use this opportunity for a brief consideration of the phenomenon of waiting.

There are different ways of waiting.

At one end of the great spectrum there is waiting for Godot, who embodies universal salvation. For many of us who lived in the communist world, waiting was something very close to this extreme position. Surrounded, bound, and as it were internally colonized by the totalitarian system, people lost the sense that there was a way out. They lost the will to do anything; they lost the feeling that there was anything they could do. They simply lost hope. But they did not and indeed could not lose the need for hope, because without hope a meaningful life is impossible. So they waited for Godot. Because they did not carry hope within them, they expected it to arrive as some kind of salvation from the outside. But Godot—at least as one who is expected—will not come, because he simply doesn't exist. He only represents hope. He is not hope itself, but an illusion. He is the product of our own helplessness, a patch over a hole in the spirit. The patch itself is full of holes. It is the hope of people without hope.

On the other end of the spectrum there is waiting of another kind: that is, patience. For us this waiting was based on the knowledge that it made sense on principle to resist by speaking the truth simply because it was the right thing to do, without speculating whether it would lead somewhere tomorrow, or the day after, or ever. This kind of waiting grew out of the faith that repeating this defiant truth made sense in itself, regardless of whether it was ever appreciated, or victorious, or repressed for the hundredth time. At the very least, it meant that someone was not supporting the government of lies. It also, of course, grew out of the faith—but this is of secondary importance—that a seed once sown would one day take root and send forth a shoot. No one knew when. But it would happen someday, perhaps for future generations.

This stance—for simplicity's sake, let us call it the dissident stance—assumed and cultivated patience. It taught us how to wait. It taught us waiting as patience, waiting as a state of hope, not as an expression of hopelessness. Whereas waiting for Godot is a meaningless form of self-deception and therefore a waste of time, this second type of waiting does have meaning; it is not a sweet lie but a bitter truth, and time spent in this kind of waiting is not wasted. To wait until good seeds sprout is not the same as waiting for Godot. Waiting for Godot means waiting for lilies we have never planted to grow.

I should make it clear that citizens of the communist world could not be divided into dissidents and those who merely waited for Godot. To a certain extent, all of us waited for Godot at times, and at other times were dissidents. It's just that some of us might have been more the former, and others more the latter.

Nevertheless, this experience can be simplified to the recognition that there are different kinds of waiting.

Obviously, I am thinking about this not because I feel a strong nostalgia for the past. I am trying to determine what this experience means for the present and for the future.

Allow me to be personal for a moment. Although I am trained in the dissident type of patience based on the awareness that waiting has a meaning, nevertheless, in the three years since our peaceful, antitotalitarian revolution I have been seized again and again by a desperate impatience. I have agonized over how slowly things were changing. My country still didn't have a new, democratic constitution; Czechs and Slovaks could not agree on whether they wished to live in one country or in two; we were not moving swiftly enough toward the Western democratic world and its structures; we were having trouble coming to terms with our own past; we were too slow to get rid of the legacy of the old regime and the moral poverty it left behind.

I longed desperately for at least some of these problems to be resolved so that I could cross them off the list and put them out of the way. I longed for some visible, tangible, indisputable evidence that something was finished, over and done with. I found it difficult to accept that politics, like history itself, is a never-ending process, in which nothing is ever definitively over.

It was as though I had forgotten how to wait, to wait in the way that has meaning.

And only now, when I have had a little time to step back and think about all this, am I beginning to understand that, in my impatience, I succumbed to precisely the thing I had criticized: the destructive impatience of contemporary technocratic civilization. This grows out of a vain belief in the primacy of reason and it assumes erroneously that the world is nothing but a crossword puzzle to be solved, that there is only one correct way—the so-called objective way—to solve it, and that it is entirely up to me whether I succeed or not. Without even being aware of it, I, too, submitted to the perverted belief that I was the master of reality, that the only task was to improve reality according to some existing recipe, that it was entirely up to me when I did it, and thus that there was no reason not to do it right away.

In short, I thought time belonged to me.

It was, of course, a big mistake.

The world, Being, and history have their own time. We can, of course, enter that time in a creative way, but none of us has it entirely in his hands. The world and Being do not heed the commands of the technologist or the technocrat, and they do not exist to do his bidding. They resist his sense of time, just as they resist a broad interpretation of their sense of time. And just as they have their own secrets and their own mystery, which is constantly catching modern enlightenment rationality off guard, they also take their own, meandering course. If we give in to the desire to eradicate this unfathomable meandering by erecting some monstrous dam, we risk a great deal, from the loss of groundwater to catastrophic changes in the biosphere.

If I consider my own political impatience, I realize with new urgency that a politician of the present and the future—allow me to use the expression "postmodern politician"—must learn, in the deepest and best sense of the word, the importance of waiting. I don't mean waiting for Godot; his waiting must be the expression of respect for the inner dynamics and tempo of Being, for the nature of things, for their integrity and their independent dynamics, which resist coercive manipulation. He must have the will to open events to the possibility of manifesting themselves as they really are, in their essence. His actions cannot derive from impersonal analysis; they must come out of a personal point of view, which cannot be based on a sense of superiority but must spring from humility.

The world cannot be brought under total control because it is not a machine. Nor can it be rebuilt from the ground up merely on the basis of a technological idea. Utopians who believe this sow even greater suffering than what they seek to alleviate. If reason is disengaged from the unique human spirit and becomes the main guide to political action, it can only lead to the use of force, to violence. The world will resist an order forced upon it by a brain that has forgotten that it is itself merely a modest aspect of the world's infinitely rich morphology. And the more systematically and impatiently the world is crammed into rational categories, the more explosions of irrationality there will be to astonish us.

Yes, even I—the sarcastic critic of all those who vainly attempt to explain the world—had to remind myself that the world cannot just be explained, it must be grasped and understood as well. It is not enough to impose one's own words on it; one must also listen to the polyphony of often contradictory messages the world sends out and try to penetrate their meaning. It is not enough to describe, in scientific terms, the mechanics of things and events; their spirit must be personally perceived and experienced. We cannot merely follow the timetable we have set for our influence on the world; we must also honor and respect the infinitely more complex timetable the world has set for itself. That timetable is the sum of the thousands of independent timetables of an infinite number of natural, historical, and human actions.

You cannot wait for Godot.

Godot will not come, because he does not exist.

In fact, you can't even fabricate Godot. A typical example of a fabricated Godot—that is, a Godot that actually shows up and is therefore a false Godot—is communism. It was supposed to save us, but it ended up only destroying us.

There was, in fact, something communistic in my impatience to renew democracy. Or, in more general terms, something of a rationally enlightened nature. I wanted to nudge history forward in the way a child would when wishing to make a flower grow more quickly: by tugging at it.

I think the art of waiting is something that has to be learned. We must patiently plant the seeds and water the ground well, and give the plants exactly the amount of time they need to mature.

Just as we cannot fool a plant, we cannot fool history. But we must water history as well, patiently and every day. We must water it not just with understanding, not just with humility, but with love.

If politicians and citizens learn to wait in the best sense of the word—that is, as a way of respecting the inner order of things we are never allowed to see into fully—if they understand that everything in the world has its own time and that, in addition to what they desire from the world and history, what the world and history themselves aspire to is also important, then humanity will not necessarily turn out as badly as it sometimes seems it might.

I come from a country that is full of impatient people. Perhaps they are impatient because they have waited for Godot for so long that they think Godot has finally come. This is an error as profound as the one on which their waiting was based. Godot did not come. And that is just as well, because any Godot that did come would be merely the imaginary Godot, the communist Godot. What came to fruition had to come to fruition. Perhaps it would have come to fruition sooner had we watered it better. But now we have a single task. We have to take this harvest, extract from it the seeds, sow them again, and patiently water them.

If we are certain that the planting was good and that we are watering regularly, we have no reason to be impatient. It is enough to realize that our waiting has a meaning.

Waiting that has meaning because it grows out of hope and not hopelessness, from faith and not despair, from humility toward the time of the world and not out of fear of its sublime tranquillity, is accompanied not by boredom but by suspense. This kind of waiting is more than just waiting.

It is life. Life as the joyous involvement in the miracle of Being.

Wrocław University

I have many friends in Poland who for years, as so-called dissidents, resisted the communist regime. I myself was in a similar position for a long time. We used to meet, aware of the closeness if not the identity of our points of departure and our aims. We felt that we were on the same boat and we tried, through all available means, to help one another and to work together. Great historical changes later carried many of us into the world of high politics, and we were forced to assume direct responsibility for the political development of our countries.

Today—roughly three years after these changes—we may observe an interesting phenomenon in Czechoslovakia and, to a certain extent, in Poland as well. People with a dissident past often meet with unexpected criticism and even resistance. In many cases their past, rather than standing in their favor, is held against them. They are no longer seen as heroes of the antitotalitarian revolutions, or even as saviors of their countries, and the evolution of democracy often pushes them out of politics altogether to make way for people who, so far, are less well known but—genuinely or not—are more realistic and thus more adaptable in everyday practical politics. This phenomenon has many different causes and could be the subject for a lengthy essay, if not a whole book.

I would like to use this occasion, when I have been named an honorary doctor of Wrocław University—an important intellectual center—for a brief discussion of a theme related to the phenomenon I have just described—that is, the theme of the intellect in politics, or, rather, the intellectual and spiritual dimension of politics. Former dissidents, or some of them at least, are criticized for being dreamers, idealists, or moralists who do not belong in real politics because—as in Baudelaire's famous poem about a poet—they are like "the prince of clouds" who is prevented by "giant wings" from walking on the earth.

This criticism may be true of some, and it may malign others. But either way, it is no accident that the theme of the spiritual or moral dimension of politics is raised here. The political substance of the so-called dissident stance was of a somewhat different nature, and had a different structure and different sources, from normal political activity in free circumstances. Against the vastly superior power of the totalitarian system stood individuals who, despite the risks involved and the uncertainty of any real changes occurring, repeated over and over that the emperor was wearing no clothes. This Sisyphean, almost quixotic stance originated mainly in the moral or existential field, in a heightened feeling of personal responsibility for the world. That is, the political activity of the dissidents had, far more obviously than it might have in conditions of freedom, a spiritual or moral dimension. Their way of thinking and behaving, their values, the claims they made, their style of work, their standards of success and failure—in short, much of what grew out of that stance—can rightly appear inappropriate, alien, impractical, and idealistic when transferred to real politics in democratic conditions.

The question I pose goes as follows: Does this mean that if we wish to pass muster in practical politics we must forget about our past, renounce our former way of thinking and acting, and completely adapt to the radical new circumstances? Or, on the contrary, does the new situation in which we find ourselves challenge us to enliven and enrich practical politics by attempting to introduce something of what had been unique to us in the past? That is, should we try—in a way appropriate to the new circumstances, of course—to reinforce precisely what is so often lacking in the politics of today: its spiritual and moral dimension? Pressured by the conventions, stereotypes, and models of behavior that commonly dominate politics today, are we to give up on the imperatives that guided us in the past and thus alter our selves? Or should we try—under the pressure of those imperatives—to change politics?

As you will certainly have guessed, I lean toward the second alternative. Naturally, the dissidents' dramatic cry from the dark depths of totalitarian conditions is indeed a somewhat different genre of human endeavor from, for example, the complex negotiation of an international agreement. Many forms of work, habit, and style simply cannot be brought from dissident activity into practical politics, and to try to do so would not only make no sense, but might even cause a great deal of harm. I'm not talking now of genres and forms, however; I'm talking about essence and substance, and even though I run the risk of providing my opponents with yet another argument for the claim that I am an incorrigible dreamer, I must say that the attempt to breathe something of the dissident experience into practical politics ought to be made. More than that, I think it is our responsibility. We went through certain experiences, we came to certain conclusions, and this, I think, enjoins us to evaluate their meaning and to enrich politics with it. Perhaps it is risky, and perhaps it won't succeed. But why should those who, in their own time, triumphed precisely because they were not afraid of risk and failure, fear them now?

Nevertheless, some things are easy to say but hard to do. For two and a half years, I was the first noncommunist president our country had had for many decades, and at the same time I was its last president: Czechoslovakia, as you certainly know, will cease to exist in nine days. So I know better than anyone else how difficult it sometimes is for a politician to stand up for his principles and his ideals when he finds himself in the middle of a dramatic clash of freely evolving political forces, at the intersection of all kinds of social pressure. If, despite my recent experience, I say what I say, perhaps people will believe that I mean it seriously.

But how are we to infuse politics with the spiritual and moral dimension I have in mind here? What does that mean in practical terms?

The dissident movement was not typically ideological. Of

course, some of us tended more to the right, others to the left, some were close to one trend in opinion or politics, others to another. Nevertheless, I don't think this was the most important thing. What was essential was something different: the courage to confront evil together and in solidarity, the will to come to an agreement and to cooperate, the ability to place the common and general interest over any personal or group interests, the feeling of common responsibility for the world, and the willingness personally to stand behind one's own deeds. Truth and certain elementary values, such as respect for human rights, civil society, the indivisibility of freedom, the rule of law—these were notions that bound us together and made it worth our while to enter again and again into a lopsided struggle with the powers that be.

By politics with a spiritual dimension, I do not understand a politics that is merely a technological competition for power, limited to what can be practically achieved and seeking primarily to satisfy this or that particular interest. Nor do I mean a politics that is concerned merely with promoting a given ideological or political conception. And I certainly do not mean a politics based on the idea that the end justifies the means. I mean, rather, a politics deriving from a strong and utterly personal sense of responsibility for the world, a politics deriving from the awareness that none of us—as an individual—can save the world as a whole, but that each of us must behave as though it were in his power to do so. I certainly don't need to emphasize that the origin of such a sense of responsibility is metaphysical.

The starting point of this politics is neither the will to power nor an ideological vision of the world but, rather, a moral stance. Everything beyond that—the whole rich palette of emphases, principles, values, and aims that can be imagined under the notion of politics with a spiritual dimension—can be explained and grasped only as a consequence of this very simple and understandable basic stance.

The politics I refer to here cannot be enshrined in or guaranteed by any law, decree, or declaration. We cannot hope that any single, specific political act might bring it about. Only the aim of an ideology can be achieved; the aim of the kind of politics I mean is never completely attainable, because this politics is nothing more than a permanent challenge, a never-ending effort that can only—in the best possible case—leave behind it a certain trace of goodness. This trace can then naturally be found, though in an imperfect form, in many different things, from the spirit of the laws, to everyday political decisions, right down to the general political climate in areas where it has had an impact.

There naturally exist many specific values, principles, ideas, and measures that can reveal the influence or impact of such a politics. Nevertheless, this politics cannot be reduced to any of that. That is, it cannot be identified with a system of theses that would entirely define it, as is the case with ideological politics. It consists in something far more subtle and difficult to grasp. It resides in a spirit or ethos that can emanate from a specific political act but that never ends with that act.

For instance, one can imagine a foreign-policy initiative that demonstrably does not merely pursue the selfish interests of a country, but instead displays a feeling of common responsibility for the fate of all of human society, its freedom, its plurality, and its life in peace. A domestic policy aimed at integration and stability and enabling mutual understanding might display the same qualities. Economic, ecological, social, and even educational and cultural policies can be imagined in which the policy-makers were obviously more concerned about general and lasting interests than about particular, momentary interests; that they were more concerned about the multiplicity of social life than about a single dimension of it; that they were more concerned about creating conditions that are human and humanly bearable than making quick political capital or implementing a particular ideological proposition. It is obvious that the center of their interest is the unique human being, not just some political theory.

It is possible to imagine thousands of tiny, inconspicuous, everyday decisions whose common denominator is precisely the spirit and ethos of a politics that is aware of the global threat to the human race and does not support general consumer resignation but, rather, seeks to awaken a deeper interest in the state of the world and rally the will to confront the threats hanging over it. Above all, however, it is possible to imagine that, through the agency of thousands of properly chosen, carefully combined, and well-timed public actions, the positive local climate in a country—that is, a climate of solidarity, creativity, cooperation, tolerance, and deepening civic responsibility—can slowly, inconspicuously, but steadily be strengthened.

What is at issue here is not a set of dogmas, postulates, and ideological theses but a political style, a political atmosphere, the inner spirit of politics. The point is that political activity ought to have human contours and aim to create conditions that display these human contours, which are not marked by an effort to serve humanity merely by serving abstract claims about what is in its interests. Human interests can never be forced into a single, unambiguous demand. All forms of generalized knowledge are important, of course, but only when their application is accompanied by things as apparently banal and mysterious as compassion, a sense of peace, taste, appropriateness, solicitude, understanding, solidarity.

I repeat again that this is easy enough to say but difficult to do. To follow this path demands infinite tenacity, infinite patience, much ingenuity, iron nerves, great dedication, and, last but not least, great courage. I am in no way claiming to know how to walk this path myself. Nevertheless, I feel that, in today's dramatic, confused, and generally endangered world, that is precisely the path we must take. And I feel that the specific dissident experience can—when carefully thought through and evaluated—provide this kind of politics with a solid foundation, with inspiration, with something to measure up to. Naturally, I do not know whether we will succeed. Only time will tell.

Advent is almost here, a time of heightened expectation, a time of great hope. For all of us, I wish that hope may genuinely return to our lives. We are awaiting a new birth. May a new and decent spirit be born as well in the public life of our two fraternal countries!

The George Washington University

WASHINGTON, D.C., APRIL 22, 1993

I remember a time when some of my friends and acquaintances used to go out of their way to avoid meeting me in the street. Though I certainly did not intend it to be so, they saw me, in a way, as a voice of their conscience. They knew that if they stopped and talked with me they would feel compelled to apologize for not openly defying the regime, too, or to explain to me why they could not do it, or to defend themselves by claiming that dissent was pointless anyway. Conversations like this were usually quite an ordeal for both sides, and thus it was better to stay away from them altogether.

Another reason for their behavior was fear that the police were following me, and that merely talking to me would cause them complications. It was easier not to go near me, for thus they would avoid both an unpleasant conversation and the potential persecution that could follow. In short, I was, for those friends, an inconvenience. And inconveniences are best avoided.

For long decades, the chief nightmare of the democratic world was communism. Today—three years after it began to collapse like an avalanche—it would seem as though another nightmare has replaced it: postcommunism. There were many, not just in the West but in the East as well, who had been looking forward to the fall of communism for years, and who had hoped that its collapse would mean that history had at last come to its senses. Today, these same people are seriously worried about the consequences of that fall. Some of them may even feel a little nostalgic for a world that was, after all, slightly more transparent and understandable than the present one.

I do not share sentiments of that kind. I think we must not understand postcommunism merely as something that makes life difficult for the rest of the world. I certainly did not understand communism that way. I saw it chiefly as a challenge, a challenge to think and to act. Postcommunism represents that kind of challenge to an even greater extent.

Anyone who understands a given historical phenomenon merely as an inconvenience will ultimately see many other things the same way: the warnings of ecologists, public opinion, the vagaries of voters, public morality. It is an easy and therefore seductive way of seeing the world and history. But it is extremely dangerous, because we tend to remain aloof from things that inconvenience us and get in our way, just as some of my acquaintances avoided me during the communist era. Any position based on the feeling that the world, or history, is merely an accumulation of inconveniences inevitably leads one to turn away from reality, and ultimately to resign oneself to it. It leads to appeasement, even to collaboration. The consequences of such a position may be suicidal.

What in fact do we mean by postcommunism? Basically, it is a term for the state of affairs in all the countries that have rid themselves of communism. But it is a dangerous simplification to put all these countries in one basket. Though it is true that they are all faced with essentially the same task—that is, ridding themselves of the disastrous legacy of communism, repairing the damage it caused, and creating, or renewing, democracy—at the same time, and for many reasons, there are great differences between them.

I will not go into all the problems encountered by postcommunist countries; experts are no doubt already writing books on the subject. I will mention only some of the root causes of the phenomena that arouse the greatest concern in the democratic West, phenomena such as nationalism, xenophobia, and the poor moral and intellectual climate which, to a greater or lesser extent, accompanies the creation of a new political and economic system.

The first of these causes lies in the fact that communism was far from being simply the dictatorship of one group of people over another. It was a genuinely totalitarian system—that is, it penetrated every aspect of life and deformed everything it touched, including all the natural ways people had developed of living together. It profoundly affected all forms of human behavior. For years, a specific structure of values and models of behavior was deliberately fostered in the consciousness of society. It was a perverted structure, one that went against all the natural tendencies of life, but society nevertheless internalized it, or, rather, was compelled to internalize it.

When communist power and its ideology collapsed, this structure collapsed along with it. But people could not immediately absorb and internalize a new structure—one corresponding to the elementary principles of civil society and democracy. The human mind and human habits cannot be transformed overnight; to build a new system of living values and to learn to identify with them takes time.

In a situation where one thing has collapsed and something new does not yet exist, many people feel hollow and frustrated. This state is fertile ground for phenomena such as scapegoat-hunting, radicalism of all kinds, and the need to hide behind the anonymity of a group, whether socially or ethnically based. It encourages hatred of the world, self-affirmation at all costs, the feeling that everything is now permitted, and the unparalleled flourishing of selfishness that goes along with this. It gives rise to the search for a common and easily identifiable enemy, to political extremism, to the most primitive cult of consumerism, to a carpetbagging morality, stimulated by the historically unprecedented restructuring of property relations, and so on and on.

Thanks to its former democratic traditions and to its unique intellectual and spiritual climate, the Czech Republic, the westernmost of the postcommunist countries, is relatively well off in this regard, compared with some of the other countries in the region. Nevertheless, we, too, are going through the same great transformation as are all the postcommunist countries, and we can therefore talk about it from inside knowledge.

Another factor that must be considered in any analysis of postcommunist phenomena is the intrinsic tendency of communism to make everything the same. The greatest enemy of communism was always individuality, variety, difference—in a word, freedom. From Berlin to Vladivostok, the streets and buildings were decorated with the same red stars. Everywhere the same kind of celebratory parades were staged. Analogical state administrations were set up, along with a whole system of centrally directed social and economic life. This great shroud of uniformity, suffocating all national, intellectual, spiritual, social, cultural, or religious variety, glossed over any differences and created the monstrous illusion that we were all the same.

The fall of communism destroyed this shroud of sameness, and the world was caught napping by an outburst of the many unanticipated identities concealed beneath it, each of which—after such a long time in the shadows—felt a natural need to draw attention to itself, to emphasize its uniqueness and its difference from others. This is the reason for the eruption of so many different kinds of old-fashioned patriotism, revivalist messianism, conservatism, and expressions of hatred toward all those who appear to be betraying their roots or identifying with different ones.

The desire to renew and emphasize one's identity, one's uniqueness, is also behind the emergence of many new states. Nations that have never had countries of their own feel an understandable need to experience independence. It is no fault of theirs that the opportunity has arisen decades or even centuries after it came to other nations.

This circumstance is related to yet another matter. For a long time, communism brought history, and with it all natural development, to a halt. Whereas the Western democracies have had decades to forge a civil society, to build internationally integrated structures, and to learn the arts of peaceful international coexistence and cooperation, the countries ruled by communism could not go through this creative process. National and cultural differences were driven into subterranean areas of social life, where they were kept on ice and thus prevented from developing freely, from taking on modern forms in the fresh air, from creating, over time, the free space of unity in variety.

At the same time, many of the nations suppressed by communism had not enjoyed freedom even before its advent, and thus had not had a chance to resolve many of the basic questions of their existence as countries. Consequently, thousands of problems have suddenly burst forth into the light of day, problems left unresolved by history, problems we had wrongly supposed were long forgotten. It is truly astonishing to discover how, after decades of falsified history and ideological manipulation and massaging, nothing has been forgotten. Nations are now remembering their ancient achievements and their ancient suffering, their ancient suppressors and their allies, their ancient statehood and their former borders, their traditional animosities and their affinities—in short, they are suddenly recalling a history that, until recently, had been carefully concealed or misrepresented.

Thus, in many parts of the so-called postcommunist world, it is not just the regional order (sometimes referred to as the Yalta order) that is being corrected. There are also attempts to correct certain shortcomings in the Versailles order, and even to go further back into history and exploit the greatest freedom some of them have ever had to make complete amends. It is an impossible desire, of course, but understandable nevertheless.

If we wish to grasp the problems of the postcommunist world, or some of them at least, then we must continually remind ourselves of something else. It is easy to deny the latent problems, ambitions, and particularities of nations. It is easy to make everything the same by force, to destroy complex and fragile social, cultural, and economic relationships and institutions built up over centuries, and to enforce a single, primitive model of central control in the spirit of a proud utopianism. It is as easy to do that as it is to smash a piece of antique, inlaid furniture with a single blow from a hammer. But it is infinitely more difficult to restore it, or to create it directly.

The fall of the communist empire is an event on the same scale of historical importance as the fall of the Roman Empire. And it has similar consequences, both positive and extremely disturbing. It heralds a significant change in the countenance of today's world. The change will be painful and will take a long time. To build a new world on the ruins of communism might be as long and complex a task as the creation of a Christian Europe—after the great migrations—once was.

What are we to do if we do not wish to understand post-communism simply as a new inconvenience that would be better avoided by sticking our heads in the sand and minding our own business?

I think the most important thing is to take account not just of external and more or less measurable phenomena like the gross national product, the progress of privatization, the stability of the political system, and the discernible degree to which human rights are observed. All of these things are important, of course, but something more is necessary. There must be an effort to understand the deep events taking place in the womb of post-communist societies, to take note of their historical meaning, and to think about their global implications.

It must be understood that these are not the curious woes of a distant and circumscribed part of the world, but events that concern everyone, and all of our present-day civilization. The temptation must be resisted to adopt a disparaging and slightly puzzled attitude, one based on a subconscious feeling of superiority on the part of observers who happen to be better off. Just as Czechs should not sneer at the problems of Tadzhikistan, no one should sneer at the problems of the Czech Republic. Any point of departure, therefore, should involve deep insight and a deep sense of co-responsibility. It is only against this background of empathy that meaningful ways of assisting can be sought.

It seems to me that the challenge offered by the post-communist world is merely the current form of the broader and more profound challenge to discover a new type of self-comprehension for man, and a new type of politics that should flow from that understanding. As we all know, today's planetary civilization is in serious danger. Modern man thinks of himself as the lord of creation and not just a part of it, and his vanity is rapidly destroying his hope of survival. Because he is not grounded in a humble respect for the order of Being, modern man allows himself to be driven by his particular interests. He is no longer capable of governing his behavior in a way that takes account of the general interest.

We are rationally capable of describing, in vivid detail, all the dangers that threaten the world: the deepening gulf between its rich and poor parts, the population explosion, the potential for dramatic confrontations between different racial and cultural groups—the arming of whom no one seems able to stop—the nuclear threat, the plundering of natural resources, the destruction of the natural variety of species, the creation of holes in the ozone layer, and unstoppable global warming. What is unsettling is that, the more we know about such dangers, the less we seem able to deal with them.

I see only one way out of this crisis. We must come to a new understanding of ourselves, our limitations, and our place in the world. We must grasp our responsibility in a new way, and re-establish a relationship with the things that transcend us. We must rehabilitate our human subjecthood, and liberate ourselves from the captivity of a purely rational perception of the world. Through this subjecthood and the individual conscience that goes with it, we must discover a new relationship to our neighbors and to the universe and its metaphysical order, which is the source of the moral order.

We live in a world in which our destinies are tied to one another more closely than ever before. It is a world with a single planetary civilization, yet it contains many cultures that, with increasing vigor and single-mindedness, resist unification, reject mutual understanding, and exist in what amounts to latent confrontation. It is a deeply dangerous state of affairs, and it must be changed.

The first step in this direction can be nothing less than a broadbased attempt by these cultures to understand one another, and to affirm one another's right to existence. Only then can a kind of worldwide pluralistic metaculture, a self-preservational minimum on which everyone can agree, begin to form. It is only in the context of such a metaculture that a new sense of political responsibility—global responsibility—can come into being. And it is only with this newborn sense of responsibility that the instruments can be created which will allow humanity to deal with all the dangers it has created for itself.

The new political self-understanding I am talking about clearly entails a definitive departure from an understanding of the world that considers history, foreign cultures, foreign nations, and ultimately all those warnings about our future as a mere agglomeration of annoying inconveniences that disturb our tranquillity.

A quiet life on the peak of a volcano is just as illusory as the notion I mentioned at the beginning: that, by avoiding an encounter with a dissident in the street, we can avoid the problem of communism and the question of how to deal with it.

Ultimately, I understand postcommunism as one of many challenges to contemporary man—regardless of what part of the world he lives in—to awaken to his global responsibilities, and to awaken to them before it is too late.

This morning I had the honor of taking part in the opening of the Holocaust Memorial Museum.

On this occasion, as I have so often before, I asked myself how this could have happened. How could people in the twentieth century—who are aware of the theory of relativity and quantum mechanics, who have penetrated to the heart of the atom and are exploring the reaches of outer space—have committed acts of horror so atrocious that to call them bestial would be an incredible disservice to all those creatures who happen not to be human? How could we have permitted it to happen?

In the context of my ruminations here, one aspect of a possible answer occurs to me. It was a failure of democracy, the politics of appeasement, giving way to evil: what in my country we call the spirit of Munich. The inability of Europe and the world to recognize the emerging evil in time and to stop it from growing to such monstrous proportions is merely a consequence of understanding the world as an agglomeration of inconvenience. The issue here is the absence of a wider sense of responsibility for the world.

Czechs remember well a statement made by a democratic statesman shortly before he signed the Munich Agreement, the real beginning of all the horrors of the Second World War. He was appalled, he said then, that his country was digging trenches and trying on gas masks "because of a quarrel in a faraway country between people of whom we know nothing." This is a classic example of how suicidal it is to try to sidestep difficulties. This politician regarded Nazism as a problem that would go away if he stuck his head in the sand, or—as it were—crossed over to the other side of the street.

And so the Chosen People were chosen by history to bear the brunt for us all. The meaning of their sacrifice is to warn us against indifference to things we foolishly believe do not concern us.

In today's world, everything concerns everyone. Communism also concerned everyone. And it is also the concern of everyone whether or not, and in what way, we manage to build a new zone of democracy, freedom, and prosperity on its ruins.

Every intellectual and material investment in the postcommunist world that is not haphazard but based on a deep understanding of what is happening here will repay the whole world many times over.

More than that, it will also be one more step on the thorny path the human race is taking toward a new understanding of its responsibility for its own destiny.

The Onassis Prize for Man and Mankind

ATHENS, MAY 24, 1993

As a man whose lifelong endeavors have been associated with the struggle for democracy in his country, I am deeply moved to find myself—for the first time in my life—in Athens, the cradle of democracy, to receive here a most prestigious award.

It is here, in this city and in this country, that the notion of democracy was born two and a half thousand years ago. Let us give thought to the question of how the meaning of this term differs now from what it meant then, and what aspects of that difference could be of interest to us at this particular time.

I shall tell you where I see the biggest difference. Ancient Greek democracy was inseparably linked with the institution of the agora, the marketplace, where political decisions were reached through dialogue as citizens enjoying equal rights talked to one another directly, face to face. Nowadays, direct conversation among citizens, and between citizens and politicians, has become a marginal phenomenon. Indirect contacts, filtered through a whole system of intermediate links, or perhaps I could even say "intermediate worlds," have a far greater weight now.

This is quite understandable. Small city-states, where all those who shared in the rights of citizenship could easily assemble in one square, and where nearly all citizens may have known one another, have given way to states with populations of dozens and sometimes hundreds of millions. Consequently contacts, including communication between members of the public and the politicians who represent them, are conveyed by a variety of instruments, such as the stratified system of representative democracy, the powerful megamachineries of large political parties, or the methods of communication most characteristic of the present times—that is, the media.

Under these circumstances, many people hardly ever see a politician as a person anymore. Instead, a politician is a shadow they watch on television, not knowing whether he is speaking impromptu or reading from a prompter hidden behind the cameras a text written for him by anonymous advisers or experts. Citizens no longer perceive the politician as a living human being, for they have never seen and will never see him that way. They respond only to his image, created for them by TV, radio, and newspaper commentators. If they want to ask a politician a question they can usually do so only in writing, and will receive a reply from a nameless member of his staff. If they decide to vote for him in an election they often cannot give their vote to him alone but must vote for a political party as well, and with it, for a number of other politicians about whom they know nothing and for whom they care nothing, on a list they could not have influenced because such lists are put together by party committees the voters neither know nor elect. Politics ceases to be a part of the citizen's immediate life and becomes something like a peculiar TV show, which could be comic or tragic, but which they can only watch passively.

From the politicians' viewpoint, citizens are equally distant. They too seem no more than a shadow, a collectivized, anonymous mass speaking in most cases only through data produced by opinion polls. It also happens, rather often, that politicians do not actually talk to each other but only to one another's shadows as they appear in the media.

I have had direct experience of this myself. Often, what the press wrote, or did not write, about a remark I made somewhere proved to be of far greater consequence than the remark itself. Democratic choice in such cases ceases to be a choice between alternatives people are familiar with and have personally tried; it becomes, instead, a choice between alternatives offered by those who run the media. And when a citizen feels the urge to take part in decision-making on matters of general interest—that is, to engage in politics—he has no choice but to join one of the existing political parties, and before he can devote his intellect to the affairs of his community he must try to secure his rise within the party. Those to whom this path is unacceptable may find that there is no place for them in politics, and, though they live in a world that claims to be based on the principle of equality of civil rights, they must resign themselves to being never entirely equal to others.

I find it fantastic that today's civilization makes it possible for the whole world to witness important events, no matter where they happen, in the same instant. It is marvelous that people can communicate with each other immediately when they want to, and that they can meet at a few hours' notice. I also deem it immensely important that politics is under the scrutiny of a free and independent press.

The only thing that worries me is the depersonalization and dehumanization of politics that has come about with the progress of civilization. An ordinary human being, with a personal conscience, personally answering for something to somebody, and personally and directly taking responsibility, seems to be receding further and further from the realm of politics. Politicians seem to have turned into puppets that only look human and move in a giant, rather inhuman theater; they appear to have become merely cogs in a huge machine, objects of a major automatism of civilization which has gotten out of control and for which nobody is responsible.

Today's world, as we all know, is faced with multiple threats. From whichever angle I look at this menace, I always come to the conclusion that salvation can come only through a profound awakening of man to his own personal responsibility, which is at the same time a global responsibility. Thus, the only way to save our world, as I see it, lies in a democracy that recalls its ancient Greek roots: democracy based on an integral human personality personally answering for the fate of the community.

I believe in face-to-face contact—the kind of communication

that prevailed at the agora. The great challenge of the present era is to seek out forms of democracy that suit the present times while they revive the very face-to-face contact that marked the birth of democracy.

The modern era has reached a point of culmination, and if we are not to perish of our modernness we have to rehabilitate the human dimension of citizenship as well as of politics. This is what I consider to be the principal challenge of our time, a challenge for the third millennium.

The Council of Europe Summit

I think that all of us—whether from the West, the East, the South, or the North of Europe—can agree that the common basis of any effort to integrate Europe should be the wealth of values and ideals we share. Among them are respect for the uniqueness and the freedom of each human being, for a democratic and pluralistic political system, for a market economy, and for the principles of civil society and the rule of law. We respect the notion of unity in diversity and share a determination to foster creative cooperation among the different nations, ethnic, religious, and cultural groups, and spheres of civilization that exist in Europe.

This intellectual and spiritual basis of European civilization is the product of thousands of years of coexistence, of the intermingling of many traditions, and of vast historical experience, both good and bad. The fall of communism has presented our continent with a unique opportunity to unite on that foundation and to become—for the first time in a very long time, if not in history—a stabilizing force in the world. Despite general agreement on the values upon which European integration should stand, this process has, four years after the fall of the Iron Curtain, encountered a number of obstacles. Many are even beginning to doubt that the process can succeed, that it can lead to the kind of Europe in which everyone will feel at ease, in which no one will feel repressed or threatened, and no one will have any reason to behave aggressively.

What are the reasons for this discrepancy between the possibilities and the reality? Why, so soon after the collapse of a bipolar Europe, and at a time when we all appear to want the same things, do we suddenly feel so much doubt? Why does a goal that seemed within reach at the beginning of 1990 now seem so distant?

There are many reasons for this state of affairs, but I feel strongly that they all have one thing in common: the erroneous belief that the great European task before us is a purely technical, purely administrative, or purely systemic matter, and that all we need to do is come up with ingenious structures, new institutions, and new legal norms and regulations. In short, we behave as though we need do no more than discuss exhaustively, or, more precisely, argue exhaustively, over technical matters, without ever attempting to change anything in ourselves or in the habitual motives and stereotypes of our behavior. Thus, the very values that were to be secured by systemic changes get lost in the tangle of debates over those changes. In other words, what was to have been no more than a means to an end becomes the central topic of discussion. This weakens our very capacity to agree.

Many of the great supranational empires and alliances in history, or at least many of those that survived for long periods of time and enriched the human history of their era in some way, not only had strong central ideas that promoted intellectual and spiritual advancement, they were also remarkably determined to stand behind these ideas and willing to make great sacrifices to bring them to fruition, because it was clear to everyone that those sacrifices were worth it. This was more than just a belief in certain values; it was a deep and generally shared feeling that those values carried with them moral obligations.

This, I fear, is precisely what is critically lacking in the Europe of today. We argue about quotas, tariffs, and interest rates. We assert our own partial and often very selfish interests, whether they concern geopolitical, ideological, economic, or other matters. We hope we can solve the problem of minorities by agreeing on how many hours children must spend learning their mother tongue in school, or which road signs should be bilingual. And so, all too often, we succumb to the notion that, should we manage to discover a formula for compromise with which everyone agrees, we will have succeeded. Yet administrative measures, general treaties, and high-sounding declarations—the products of long negotiations among specialists—will hardly save us if they are not the expression of a common European purpose. Only such a purpose can guarantee that the agreements and measures we do adopt will not remain just scraps of paper.

The greatness of the idea of European integration on democratic foundations consists in its capacity to overcome the old Herderian idea of the nation-state as the highest expression of national life. Thus, European integration should—and must, if it is to succeed—enable all the nationalities to realize their national autonomy within the framework of a broad civil society created by the supernational community. The greatness of this idea lies in its power to smother the demons of nationalism, those instigators of modern wars, and to enable nations to live in peace, security, freedom, and prosperity by forgoing some of their immediate interests in favor of the far greater benefits of realizing their long-term interests.

To put it more succinctly, Europe today lacks an ethos; it lacks imagination, it lacks generosity, it lacks the ability to see beyond the horizon of its own particular interests, be they partisan or otherwise, and to resist pressure from various lobbying groups. It lacks a genuine identification with the meaning and purpose of integration. Europe appears not to have achieved a genuine and profound sense of responsibility for itself as a whole, and thus for the future of all those who live in it.

Are we really so incorrigible? Twice in this century all of Europe has paid a tragic price for the narrow-mindedness and lack of imagination of its democracies. These democracies first failed when confronted with Nazism; they retreated and refused to resist this evil in the bud, only to have to pay a million times more in the struggle against Nazism in full bloom. They failed a second time when they allowed Stalin to swallow up half of our continent and bring history there to a halt. Today, this failure is tragically coming back to haunt not only those who have recently escaped from Soviet tyranny, but everyone.

There is a saying: "Everything good and evil comes in threes." Democratic Europe cannot afford a third failure.

And yet I am afraid a third such failure is looming. I am thinking not only of the caution and indecision that mark the attitudes of the developed countries of Western Europe toward the postcommunist countries. I am thinking chiefly of how they have behaved so far in relation to events in Bosnia and Herzegovina, and in the whole of the former Yugoslavia. The aim of the peace talks ought to be a comprehensive defense of precisely those values on which the future Europe should stand—that is, the values of a civil society based on the peaceful coexistence of various ethnic groups and cultures. Instead they are, more and more blatantly, an occasion to argue over the borders of ethnically purified ministates, as defined by clashes between illegal armies. An internationally recognized multinational state is being divided into parcels according to the dictates of fanatical warlords.

Such behavior, regardless of how well intentioned—and didn't Chamberlain have the best of intentions?—sanctifies the idea of the "ethnically pure state" and gives up on the idea of the civil society. We talk and talk, we drown in compromises, we redraw the maps, we read the lips of the ethnic cleansers, and, with increasingly serious consequences, we forget the fundamental values upon which we would like to shape the future of our continent. We are cutting off the very branch we are sitting on.

The reason for this sad state of affairs is simple. It lies in the erroneous belief that we can somehow outwit history and in the ostrichlike belief that the need for generous and dedicated commitment can be met by appeasing warring factions and by giving in to their demands.

The former Yugoslavia is the first great and, at present, the most visible testing ground for Europe in the era that was initiated by the end of the Cold War. But it is not, of course, the only one.

Another one consists in how we deal with the temptation to open the back gate to the demons of nationalist collectivism with an apparently innocent emphasis on minority rights, especially the right of minorities to self-determination. At first sight, this emphasis would seem harmless and beyond reproach. But one real consequence could be new unrest and tension, because demanding self-determination inevitably leads to questioning the integrity of the individual states and the inviolability of their present borders and even the validity of all postwar peace treaties. Attempts of this kind are dangerous chiefly because they look not to the future but to the past, and because they disregard the certainty that only democracy, individual human rights and freedoms, and the civic principle can guarantee the genuinely full development of even that aspect of one's identity represented by membership in a nationality.

There are countless such tests and pitfalls in Europe today. We cannot expect to stand up to the tests or avoid the pitfalls if we continue to believe that we need not forgo any of our particular interests, or accept the new Europe as a radical moral imperative; if we believe that it is enough—within the framework of established political practice—to negotiate, argue, appoint commissions, and go from conference to conference with attaché cases brimming with paper that wraps base and narrow-minded interests in noble, high-sounding words.

If some Western states cannot rid themselves of their subconscious drive for a dominant position, if they don't stop trying to reduce the idea of Europe to a noble backdrop against which they continue to defend their own petty concerns, and if the postcommunist states do not make radical efforts to exorcise the ghosts their newly won freedom has turned loose, then Europe will only with great difficulty be able to respond to the challenge of the present and grasp the opportunities that lie before it.

The Council of Europe, the oldest existing pan-European

institution, exists to cultivate the values from which the spirit and ethos of European integration might grow, and to ensure that these values are embodied in international legal standards. If, as I contend, the main task of Europe today is to grasp the spirit of its own unification, to understand the moral obligations that flow from that, to assume—genuinely, and not just super-ficially—a new type of responsibility for itself, then the Council of Europe can play a unique and indispensable role in carrying out this complex task.

The Czech Republic would welcome this and is prepared to do everything in its power to make it happen.

The Co-responsibility
of the West

(AN ARTICLE WRITTEN FOR *FOREIGN AFFAIRS*)
DECEMBER 22, 1993

Four years after the fall of communism, it can be said without much exaggeration that this momentous historical event has caused the democratic West some major headaches. For all we know, many a Western politician may occasionally wonder, in the privacy of his mind, whether it might not have been a mistake to support the struggles for self-liberation within the Soviet bloc (even though that support was mainly verbal and moral) and whether the West should not have done more to prolong the existence of communism. After all, the world used to be so simple. There was a single adversary who was more or less understandable, who was directed from a single center, and whose sole aim in its final years (not counting some predictable exceptions) was to maintain the status quo. At the same time, the existence of this adversary drew the West together as well, because, faced with this global and clearly defined danger, it could always somehow agree on a common approach.

All that has vanished. The world has suddenly become unusually complex and far less intelligible. The old order has collapsed, but no one has yet created a new one. And at the same time, the "postcommunist world" is constantly springing new surprises on the West: nations hitherto unheard of are awakening and want countries of their own. Highly improbable people from God-knows-where are winning elections. It is not even clear whether some of the same people who four years ago so astonishingly roused themselves from their torpor and overthrew communism do not actually miss that system today.

The unwitting nostalgia in the West for the old order may be discerned even in such superficial matters as how they refer to our countries. From the Czech Republic to Kazakhstan, we are, and will no doubt remain for some time to come, "post-communist countries" and "former members of the former Warsaw Pact." I am guilty of having used these expressions myself, but I must admit an increasing aversion to them. After all, we did not go to the trouble of getting rid of communism only to have it remain—even with a prefix—forever sewn to our coats. Nor did we go to the trouble of liquidating the Warsaw Pact only to bear forever the stigma of our former membership in it. (Not long ago I observed, somewhat undiplomatically, that we do not refer to the United States as "a former British colony.") These formulations betray both the need to categorize us and the inability to find a key to understanding us other than the old familiar one.

Indeed, I sometimes feel sorry for Western statesmen when I observe the unease and surprise with which they listen to the widely divergent geopolitical and historical homilies delivered by various representatives of our part of Europe. The Pole still goes on about the 1941 division of Poland by Germany and Russia, almost as though he expected it to happen again to-morrow; the Hungarian refers to the Treaty of Trianon in 1920 as a historical wrong done to his people and deplores that, as a consequence, an enormous number of Hungarians no longer live in Hungary proper; a Czech will complain about Munich and Yalta and the other betrayals of his poor country by the West; and a Slovak will talk about what a historical injustice it was that no one ever perceived the Slovaks as a separate nation. At such moments I realize how much easier it must have been for Western politicians when they were faced with a homogeneous Soviet mass and didn't have to worry about distinguishing one nation from another.

I well understand the unease with which the West follows what for it are the strange problems of all those "postcommunist" countries, and I well understand all the real (though often unexpressed) reasons that lead the West to behave reticently toward them. Still, I am strongly persuaded that this reticence is extremely short-sighted and that over time it may even become quite dangerous, for it is not, as it may seem, a sign of sober judgment alone but also of an inability to comprehend the essence of the new situation and a lack of imagination and courage in the search for new solutions commensurate with the new circumstances.

If the West, along with all the other democratic forces in the world, is incapable of rapidly engaging in the common creation of a new order in European and Euro-Asian affairs—a better order than the old bipolar one—then someone else might well begin to do the job, and the order thus created could be far worse than the one preceding it. I am thinking not so much of a new Stalin as of the "order" that could emerge from the violent clash of the many different and impenetrable forces that the disorganized state of the world today may bring to life, not only in the East but in the West as well.

Such an outcome would inevitably lead to new conflicts and new suffering, perhaps far greater than what came before. It could also ultimately demonstrate that the democratic West had lost its ability realistically to foster and cultivate the values it has always proclaimed and undertaken to safeguard, to which end it has built its arsenal of weapons. This state of affairs would be far more than just a crisis of the East; it would also be a crisis of the West, a crisis of democracy, a crisis of Euro-American civilization itself. Let events in the former Yugoslavia stand as a warning. This is not just a Balkan predicament. The inability of Europe and the United States to intervene effectively in defense of the basic values of civilization that are being so drastically destroyed in the Balkans (and, what is more, in an area that was always an integral part of Europe) tells us something about the democratic world as well.

If we in these "postcommunist" countries call for a new

order, if we appeal to the West not to close itself off to us, and if we demand a radical re-evaluation of the new situation, this is not only because we are concerned about our own security and stability, and not only because we feel that the security of the West itself is at stake. The reason is far deeper. We are concerned about the destiny of the values and principles that communism denied, and in whose name we resisted communism and ultimately brought it down.

I recognize that this rather bold claim calls for an explanation.

Well, then: Many years of living under communism gave us certain experiences that the noncommunist West fortunately did not have to live through. We came to understand (or, to be precise, some of us did) that the only genuine values are those for which one is capable, if necessary, of sacrificing something. (The Czech philosopher Jan Patočka, at the end of his life, devoted considerable thought to this question.) The traditional values of Western civilization—such as democracy, respect for human rights and for the order of nature, the freedom of the individual and the inviolability of his property, the feeling of co-responsibility for the world, which means the awareness that if freedom is threatened anywhere it is threatened everywhere—all of these things became values with moral, and therefore metaphysical, underpinnings. Without intending to, the communists taught us to locate the truth of the world not in mere information about it, but in an attitude, a commitment, a moral imperative.

I have the impression that precisely this awareness is sadly lacking in the present-day West, the "non-postcommunist" West (but, with increasing obviousness, in the "postcommunist" West as well). Naturally, all of us continue to pay lip service to democracy, human rights, the order of nature, and responsibility for the world, but apparently only insofar as it does not require any sacrifice. By that I of course do not mean merely sacrifice in the form of fallen soldiers. The West has made, and continues to make, such sacrifices, though some instances may be more meaningful than others. I have in mind, rather, sacrifice in a less conspicuous but infinitely broader sense—that is, a willingness to sacrifice for the common interest something of one's own particular interests, including even the quest for larger and larger domestic production and consumption. The pragmatism of politicians who want to win the next election, for whom the highest authority is therefore the will and the mood of a rather spoiled consumer society, makes it impossible for those people to be aware of the moral, metaphysical, and often tragic dimensions of their own program.

Why has the West lost its ability to sacrifice? There are probably many reasons for this, some completely random political ones, others that might be called philosophical. One example of a random political reason would be a deceptive impression that has apparently gained wide currency in the United States. Since the fall of communism is considered by many an American victory, now that the Cold War is over the sentiment is that the headaches it caused should be over, too. But the headaches are never over. If the West has indeed won the Cold War, then today it faces perhaps an even more difficult task: winning the peace as well. But there are also reasons, as I have said, that run considerably deeper. The economic advances of Euro-American civilization, based as they are on advances in scientific and technical knowledge, have gradually altered man's very value systems. Respect for the metaphysical horizons of his being is, to an increasing extent, pushed aside to make room for a new deity: the ideal of the perpetual growth of production and consumption.

This is the source of that protectionism, that fear in the West of cheap Eastern goods, that reluctance to get more deeply involved anywhere that there are no immediate gains, that caution, that lack of imagination and courage, that love of the status quo which ultimately leads many to call the part of Europe that has freed itself from communism in the name of democracy if not "current" then at least "former members of the former Warsaw Pact," "former members of COMECON," or "immature and unstable democracies," and, as far as possible, to lock themselves up in the world to which they have become accustomed.

A liberal market economy? Yes, but only for us. Security?

Yes, but only for us. National interests? Yes, but only our own. No, I am not speaking out of a sense of injury or unrequited love. If you will pardon me for saying so, I know more about the immaturity of Czech democracy than anyone in the West. I am simply making some general observations, nothing more. The Western way of affirming Western values, in short, seems to me to have seriously cooled off.

Is it any wonder that, in more than one "postcommunist" country, "postcommunists" have done well in elections? This might even be attributable to the "non-postcommunist West," which is doing so much to make the "postcommunist West" or the "East" itself disappointed in the atmosphere of the world in which it placed so much hope during the time of resistance to communism.

Let me make myself clear. I do not at all think that the main role of the democratic West is to solve all the problems of the "postcommunist world." Our countries (whether those that declare themselves to be, and evidently are, a part of the Western European sphere of civilization, or those that belong to the "Central Asian" sphere of civilization, or to any other) must deal with their own immense problems themselves. The "non-postcommunist West" should not, however, look on as though it were a mere visitor at a zoo or the audience on the edge of their seats at a horror movie. It should perceive these processes at the very least as something that intrinsically concerns it, that somehow decides its own fate, that demands its own active involvement and challenges it to make sacrifices in the interest of a bearable future for us all.

The creation of a new order can have dozens of variations. It is a matter of evolution, and calls for and assumes great judgment and a profound capacity to understand. No one will get anywhere these days with the designation "former members of the former Warsaw Pact"; in fact, insisting on this formulation may only cause further damage. For instance, on the matter of security arrangements, the nature and substance of the "Partnership for Peace" project will be one thing if we are talking about the Central Asian republics that are today members of the Commonwealth of Independent States, and something entirely different in the case of such countries as Hungary, the Czech Republic, Slovakia, and Slovenia. By virtue of their entire history, spiritual and intellectual traditions, culture, atmosphere, and geopolitical position, the latter countries belong to the classical European West, and any separation of them from that West would be suicidal for the whole of Europe, something anyone with even a rudimentary knowledge of European history should understand.

I am not criticizing the "Partnership for Peace" proposal. On the contrary, I consider it a very reasonable starting point. (If I can fault it for anything, it would only be for not having come into existence two or three years ago.) I am merely saying that everything now will depend on how it is carried out. This will be the real test of the West's resolve. Specifically, I believe that, for the Central European countries, and later for other European countries, full membership should clearly and quickly become the goal. NATO would thus gradually outgrow its present role to become a genuinely pan-European security structure. But this expansion of NATO should take place against the background of a clearly defined and genuinely cooperative relationship with Russia (or the Commonwealth of Independent States) as a great Euro-Asian nuclear power that is, in all respects, in a radically different position from the small Central European countries. The "Partnership for Peace" proposal could also provide a starting point for this specific relationship.

At this moment, however, my concern is not with concrete proposals for a new architecture of Atlantic-European-Asian relations, even though I have my own specific opinions about them, but with something else: the very unwillingness of the "non-postcommunist West" to join in the creation of such proposals, its unwillingness to hear the warning voices coming from our part of the world. My concern is that the West come to understand that the great task of self-defense against the communist menace has been supplanted today by an even more difficult task: to assume courageously, in its own interests and in the general interest, its share of the responsibility for the new organization of things in the entire Northern Hemisphere.

To make my point briefly and simply, it seems to me that the fate of the so-called West is today being decided in the so-called East. If the West does not find a key to us, who were once violently separated from the West (with no great resistance on its part), or to those who somewhere far away have likewise extricated themselves from communist domination, it will ultimately lose the key to itself. If, for instance, it looks on passively at "Eastern" or Balkan nationalism, it will give the green light to its own potentially divisive nationalism, which it was able to deal with so magnanimously in the era of the communist threat. If it closes its eyes to the postcommunist ecological catastrophe, it will sooner or later bring on its own ecological catastrophe, and ultimately a global one. If it does not learn from our experience of where human pride can lead, from the hubris of people who invented a rational utopia for themselves and tried to create a paradise on earth, if it persists in its anthropocentric understanding of the earth, it will bear the consequences, and so will the whole world. If its own consumer affluence remains more important to it than the laudable foundations of the affluence, it will soon forfeit that affluence.

Today, more than ever before in the history of mankind, everything is interrelated. Therefore, the values and the prospects of contemporary civilization are subjected everywhere to great tests. Because of this, the future of the United States and the European Union is being decided in suffering Sarajevo and Mostar, in the plundered Brazilian rain forests, in the wretched poverty of Bangladesh and Somalia. Theoretically, almost everyone now knows this. But how does the knowledge find expression in practical politics? In the practical politics of each one of us?

People today know that they can be saved only by a new type of global responsibility. Just one small detail is missing: that responsibility actually has to be undertaken.

New Year's Address to the Nation

A year ago, when the Czech Republic became independent, it was for most of us an occasion more for sober reflection than for celebration. What, we asked ourselves, will this division of the country that has been our home mean for us all—Czechs and Slovaks? What will it mean for Central Europe? Are we to understand this as an achievement of our political representatives, or as a defeat in the struggle for a common country?

The first year of our new existence as a state has dissipated most of last year's fears. Our republics did not collapse, and our separation did not rock the foundations of Central Europe. Czech society accepted this change matter-of-factly and with understanding. It did not succumb to despondency or defeatism. It did not come to resent the Slovaks and, without much delay, got on with creating new conditions within the dimensions of the Czech state. We soon understood that the pain that the separation of Czechoslovakia brought many of us was a price we had to pay for our post-November freedom.

What this division will actually mean historically, and what it will bring with it, again depends mainly on us alone. The meaning of European unification lies in a new type of coexistence and cooperation between all its autonomous parts. We ought therefore to accept the fact that we will be participating in this unification as two sovereign states, linked by a wealth of common Czechoslovak experience, as no more than a new and different kind of challenge to fulfill this European aim. If we succeed, it will mean that we have proved ourselves in a historic test.

We certainly have the means to do so. Most important, the Czech Republic managed immediately to establish a continuity with what was good in both the more remote and the more immediate aspects of our Czechoslovak heritage. We declared allegiance to the humanistic and democratic traditions of our recent history, expressing this symbolically by assuming the Czechoslovak national holiday [October 28] as our own, and we continued uninterrupted the great work of transformation begun in November 1989.

Because of all that, our Parliament was able to pass a new democratic constitution in time, as well as countless other laws necessary to continue the fundamental restructuring of our entire legal system. The new constitution has gradually been brought to life: a president was elected and a Constitutional Court established, and this year the process will be completed with the election of a Senate. Our government enjoys the continuing support of Parliament and of most citizens. Thanks as well to the orderly way Czechoslovakia was divided, the Czech Republic quickly received full recognition from the international community. It soon stood on its own two feet in foreign policy and, in a way appropriate to the new situation, creatively perpetuated the spirit of foreign-policy initiatives taken by post-November Czechoslovakia.

The clearest achievement of the Czech Republic undoubtedly is that it has been able to maintain the tempo of economic transformation without deviating from its original conception, thus demonstrating that the approach taken after initial discussions was the right one. As is generally known, all the main macroeconomic indicators are positive today, the basic institutions and relationships of the market economy are beginning to work, and privatization is proceeding well. This year, its second wave will take place, after which an absolute majority of companies will have new, specific owners. When and how quickly production will again begin to increase will depend no longer on the economic policies of the government but on the creativity of the entrepreneurial sphere. On the whole, it can be said that the basic systemic changes in our economy have been made, and thus its transformation can now be considered irreversible.

This said, I know well about all the difficult and often painful things that are being caused in your everyday lives by the great changes occurring today. I know of your fear of the growing crime rate. I know about the problems that many of you, particularly those who are older, face because of the transformation of the social-assistance and health-care systems. I know about the risks connected with running your businesses. All the more, therefore, do I admire your acceptance of the sense these changes make, and the patience with which you are coming to terms with the burdensome phenomena they bring with them. Again and again, I have occasion to admire the courage with which so many of you fill the new conditions of our life with creative work.

The speed and the outcome of our social transformation are not merely an achievement of the government and Parliament; it is, above all, you, the citizens of the Czech Republic, who have brought them about.

I know you do not expect from me a detailed discussion of the situation, the achievements, and the shortcomings in each individual area of our lives. More properly, you expect from me some comments on what awaits us in the new year.

The common denominator of the several important tasks we should concern ourselves with now is the creation of a genuine, open, and multilayered civil society.

The massive disengagement of the state from the economy must, in my opinion, quickly find its counterpart in civic and public life. Faith in the individual as a genuine creator of economic prosperity should be deliberately extended, and far less timorously than has so far been the case, to include faith in the individual as a citizen capable of assuming his share of responsibility for the affairs of society.

Naturally, there are duties that only the state can and must carry out if the state is to have any meaning at all. There may be even more of them than our present government will admit. At the same time, however, there are many other functions that might and should be carried out to a far greater extent by citizens themselves, that they can in fact carry out better than the state. The central rationality of the state—be it ever so enlightened—cannot continue to take the place of the pluralistic richness of ideas, the knowledge, the experience, and the inventiveness of individuals and the great variety of associations they naturally create.

By its very nature, life is infinitely colorful and varied. We are constantly being astonished by something new in the rich fabric of social relations, interests, and activities. It simply cannot be predicted, let alone planned for or regulated. To try to do so would be to suffocate life and thus risk a confrontation with it. The more varied civil society is, the better it corresponds to the very essence of human life and permits the positive dimensions of the human spirit to express themselves. Ultimately it makes possible a richer life.

Democracy is a system based on trust in the human sense of responsibility, which it ought to awaken and cultivate. Democracy and civil society are thus two sides of the same coin. Today, when our very planetary civilization is endangered by human irresponsibility, I see no other way to save it than through a general awakening and cultivation of the sense of responsibility people have for the affairs of this world.

The development of civil society naturally depends above all on the citizens themselves. But it depends on far more than them as well. What can the state do to promote this? Out of many possible examples, I will mention at least two that seem to me particularly relevant at this moment.

There is much discussion today about reform of the civil service. This confronts the state with a typical challenge of this age, a challenge that has a deeper significance than might appear at first glance. If the civil service finds the courage to decentralize itself in time, and, in a well-considered fashion, to devolve dif-

ferent types of decision-making to the lowest level of government capable of effectively assuming them, and to allow more
room for self-administration—on a higher level than merely the
municipalities—then this can contribute significantly to the creation of a genuine civil society. After all, there are countless
things handled today by the ministries that people on the level of
the districts or the natural regions could deal with themselves far
more flexibly and with better knowledge of the specific circumstances. Much of what the districts handle today could be dealt
with more quickly and efficiently by municipalities. And an
even more daring decentralization in the redistribution of funds
would only encourage more sensitive responses to the multi-
farious needs of life, which can scarcely be centrally monitored.
A well-established network of local administrations should not
complicate life for the central authorities, but on the contrary
should make life easier, releasing them from the obligation to
play the game of omniscience.

Another area in which civic participation in public life ought
to be significantly strengthened is in the extensive network of
organizations, mostly neither private nor state-controlled, whose
purpose is not to make a profit, yet which are vitally important
to society. Hundreds of schools, health centers, cultural institutions, and foundations are waiting for a law or laws to clarify
their position under the new conditions, define their relationship
to their founders, set the ground rules for fund-raising, the
administration of their monies, and of course, their public
accountability.

The flourishing of this nonprofit sector is another of the
essential elements of a mature civil society. Even more than this:
it is one of the direct indicators of such a society's maturity.
Genuine plurality in this field naturally depends again on the
plurality of the sources that nourish it. The state ought not to be
established on the notion that it alone knows best what society
needs, and that it alone should finance the nongovernmental
sector from taxes. Financing from the center leads inevitably to

control from the center. Here, too, citizens must be trusted more and encouraged to assume greater responsibility. This means nothing less than a thoughtful devolution to other organizations of some of the redistributive function of the state.

Naturally, there is a risk that these organizations will not always behave as purposefully as the state, but that risk is far outweighed by the fact that only a very complex structure of many independent sources can provide for the varied and constantly changing needs of public life and bring about genuine plurality and competition. Even more important, it is essential that the expansion of possibilities I am speaking of here deepen in society a sense of civic solidarity and an interest in public affairs and give people the experience of participating in them, a feeling of responsibility for the whole, and thus, indirectly, good relations with their own country.

The issue here is not very complicated. To put it simply, if our daring economic reforms are not accompanied by the purposeful development of all aspects of civil society, our life will soon become one-dimensional and arid, limited to a race for profits, accompanied by an apathy toward public affairs and a dependence on the state to do everything for us.

A modern democratic state cannot consist merely of civil service, political parties, and private enterprises. It must offer citizens a colorful array of ways to become involved, both privately and publicly, and must develop very different types of civic coexistence, solidarity, and participation. In a richly layered civil society, a vital and inimitable role is played not only by the organs of administration and nonprofit organizations, but also by the churches, the trade unions, the widest possible array of civic associations, groups, and clubs. All of this together is what creates the life-giving environment for politics and its main components, political parties. A genuine civil society is, moreover, the best insurance against various kinds of social tension and political or social upheavals: it makes it possible for various problems to be solved immediately, when and where they arise, before they turn septic somewhere under the skin of society and fester to the point where they might have a dangerous impact on the life of society as a whole.

Today we often hear the word "standard": we are building a standard market economy, a standard political system, and standard political parties; we are promulgating standard laws, norms, and principles; we watch standard advertising on television.

I have nothing against this if "standard" means that something has passed the test of experience and has been found good. We should, however, guard against recognizing "standardness" as such, "standardness" in itself, and ultimately against the illusion that everything standard, everything usual, is automatically good as well. There are things that, by their very nature, cannot be standard and that, were we to standardize them, would merely become flat and all the same. This would be unforgivable. After all, life itself is a phenomenon that is intrinsically nonstandard, and I would be horrified by a world that demanded I have a standard wife, a standard smile, or a standard soul, or that I be a standard president. Yes, I am calling for a "standard" civil society. But what does that mean? Nothing less and nothing more than respect for everything that is nonstandard, unique, personal, unusual, even provocative. It simply means respect for life and its mystery, confidence in the human spirit, and an opportunity for all nonstandard beings who derive pleasure from occasionally doing something that gives pleasure to others.

Talk about civil society is, of course, talk about the character of the state.

My feeling is that the Czech nation—just like other mature European nations—has already outgrown the diapers of its modern national awakening and has come to the awareness that its "Czechness" cannot be the sole or even the chief meaning of its existence, and that the state must be something a little different and a little more than the mere pinnacle of the nation's being. Naturally, we all acknowledge our nation; we acknowledge its history, its traditions, its culture, and its good customs. We love our language, our landscape, the cities and towns in which we live, and the intellectual and spiritual climate of our country. In the same way, however, we acknowledge other levels of belonging: we are members of our family, our church, our community, our profession, our enterprise, our club or political party, the company of those with whom we share a world-view.

I think most of us now understand that none of these affiliations, regardless of how comparatively rich they may be, can be raised in importance above any other, or exchanged in any determining sense for state existence. During the Second World War, we saw where the idea of the ethnically pure state led, and today we watch with helpless horror as that conception plays itself out in the former Yugoslavia. During the era of communism, we saw where the idea of an ideological class-based state led. Where the idea of a strictly religious state leads we can see today in exponents of fundamentalism who are trying to seize power in some of the Islamic countries. Attempts to establish a state exclusively on what differentiates some from others, and thus on what separates people, always leads to violence.

Today, the only alternative to the programmatic national state as it has emerged in various forms in Europe over the past centuries is a state founded on the civic principle, a principle that unites people rather than separating them, without of course denying them any of their other affiliations. In fact, this is the only principle that enables people, freely and in concert with others, to give substance to all their affiliations. A truly civic state, shored up by democratic law, is based on an understanding and acceptance of others, not on resistance to them.

Building a state on the civic principle, however, can only be accomplished by building a genuinely civil society. This ought to be the route the Czech Republic takes. It will not lead to the loss of national identity, or any other identity; on the contrary, it will lead to such identity's peaceful evolution.

Europe was a political reality long before nations in the modern sense of the word began to take shape. At the same time, its inner order always derived from a certain balance of power. That balance was mostly imposed upon Europe by those who were more powerful, and those who were less powerful paid the price. The individual parts of Europe never lived simply and entirely for themselves, independent of the others.

Today, Europe is attempting to create a historically new kind of order by a process we refer to as unification. The point is not for all European nations, ethnic groups, cultures, and regions to merge in some amorphous pan-European sea, nor is it to create a kind of monstrous superstate. The point is to create a theater of close and equitable cooperation among the autonomous elements of Europe—that is, to build a Europe in which no one more powerful could any longer suppress anyone less powerful, in which it would no longer be possible to settle disputes by force. This is a complex process, and undoubtedly many mistakes will be made as it proceeds. Nevertheless, it's a worthy attempt.

The basic principle that will make this integration at all possible is again, of course, the civic principle, which should guarantee that national rancor will never again triumph over normal civic cooperation. The many different civil societies in the democratic European countries will, together, create the great European civil society. I see no other and no better possibility for us than to accept this spirit of a civic Europe. It is the only alternative that can rid us once and for all of the fear of others.

The relationship between citizens and their politicians in a democratic society is always two-way: politics reflects the will and the mood of the citizens, and the behavior of politicians, in turn, influences the behavior of citizens. A political power determined to create a civil society will be concerned not merely with issuing appropriate laws but also with forging what is understood as political culture. To be specific, if politicians wish to awaken in citizens their strengths and best characteristics, their will to serve the whole of society, and their responsibility toward it, then they themselves should think less about making their mark and belittling others and more about the common good. A positive political climate is one of the most important conditions of a positive social climate.

After all the upheavals brought about by the shock of our newly attained freedom, it is time for good will, tolerance, decency, interest in others, faith in the good in humanity, respect for life, natural responsibility, modesty, and an amicable view of the world to return to our social climate. The more successfully this is done, the better we will all live.

Four years ago on this day, I said that our country was not flourishing. What can I say today? I would not be so bold as to say that it is now flourishing. But I would certainly not hesitate to say that in many places it has begun to put forth shoots: because the shoots of something new, something promising, something hopeful, can be seen almost everywhere. And every time I meet people whose work displays enterprise, solidarity with the suffering, concern with our cultural heritage, or a simple respect for nature, my faith in the future of this country grows.

All such people deserve our gratitude, and the greater the difficulties they must overcome, the greater our gratitude should be.

Everything new and good that is beginning to flourish around us we need to cultivate with great care, to water daily and watch closely.

For the new year, I wish you all satisfaction in your private lives, success in your work and in public life, peace of mind, congenial surroundings, and, above all, faith in the meaning of our common efforts.

The Indira Gandhi Prize

One evening years ago, I was listening to the radio and heard the news that Mrs. Indira Gandhi had been assassinated. I was so upset that sleep was out of the question, and there was only one way to calm myself: I sat down and wrote a short essay on the state of the world. It was called "Thriller."

The news of the assassination of her son Rajiv found me, as president of my country, on a visit to Oslo—the city where the Nobel Peace Prize is presented—in the company of Mrs. Gro Harlem Brundtland, a laureate of the prize I am being honored with today. We shared our regret and our outrage, and we honored the memory of the murdered man with a moment of silence.

Twice in the recent history of India—which has contributed so much to the spiritual richness of the world, especially the idea of tolerance and nonviolent opposition to tyranny—violence and hatred triumphed. In both cases, however, it was a two-edged victory, for the death of the victims, mother and son, challenged the world's conscience. Paradoxically, the impact of their deaths brought their life's work, in the spirit of Mahatma Gandhi, to fulfillment.

I am moved and deeply honored to be receiving the Indira Gandhi Prize today. To me, it is a way of honoring all the citizens of my country who for years engaged in nonviolent opposition to the totalitarian regime. It is also an honor to everyone who ultimately helped overthrow that regime without the spilling of a single drop of blood. It was because of this that our antitotalitarian revolution was dubbed "gentle" and "velvet" by the world press. In the name of all those fellow citizens of mine

I would like to thank India for the recognition they are receiving today.

With your permission, I would like to use this occasion to make some observations on the state of the world today. That is, I would like to respond to this great honor somewhat in the way I responded years ago to the news of Indira Gandhi's death.

Let me begin with a memory from long ago. In the 1960s, when I was traveling in the Central Asian republics of what was then the Soviet Union, I had the powerful feeling that I was passing through the world's last great colonial empire. It was obvious to me that the process of liberation going on in the rest of the world must one day assert itself in this empire, too. My guess then was that it would take about fifty years. It happened in twenty-five. I mention this to emphasize the connection between the two most important events of the second half of the twentieth century: decolonization and the fall of communism. From the world's point of view, of course, the fall of communism has many dimensions of meaning. One of them is that the fall of communism was the final stage in the process of decolonization.

This is not the only connection between those two world-shaking events. Another follows from the first, or is related to it: like the fall of communism, decolonization has made our world a multipolar one. If decolonization brought an end to the long European domination of the planet, then the fall of communism brought an end to the injustice into which that earlier injustice—colonialism—became transformed in the twentieth century, a bipolar division of the world. Thus, both events— decolonization and the fall of communism—can be understood as great, interrelated steps toward genuine cultural and political plurality in the world. And thus it can be said without much exaggeration that it is only now, at the end of the twentieth century, that a genuinely new era of modern human history is beginning—an era during which a single culture, or the two great powers that emerged from it, no longer dominate everyone, making room for real multiplicity. What specific shapes and forms this new epoch will assume over time, and what system of world organization will gradually be created, we of course do not know at this moment. Our progeny, those who will live in the next century, will know more about it.

Multiculturalism and multipolarity are nothing new in history. On the contrary, for thousands of years different cultures and civilizations have lived parallel lives on our planet. Some of them knew almost nothing about anyone else; some simply took no notice of others; some waged war with one another; some influenced one another. But none of them could, in and of themselves, determine or influence the fate of our planet as a whole.

The multicultural era on whose threshold we find ourselves today will differ radically from all eras preceding it. It comes to life within the framework of a single global civilization. Whether the expression of it is good or bad, it can fundamentally affect the state of the world. In this lies its absolute historical originality, making it a watershed not only in modern history, but in the history of the entire human race.

This originality of the coming epoch naturally places—and will continue to place—entirely new and as-yet-unknown demands on humanity and on each individual. It is a historically unprecedented challenge to the human race. Faced with this challenge, we have a chance to pass our greatest test so far. I surely do not need to paint in lurid colors the apocalyptic consequences that failure to pass this test could bring. I shall merely try to outline briefly the situation in which we find ourselves on the threshold of this new era.

Today's global civilization undoubtedly began with the European modern age, with its reliance on rational cognition, the idea of progress, and the development of science and technology. This modern European age grew rapidly to become a phenomenon that we might call Euro-American civilization.

Through its influence, and its often predatory expansion (which, however, is a product of its spirit), it came to encompass the whole world. Thanks to television and other communications systems, far-flung individuals today are better linked informationally than, until recently, a small country used to be. The whole world is crisscrossed with thousands of networks of commercial and currency relationships that form the basis of a single integrated economic system. Whatever happens in an important bank or an important stock market anywhere in the world has instant repercussions everywhere else. Identical or similar manufactured goods, industrial technologies, means of transportation, and infrastructure systems now cover practically the entire planet. Not only that: this informational and economic globalization necessarily leads to standardization of social behavior, of habits and life-styles, and of environments. In the big cities of the world, similar skyscrapers have sprung up. Advertising is similar. People from the most diverse corners of the earth long for the same standard of living.

Precisely because of this globalization, our planet is in graver danger today than ever before. For just as the benefits of civilization are global today, so are all the dangers of that civilization, be they economic, social, demographic, ecological, or any other. In short, all of humanity is in the same boat, and almost everything that happens anywhere directly or indirectly touches everyone.

This completely new circumstance makes new demands on the human spirit. It requires something that has never in history been required of it with such urgency, and that, moreover, goes quite beyond the spiritual framework of the very civilization that has created these requirements. It demands a completely new type of responsibility.

It is not my intention today to explain why this demand goes beyond the standard horizon of our present rationalistic and—as many would say—materialistic civilization, nor to analyze this demand or speculate on ways to satisfy it. It is enough, in the context of what I want to say today, merely to state that it exists.

My concern today is with a single aspect of the present situation, one I already mentioned: the question of multipolarity and multiculturalism within the context of a single global civilization.

One of the serious threats to the world today is the increasing number of conflicts among nations, ethnic groups, cultures, and religions. These conflicts are especially dangerous now because of their great potential to spread. Many quarrelsome factions would have no problem acquiring an atomic weapon, and any local conflict can, thanks to television, instantaneously mobilize a million more people who in another era would probably never have heard of the conflict. There are, of course, many different reasons, from social to historical, for these conflicts. I would like to mention just two.

The first is more or less external: the order in the world created by colonialism and the hegemony of Europe. It was, of course, an unnatural order, often enforced by violence on whole continents, an order that suppressed the autonomy of many parts of the world and forced an entirely different culture on them. Still, it was an order of sorts and as such it tended to limit the possibility of conflict. The sole latent conflict—that is, the conflict between the ruling power and the suppressed—in fact pushed almost all other conflicts into the background.

The same thing was true of the era of the bipolar division of the world. This division, too, was a kind of order (or, to put it more precisely, a pseudo-order) imposed upon the world, and it necessarily muted a variety of conflicts that—had the world not been divided in this bipolar way—might have exploded with far more force.

Thus, decolonization and the fall of communism also meant the end of an artificial world order. That order, however, has not yet been replaced by another, more natural order. It could be said that at this point the world is going through a transitional phase that allows all latent conflicts to come out in the open.

The upsurge in these conflicts, however, has in my opinion another, far deeper cause; somewhat paradoxically, it is the circumstance that our world is now enveloped by what is essentially a single civilization. Not only does this civilization bring everyone closer together, it—if I may put it this way—pushes everyone almost too close together. A logical result of this is the growth of intolerance. Compare two people in a hotel room and two people in a prison cell. In the hotel room, they would certainly not get on each other's nerves as much as they would in a cell, where they might have to spend months in close physical proximity with no chance to escape, even for a moment, into solitude. This homogenization and "enforced proximity" brought about by the integrating nature of the civilization in which we all—whether we wish it or not—find ourselves, and from which there is practically no escape, clearly induces a higher awareness of mutual "difference." If the autonomy and identity of various cultural spheres are smothered, if these spheres are pushed together, as it were, by thousands of civilizational pressures and forced to behave in a more or less uniform way, then an understandable response to this pressure is an increased emphasis in these communities on what is proper to them and what makes them different from others.

As a result, their antipathy to other communities grows stronger as well. The more the diverse, autonomous cultures are drawn into the single vortex of contemporary civilization, the more vigorous is their need to defend their original autonomy, their otherness, their authenticity. But against whom are they to defend it? Against civilization as such? That is truly difficult to do and would scarcely make any sense. So they defend their authenticity against a substitute enemy—against the authenticity of another. Again, I would compare it to conditions inside a prison. When I was there, I often observed that the prisoners took their hatred of prison or their jailers out on one another.

What is the way out of this vicious circle?

If the world today is not to become hopelessly enmeshed in increasingly horrifying conflicts, it has, I think, only one possible course of action. It must deliberately breathe the spirit of multicultural coexistence into the civilization that surrounds it. There is no need at all for different peoples, religions, and cultures to adapt or conform to one another. It is enough if they accept one another as legitimate and equal partners. If they respect one another and respect and honor one another's differences, they need not even understand one another. In any case, if mutual understanding is ever to come about anywhere, it can happen only on the terrain of mutual respect.

Many Europeans and Americans today are painfully aware that Euro-American civilization has undermined and destroyed the autonomy of non-European cultures. They feel it was their fault, and thus feel they must make amends through a kind of emotional identification with others, by accommodating them, by trying to ingratiate themselves, through a longing to "help" these others in one way or another. To my mind, this is a false solution, which can lead only to further unhappiness. It contains—albeit in a hidden and somewhat negative fashion—the same familiar feeling of superiority, paternalism, and a fateful sense of mission to help the "rest of the world." It is, again, that feeling of being "the chosen." It is, in fact, the flip side of colonialism. It is an intellectual dead end. I think we will all help one another best if we make no pretenses, remain ourselves, and simply respect and honor one another, just as we are.

The salvation of the world cannot begin with the invention of mechanisms for coexistence, that is, through the technology of world order. The only way to begin is by seeking a new spirit and a new ethos of coexistence. It is only from this that the techniques and mechanisms can gradually emerge, by which I mean the appropriate international organizations and negotiating systems. Only on the basis of respect for one another can we seek what will unite all of us, a kind of common, worldwide minimum whose binding nature will make it possible for mankind to coexist on a single planet. This will work only if the commitment grows out of a climate of equality and a common quest. It is no longer possible for one group to impose it upon others. The only kind of imposition that makes sense is when the reasonable and more responsible majority of humanity demands those standards from the unreasonable and less responsible minority, something that happens within every nation and in every culture.

It seems to me that we are already seeing the first signs of the multicultural climate I am talking about. I have observed more than once, in various parts of the world, that the dramatic and terrifying conflict between the original culture and the universal civilization suddenly begins to transcend itself and grow into what I would call an amalgamation of cultures. Things originally quite heterogeneous seem suddenly to be able to coexist side by side and radiate a new and unusual quality, a kind of postmodern culture of coexistence. This coexistence derives its meaning and its order precisely from the fact that no individual, no enlightened spirit, has attempted to give it a unifying meaning and order. Such indications, I feel, are the signs of a new world spirit, a spirit of peaceful coexistence of cultures in a single global civilization. The spirit of a multicultural and truly multipolar world. The spirit from which a new world order should gradually emerge, in which there will still be the large and the small, but in which no one will interfere with anyone else, let alone stifle others simply because they are different.

As I have already said, if our world is to face up to the great threat looming over it, we must find within ourselves the strength for a new type of global responsibility. The climate of multicultural coexistence, if it can be created, could be the first expression of this new responsibility, and could at the same time provide a proper environment for its development.

I am one of Mahatma Gandhi's admirers and, if I may be so bold, I believe that a reflection of his life's work might even be seen in the attempt my friends and I made, in Charter 77, to create a nonviolent opposition to the totalitarian regime in our country. This aspect of our activity later had a positive influence on the course of our antitotalitarian revolution in 1989.

If I were to say what fascinated me most about Gandhi's life, I would have to mention his stance immediately after your country gained independence, when, entirely alone, he placed himself in the path of the bloody battles between the Hindus and the Moslems and was able—in Calcutta, for example, but later here in Delhi as well—to end those merciless conflicts and compel the warring factions to shake hands.

I do not believe that man is by nature evil, or that violence and evil are a necessary part of human history. The human spirit is a mixture of all kinds of qualities and potential dispositions, from the worst to the best, and it is immensely important which of those qualities the world gives rein to, which of them political leaders inspire, and which of them they rely on in their work. Gandhi, face to face with an incredible explosion of violence and cruelty, was able to speak to the best in his fellow citizens. He was able to awaken their better qualities and let the good in them triumph over the bad. It was a great victory of the spirit over raw power—which, by the way, is a slogan that twice in recent history could be read on the walls of Czech cities—in 1968, after the Soviet occupation, and again in 1989. Gandhi's act was a triumph of human charisma over mob passions. It was a great victory for the ideas of nonviolence, tolerance, coexistence, and understanding. It was a great victory for what I would call the moral minimum, which links people of all cultures, over the mutual antipathy that can spring from differences of faith and cultural traditions.

The spiritual ethos that came to fruition in the work of Gandhi was a thousand years in the making on the great Indian subcontinent. This work is one of the major contributions of your country to modern history. It is an inspiring contribution, the impact of which can be observed again and again in all corners of the globe. I am convinced that the creation of the multicultural civilization I have talked about, the creation of conditions based on mutual respect and tolerance of different cultures, as well as the creation of a new human responsibility that alone can save this threatened and sorely tried planet, will always find one of the most important sources of its vitality in Gandhi's work.

Without the heritage of Gandhi and his Indian precursors and followers, there would be considerably less hope in the world than there is today.

International Theater Day

PRAGUE, MARCH 27, 1994

For the first time in the history of man, the planet he inhabits is encompassed by a single global civilization. Because of this, anything that happens anywhere has consequences, both good and ill, for everyone everywhere. This civilization is composed, however, of an enormous number of peoples or ethnic groups with widely diverse customs and traditions, and of many cultures, or cultural spheres, both large and small, and of many religious worlds, and many different kinds of political culture.

It seems that, the more tightly this variegated community is crowded together by contemporary civilization and compelled to accept common values and modes of behavior, the more powerfully will various groups feel the need to defend their national, racial, and cultural autonomy and identity. Many dangerous conflicts in the world today can be explained by the simple fact that, the closer we are to one another, the more we notice our differences.

Moreover, we are living at a time when various artificial orders have collapsed, whether these orders were formed by the colonial system or by the bipolar system dominated by two superpowers. The world is becoming genuinely multicultural and multipolar and is only now beginning to seek a new, genuinely just order, one that meets the needs of the present.

All of this makes the modern world an especially dramatic place, with so many peoples in so many places resisting coexistence with one another. And yet its only chance for survival lies precisely in such coexistence.

It is not true that, because of television, film, video, and the other great achievements of this era, theater is dwindling in importance. I would say that exactly the opposite is true, that theater is better suited than any other medium to reveal, in genuinely compelling and challenging ways, not only all the dark forces that are dragging the world down, but also everything bright and luminous in which its hopes are contained.

In today's dehumanizing technological civilization, theater is one of the important islands of human authenticity; that is, it is precisely what—if this world is not to end up badly—must be protected and cultivated. After all, the return of irreplaceable human subjectivity, of the particular human personality and its particular human conscience, is precisely what this world of megamachinery and anonymous megabureaucracy needs. Only man is capable of confronting all the dangers that face the world, confronting them with his renewed responsibility, his aware-ness of connections—in other words, precisely with something within him that not even the best network of modern computers can replace. The hope of the world lies in the rehabilitation of the living human being.

Theater is not just another genre, one among many. It is the only genre in which, today and every day, now and always, living human beings address and speak to other human beings. Because of that, theater is more than just the performance of sto-ries or tales. It is a place for human encounter, a space for au-thentic human existence, above all for the kind of existence that transcends itself in order to give an account of the world and of itself. It is a place for living, specific, inimitable conversation about society and its tragedies, about man, his love and anger and hatred. Theater is a point at which the intellectual and spiri-tual life of the human community crystallizes. It is a space in which the community can exercise its freedom and come to understanding.

In the global technical civilization created by so many au-tonomous cultures and threatened by conflicts between them, theater is—I firmly believe—a telescope into the future and a means of giving shape to our hope. Not because its purpose is to describe a world better than the one that exists, or to construct a vision of a better future, but because it embodies the main hope of humanity today, which is the rebirth of a living humanity. For, if theater is free conversation, free dialogue, among free people about the mysteries of the world, then it is precisely what will show humankind the way toward tolerance, mutual respect, and respect for the miracle of Being.

I appeal to you all, people of the theater, to remember your colleagues in Sarajevo. They are doing precisely what I have been talking about. Through the exercise of freedom of the spirit, through the cultivation of dialogue and the creation of a space for real human communication, they are confronting the terrible war in their country. Ethnic fanatics and thugs are casting the world back into its darkest past. People of the theater who engage their audiences in a dialogue about the dramas of today's world and the dramas of the human spirit point the way to the future.

There is another war going on in Sarajevo besides the one we see on television. It is an unarmed conflict between those who hate and kill others only because they are different, and people of the theater who bring the uniqueness of human beings alive and make dialogue possible. In this war, the people of the theater must win. It is they who point toward the future as a peaceful conversation among all human beings and societies about the mysteries of the world and Being.

These people of the theater are serving peace, and they remind us that theater still has meaning.

The Philadelphia Liberty Medal

PHILADELPHIA, JULY 4, 1994

I take this occasion—in front of this historic building, where you have paid me the high honor of awarding me the Philadelphia Liberty Medal—as an invitation to set my own sights equally high. I would like, therefore, to turn my thoughts today to the state of the world and the prospects that lie before it. I have also decided to do something that personally I find just as demanding: I will attempt to address you in English. I hope you will understand me.

There are thinkers who claim that, if the modern age began with the discovery of America, it also ended in America. This is said to have occurred in the year 1969, when America sent the first men to walk on the moon. From this historic moment, they say, a new age in the life of humanity can be dated.

I think there are good reasons for suggesting that the modern age has ended. Today, many things indicate that we are going through a transitional period, when it seems that something is on the way out and something else is being painfully born. It is as if something were crumbling, decaying, and exhausting itself, while something else, still indistinct, were arising from the rubble.

Periods of history when values undergo a fundamental shift are certainly not unprecedented. This happened in the Hellenistic period, when from the ruins of the classical world the Middle Ages were gradually born. It happened during the Renaissance, which opened the way to the modern era. The distinguishing features of such transitional periods are a mixing and blending of cultures, and a plurality or parallelism of intellectual and spiritual worlds. These are periods when all consistent value systems collapse, when cultures distant in time and space are discovered or rediscovered. These are periods when there is a tendency to quote, to imitate, and to amplify, rather than to state with authority or to integrate. New meaning is gradually born from the encounter, or the intersection, of many different elements.

Today, this state of mind or of the human world is called postmodernism. For me, a symbol of that state is a Bedouin mounted on a camel and clad in traditional robes under which he is wearing jeans, with a transistor radio in his hands and an ad for Coca-Cola on the camel's back. I am not ridiculing this, nor am I shedding an intellectual tear over the commercial expansion of the West which destroys alien cultures. I see it, rather, as a typical expression of this multicultural era, a signal that an amalgamation of cultures is taking place. I see it as proof that something is happening, something is being born, that we are in a phase when one age is succeeding another, when everything is possible. Yes, everything is possible, because our civilization does not have its own unified style, its own spirit, its own aesthetic.

This is related to the crisis, or to the transformation, of science as the basis of the modern conception of the world.

The dizzying development of this science, with its unconditional faith in objective reality and its complete dependency on general and rationally knowable laws, led to the birth of modern technological civilization—the first civilization in the history of the human race to span the entire globe and firmly bind together all human societies, submitting them to a common global destiny. It was this science that enabled man, for the first time, to see Earth from space with his own eyes, that is, to see it as another star in the sky.

At the same time, however, the relationship to the world that modern science fostered and shaped now appears to have exhausted its potential. It is increasingly clear that, strangely, the relationship is missing something. It fails to connect with the most intrinsic nature of reality, and with natural human experience. It is now more of a source of disintegration and doubt than a source of integration and meaning. It produces what amounts to a state of schizophrenia, completely alienating man as an observer from himself as a being. Classical modern science described only the surface of things, a single dimension of reality. And the more dogmatically science treated it as the only dimension, as the very essence of reality, the more misleading it became. Today, for instance, we may know immeasurably more about the universe than our ancestor did, yet it increasingly seems that they knew something more essential about it than we do, something that escapes us. The same thing is true of nature and of ourselves. The more thoroughly all our organs and their functions, their internal structures, and the biochemical reactions that take place within them are described, the more we seem to fail to grasp the spirit, purpose, and meaning of the system that they create together and that we experience as our unique "self."

And thus today we find ourselves in a paradoxical situation. We enjoy the achievements of modern civilization that have made our physical existence on this earth easier in so many important ways. Yet we do not know exactly what to do with ourselves, where to turn. The world of our experiences seems chaotic, disconnected, confusing. There appear to be no integrating forces, no unified meaning, no true inner understanding of phenomena in our experience of the world. Experts can explain anything in the objective world to us, yet we understand our own lives less and less. In short, we live in the postmodern world, where everything is possible and almost nothing is certain.

This state of affairs has its social and political consequences. The single planetary civilization to which we all belong confronts us with global challenges. We stand helpless before them, because our civilization has essentially globalized only the surface of our lives. But our inner selves continue to have a life of their own. And the fewer answers the era of rational knowledge provides to the basic questions of human Being, the more deeply it would seem that people—behind its back, as it were—cling to the ancient certainties of their tribe. For this reason, individual cultures, increasingly lumped together by contemporary civilization, are realizing with new urgency their own inner autonomy and the inner differences of others. Cultural conflicts are increasing and are understandably more dangerous today than at any other time in history. The end of the era of rationalism has been catastrophic. Armed with the same supermodern weapons, often from the same suppliers, and followed by television cameras, the members of various tribal cults are at war with one another. By day, we work with statistics; in the evening, we consult astrologers and frighten ourselves with thrillers about vampires. The abyss between the rational and the spiritual, the external and the internal, the objective and the subjective, the technical and the moral, the universal and the unique, grows constantly deeper.

Politicians are rightly worried by the problem of finding the key to the survival of a civilization that is global and at the same time clearly multicultural; of how generally respected mechanisms of peaceful coexistence can be set up, and on what set of principles they are to be established.

These questions have been highlighted with particular urgency by the two most important political events in the second half of the twentieth century: the collapse of colonial hegemony and the fall of communism. The artificial world order of the past decades has collapsed, but a new, more just order has not yet emerged. The central political task of the final years of this century, then, is the creation of a new model of coexistence among the various cultures, peoples, races, and religious spheres within a single interconnected civilization. This task is all the more urgent because other threats to contemporary humanity, brought about by the one-dimensional development of civilization, are growing more serious all the time.

Many believe this task can be accomplished through technical means; that is, they believe it can be accomplished through the invention of new organizational, political, and diplomatic instruments. Yes, it is clearly necessary to invent organizational structures appropriate to the present multicultural age. But such efforts are doomed to failure if they do not grow out of something deeper, out of generally held values.

This, too, is well known. And in searching for the most natural source of a new world order, we usually look to the traditional foundation of modern justice: to a set of values that—among other things—were first declared in this building and that are a great achievement of the modern age. I am referring to respect for the unique human being and for his or her liberties and inalienable rights, and the principle that all power derives from the people. I am, in short, referring to the fundamental ideas of modern democracy.

What I am about to say may sound provocative, but I feel more and more strongly that not even these ideas are enough, that we must go further and deeper. The point is that the solution they offer is still, as it were, modern, derived from the climate of the Enlightenment and from a view of man and his relation to the world that has been characteristic of the Euro-American sphere for the last two centuries. Today, however, we are in a different place and facing a different situation, one to which classically modern solutions in themselves do not give a satisfactory response. After all, the very principle of inalienable human rights, conferred on man by the Creator, grew out of the typically modern notion that man—as a being capable of knowing nature and the world—was the pinnacle of creation and lord of the world. This modern anthropocentrism meant that He who allegedly endowed men with his inalienable rights inevitably began to disappear from the world. He was so far beyond the grasp of modern science that He was gradually pushed into a sphere of privacy of sorts, if not directly into a sphere of private fancy—that is, into a place where public obligations no longer apply. The existence of an authority higher than man himself simply began to get in the way of human aspirations.

The idea of human rights and freedoms must be an integral part of any meaningful world order. Yet I think it must be anchored in a different place, and in a different way, from what has been the case so far. If it is to be more than just a slogan mocked by half the world, it cannot be expressed in the language of a departing era, and it must not be mere froth floating on the subsiding waters of faith in a purely scientific relationship to the world.

Paradoxically, inspiration for the renewal of this lost integrity can once again be found in science. In a science that is new—let us say postmodern; a science producing ideas that in a certain sense allow it to transcend its own limits. I will give two examples.

The first is the Anthropic Cosmological Principle. Its authors and adherents have pointed out that, from the countless possible courses of its evolution, the universe took the only one that enabled life to emerge. This is not yet proof that the aim of the universe has always been that it should one day see itself through our eyes. But how else can this matter be explained?

I think the Anthropic Cosmological Principle brings us to an idea perhaps as old as humanity itself: that we are not at all just an accidental anomaly, the microscopic caprice of a tiny particle whirling in the endless depths of the universe. Instead, we are mysteriously connected to the entire universe; we are mirrored in it, just as the entire evolution of the universe is mirrored in us. Until recently it might have seemed that we were an unhappy bit of mildew on a heavenly body whirling in space among many that have no mildew on them at all. This was something that classical science could explain. Yet, the moment it begins to appear that we are deeply connected to the entire universe, science has reached the limits of its powers. Because it is founded on the search for universal laws, it cannot deal with singularity— that is, with uniqueness. The universe is a unique event and a unique story, and so far we are the unique point of that story. But unique events and stories are the domain of poetry, not science. With the formulation of the Anthropic Cosmological

Principle, science finds itself on the border between formula and story, between science and myth. In that, however, science has paradoxically returned, in a roundabout way, to man, and offers him—in new clothing—his lost integrity. It does so by anchoring him once more in the cosmos.

The second example is the Gaia Hypothesis. This theory brings together proof that the dense network of mutual interactions between the organic and inorganic portions of the earth's surface form a single system, a kind of megaorganism, the living planet Gaia—named after an ancient goddess who is recognizable as an archetype of the Earth Mother in perhaps all religions. According to the Gaia Hypothesis, we are parts of a greater whole. Our destiny is not dependent merely on what we do for ourselves but also on what we do for Gaia as a whole. If we endanger her, she will dispense with us in the interests of a higher value—that is, life itself.

What makes the Anthropic Principle and the Gaia Hypothesis so inspiring? One simple thing: both remind us, in modern language, of what we have long suspected, of what we have long projected into our forgotten myths, and of what perhaps has always lain dormant within us as archetypes—that is, the awareness of being anchored in the earth and the universe, the awareness that we are not here alone or for ourselves alone, but are an integral part of a higher, mysterious entity against whom it is not advisable to blaspheme. This forgotten awareness is encoded in all religions. All cultures anticipate it in various forms. It is one of the things that form the basis of man's understanding of himself, of his place in the world, and ultimately of the world as such.

A modern philosopher once said: "Only a God can save us now."

Yes, the only real hope for people today is probably a renewal of our certainty that we are rooted in the earth and, at the same time, in the cosmos. This awareness endows us with the capacity for self-transcendence. Politicians at international forums may reiterate a thousand times that the basis of the new world order must be universal respect for human rights, but it will mean nothing as long as this imperative does not derive from respect for the miracle of Being, the miracle of the universe, the miracle of nature, the miracle of our own existence. Only someone who submits to the authority of the universal order and of creation, who values the right to be a part of it and a participant in it, can genuinely value himself and his neighbors, and thus honor their rights as well.

It logically follows that, in today's multicultural world, the truly reliable path to coexistence, to peaceful coexistence and creative cooperation, must start from what is at the root of all cultures and what lies infinitely deeper in human hearts and minds than political opinions, convictions, antipathies, or sympathies. It must be rooted in self-transcendence: transcendence as a hand reaching out to those close to us, to foreigners, to the human community, to all living creatures, to nature, to the universe; transcendence is a deeply and joyously experienced need to be in harmony even with what we ourselves are not, with what we do not understand, with what seems distant from us in time and space, but with which we are nevertheless mysteriously linked because, together with us, all this constitutes a single world; transcendence as the only real alternative to extinction.

The Declaration of Independence, adopted 218 years ago in this building, states that the Creator gave man the right to liberty. It seems that man can realize that liberty only if he does not forget the One who endowed him with it.

The Jackson H. Ralston Prize, Stanford University

STANFORD, SEPTEMBER 29, 1994

The honor I receive today from your university, this important intellectual center, presents me with an opportunity to set aside the political cares of the day and attempt to make several observations on a very general theme—the theme of civilization as a context for contemporary politics.

Recently I read a remarkable book from the pen of a Czech-American psychotherapist. In it, the author describes in great detail and with great veracity methods that have enabled him, over the years, to recover from the human unconscious experiences that, until recently, very few were aware of at all: the prenatal experiences of the human embryo from conception until the moment of birth. The author then demonstrates that these experiences correspond remarkably with the basic archetypes and archetypal visions or stories we find—in thousands of specific forms—in ancient myths, in legends and fairy tales, and above all in all religions. Cultures formed many thousands of years ago, cultures that developed their myths and ritual practices quite independently of one another, operate with the same basic archetypes, the prefigurations of which modern science is now discovering in the depths of the human unconscious as prenatal experiences. Naturally, no claim is made that prenatal experience is the only source of those archetypes or of all the tidings contained in the different religions. It is probably only an incidental, secondary source of inspiration, one that helps us fill in the broader picture. Still, I was unusually taken with this finding. It shows that there exist deep and fundamental experiences shared by the entire human race, and that traces of such experiences can be found in all cultures, regardless of how distant or how different they are from one another.

This, of course, is only a single example, taken from my recent holiday reading. From many other modern studies—and even from comparisons any unprejudiced layman can make for himself—it follows that all human cultures and religions have infinitely more in common than that, infinitely more that is hidden somewhere deep in their sources and foundations. There are principles, experiences, and what we might call prescientific knowledge that are more essential and mysterious than our prenatal experiences. At the same time—somewhat paradoxically—it often happens that the leading discoveries of contemporary science themselves provide confirmation of this and so, by a circular route, bring human understanding back to something that all cultures have known intuitively since the dawn of time, something that until recently science has treated as no more than a set of illusions or mere metaphors.

It turns out, for example, that many other experiences, far more difficult to explain, slumber in our collective unconscious. In various forms, these experiences surface again and again in the cultural achievements of humanity and often in individual human adventures. In a way that we scarcely understand, they transcend what a person could know himself or inherit from his ancestors. It is as if something like an antenna were picking up signals from a physically indeterminable transmitter that contains the experience of the entire human race.

Or another thing: it would appear that the whole history of the cosmos, and especially of life, is mysteriously recorded in the inner workings of all human beings. This history is projected into man's creations and is, again, something that joins us together far more than we think.

But something else seems to be the most essential of all: it cannot be an accident, or a mere concord of countless misperceptions, if after thousands of years people of different epochs and cultures feel that they are somehow parts and partakers of the same integral Being, carrying within themselves a piece of the infinity of that Being, whose very relative aspects are categories not just of space and time, but of matter and consciousness as well. I do not believe it is merely by chance or with no good reason that all cultures assume the existence of something that might be called the "Memory of Being," in which everything is constantly recorded, or that they assume the related existence of suprapersonal authorities or principles that not only transcend man but to which he constantly refers, and which are the sole, final explanation of a phenomenon as particular as human responsibility. Nor do I believe that so many modern scientists who in their work have touched on matters difficult to understand, such as the mysteries of the origin and history of the cosmos, the secrets of matter and of space-time, and the miracle of life, have taken leave of their senses when they speak of transcendence. On the contrary: it seems to me that such philosophical speculations are inseparable from their findings.

I know that by saying all this here I am running the risk that armies of scientists and journalists will label me a mystic who is abusing this renowned university forum to spread his obscure opinions. I will not hold it against them, because I am well aware that in the eyes of modern man thoughts of this nature inevitably carry with them a hint of obscurity, and many times this attitude brings complications into my own life: I know that, to my own detriment, I am too suspicious of many things. The risk of ridicule, however, is insufficient reason for me to remain silent about something I am constantly persuaded is true.

But, to sum up, it seems to me that one of the most basic human experiences, one that is genuinely universal and unites—or, more precisely, could unite—all of humanity, is the experience of transcendence in the broadest sense of the word.

In the United States, but elsewhere, too, discussions are beginning to take place about the conflict of civilizations as the most probable future course of humanity.

I am not sure that "civilization" is the correct term to use in this context. What we usually mean by "civilization" is historically and geographically defined, and distinguished by high degrees of autonomy. In the traditional sense of the word, civilizations tended to have very limited mutual contact, and if they did influence one another, it happened only very slowly and indirectly. Many civilizations had no idea that others existed. Today the situation is radically different. Practically the entire world is now connected by thousands of political and economic bonds and by elaborate communication networks. We are all aware of one another, and we have thousands of common habits, technologies, modes of behavior, civic forms, and aims. It seems to me more appropriate, therefore, to understand the world of today as a single global civilization, and I would call the conflicts that loom in the future conflicts between individual cultures or spheres of civilization.

In any case, one of the countless sources of growing tension between these spheres is that they are being forced to live closer and closer together within a single civilization, and thus they are becoming more and more clearly aware of their mutual differences, or of their own particular "otherness." I myself have compared this to life in a prison cell, in which the inmates get on one another's nerves far more than if they saw each other only occasionally.

Let me give you an example. In Europe today, thanks to the recent liberation of a large number of its nations, the border between the world of Orthodox Christianity and the world with Catholic or Protestant traditions is suddenly becoming more obvious than before. When I travel around Greece, for instance, I feel strongly that I am surrounded by different historical, cultural, and political traditions from those I know from my own country. Yet I would never dare to say that Greece belongs to a different civilization from the Czech Republic.

This modification in terminology, however, does not alter the fact that the differences between individual cultures or spheres of civilization are playing an ever-greater role in the modern world and are even beginning to show up in international politics. This process was accelerated sharply by the fall of communism and the end of the bipolar division of the world. This unnatural duality imposed upon the world, which concealed or directly suppressed historical and cultural differences, has collapsed. And these differences are now manifesting themselves with sudden and nearly explosive force, not just in the postcommunist world but also in the West and many other areas of the globe. I fully agree with those who spot in this reality one of the most serious threats to humanity in the coming era.

The role of the intellectual is, among other things, to foresee, like Cassandra, various threats, horrors, and catastrophes. The role of the politician is to listen to all the warning voices, take stock of the dangers, and at the same time think intensively about ways to confront or avert them. I cannot imagine that a politician could simply live with the knowledge that everything will turn out badly and still go on being a politician. That is why I, too, think often about ways to avert the threat that has been called the "conflict of civilizations."

At first glance, the solution is so simple and so obvious that it appears banal: the only salvation of the world today, now that the two biggest and most monstrous totalitarian utopias humanity has ever known—Nazism and communism—have fortunately collapsed, is the rapid dissemination of the basic values of the West, that is, the ideas of democracy, human rights, the civil society, and the free market. The most dynamic civilization of the last millennium, having evolved from a blending of classical, Christian, and Jewish elements, has spread and imprinted its character on the entire global civilization. It has created and developed these values and demonstrated that respect for them will guarantee the greatest degree of human freedom, justice, and prosperity.

Yet, even if this blueprint appears to Western man as the best and perhaps the only one possible, it has left much of the world unsatisfied. In such a situation, to hope that democracy will be easily expanded and that this in itself will avert a conflict of cultures would be worse than foolish.

It may, for instance, be observed that many politicians or regimes espouse these ideas in words but do not apply them in practice. Or they may give the ideas an entirely different content from those in the West. Very often we hear it said that these concepts are so closely bound to the Euro-American cultural tradition that they are simply not transferable to other milieux, or that they are only a lofty-sounding disguise for the demoralizing and destructive spirit of the West. The main source of objections would seem to be what many societies see as the inevitable product or by-product of these values: moral relativism, materialism, the denial of any kind of spirituality, a proud disdain for everything suprapersonal, a profound crisis of authority and the resulting general decay of order, a frenzied consumerism, a lack of solidarity, a selfish cult of material success, the absence of faith in a higher order of things or simply in eternity, an expansionist mentality that holds in contempt everything that in any way resists the dreary standardization and rationalism of technical civilization. People in many parts of the world are of two minds. On the one hand, they long for the prosperity they see in the West; on the other, they reject the importation of Western values and life-styles as the work of the devil. And if some distant culture does adapt to contemporary technical civilization and prospers, it frequently happens in a way that gives Western democrats goosebumps.

In short, democracy in its present Western form arouses skepticism and distrust in many parts of the world.

I admit that I, too, am not entirely satisfied with this recipe for saving the world, at least not in the form offered today. Not because it is bad, or because I would give preference to other values. It does not satisfy me because it is hopelessly half-baked. In fact, it is really only half a recipe. I am convinced that, if this were not the case, it would not evoke the great distrust that it does.

The reason for this distrust does not, I think, lie in some kind of fundamental opposition in most of the world to democracy as such and to the values it has made possible. It lies in something else: the limited ability of today's democratic world to step beyond its own shadow, or, rather, the limits of its own present spiritual and intellectual condition and direction, and thus its limited ability to address humanity in a genuinely universal way. As a consequence, democracy is seen less and less as an open system that is best able to respond to people's basic needs; as a set of possibilities that must be continually rediscovered, redefined, and brought into being. Instead, democracy is seen as something given, finished, and complete as is, something that can be exported like cars or televisions, something that the more enlightened purchase and the less enlightened do not.

In other words, it seems to me that the mistake lies not only with the backward consumers of exported democratic values, but in the very form or understanding of those values at present, and in the climate of the civilization with which they are directly connected, or appear to be connected in the eyes of a large part of the world. And that means of course that the mistake also lies in the way those values are exported, which often betrays an attitude of superiority and contempt for all those who hesitate to accept the offered goods automatically.

Where, then, is that other, missing side of the democratic solution? What is lacking in the only meaningful way of dealing with the future conflict of cultures? How can we restore that forgotten dimension of democracy that could give it universal resonance?

I am deeply convinced that it lies in what I have already tried to suggest—in the spiritual dimension that connects all cultures and in fact all humanity. If democracy is not only to survive but to expand successfully and resolve those conflicts of cultures, then, in my opinion, it must rediscover and renew its own transcendental origins. It must renew its respect for the nonmaterial order that is not only above us but also in us and among us, and which is the only possible and reliable source of man's respect for himself, for others, for the order of nature, for the order of humanity, and thus for secular authority as well. The loss of this respect always leads to loss of respect for everything else—from the laws people have made for themselves to the life of their neighbors and of our living planet. The relativization of all moral norms, the crisis of authority, the reduction of life to the pursuit of immediate material gain without regard for its general consequences—the very things Western democracy is most criticized for—originate not in democracy but in that which modern man has lost: his transcendental anchor, and along with it the only genuine source of his responsibility and self-respect. It is because of this loss that democracy forfeits much of its credibility.

The separation of executive, legislative, and judicial powers, the universal right to vote, the rule of law, freedom of expression, the inviolability of private ownership, and all the other aspects of democracy as the system that ought to be the least unjust and the least capable of violence—these are merely technical instruments that enable man to live in dignity, freedom, and responsibility. But in and of themselves, they cannot guarantee his dignity, freedom, and responsibility. The source of this basic human potential lies elsewhere: in man's relationship to that which transcends him. I think the fathers of American democracy knew this very well.

Were I to compare democracy to the sun's life-giving radiation, I would say that, though from the political point of view it is the only hope for humanity, it can have a beneficial impact on us only if it resonates with our deepest inner nature. And if part of that nature is the experience of transcendence in the broadest sense of the word—that is, man's respect for that which transcends him, without which he would not exist, and of which he is an integral part—then democracy must be imbued with the spirit of that respect if it is to succeed.

In other words, if democracy is to spread successfully throughout the world, and if civic coexistence and peace are to spread with it, then this must happen as part of an endeavor to find a new and genuinely universal articulation of that global human experience which even we, Western intellectuals, are once more beginning to recollect, one that connects us with the mythologies and religions of all cultures and opens a way for us to understand their values. It must expand simply as an environment in which we may all engage in a common quest for the general good.

That possibility of course presupposes that, first, our own democracies will once more become a place for quest and creation, for creative dialogue, for realizing the common will, and for exercising responsibility, and that they will cease to be mere battlegrounds of particular interests. Planetary democracy does not yet exist, but our global civilization is already preparing a place for it: it is the very earth we inhabit, linked with heaven above us. Only in this setting can the mutuality and commonality of the human race be newly forged, with reverence and gratitude for that which transcends each of us, and all of us together. The authority of a world democratic order simply cannot be built on anything else but the revitalized authority of the universe.

The effective expansion of democracy therefore presupposes a critical self-examination, a process that will lead to its internalization. This seems to be the key to saving today's global civilization as a whole, not only from the danger of a conflict of cultures but from the many other dangers that threaten it.

Obviously, this is easy to say but hard to bring about.

Unlike many ideological utopians, fanatics, dogmatists, and a thousand more or less suspect prophets and messiahs who wander about this world as a sad symptom of its helplessness, I do not possess any special formula to awaken the mind of man to his responsibility to the world and for the world.

Two things, however, appear to me to be certain.

In the first place, this indispensable internalization of democracy can scarcely take the form of some new doctrine, a collection of dogmas and rituals. That probably would have exactly the opposite effect: to all the mutually distrustful cultural currents would only be added others, all the more artificial because they would not have grown out of the nourishing soil of myth-making eras. If a renaissance of spirituality does occur, it will far more likely be a multileveled and multicultural emanation, with a new political ethos, spirit, and style, and ultimately will give rise to a new civic behavior.

And secondly, given its fatal incorrigibility, humanity probably will have to go through many more Rwandas and Chernobyls before it understands how unbelievably shortsighted a human being can be who has forgotten that he is not God.

The World Congress of the International PEN Club

Several times in my life I have had the honor of being invited to a world congress of the International PEN Club. But the communist regime always made it impossible for me to attend. I had to live to the age of fifty-eight, experience a revolution in my country, become the nation's president, and see the world congress held in Prague before participating in this important event for the first time in my life. I am sure you will understand, therefore, how moving this moment is for me.

I also know you will understand that I must welcome you all to Prague first and foremost as a colleague who is delighted to be able to meet so many authors I have long held in high esteem, and only secondarily as a representative of the Czech Republic, which has the honor of hosting your gathering. I trust that your presence will introduce important spiritual and intellectual stimuli into this sometimes too materialistic and somewhat provincial setting, and that for a while at least you will help draw the attention of my fellow citizens to matters that transcend the narrow horizon of their everyday cares and concerns.

To you, then, I extend the wish that your stay here be a pleasant one, that your debates be lively and fruitful, and that you also find some time to explore this magic city, whose streets were once trod by such fascinating people as Rabbi Loew, Tycho Brahe, Johannes Kepler, Arcimboldo, Gustav Meyrink, Franz Kafka, Franz Werfel, and Jaroslave Hašek.

This congress is to be devoted to the theme of tolerance,

and it will therefore have to deal with the theme of intolerance as well.

National, racial, religious, social, and political intolerance has been the lot of humanity for millennia, and it is unfortunately rooted deeply in the human psyche, and in the spirit of entire human communities. The problem is that, like many other things, this phenomenon—now that we live in a world with a single global civilization—is far more dangerous than it has ever been before. The time when conflicts between peoples, empires, cultures, and individual civilizations had only local impact is gone forever. On today's overpopulated planet, girdled by dense networks of political and economic relations and supersaturated with information and communication, everything that happens inevitably touches and concerns us all far more and in far different ways than it ever did before. The many horrors of the world today have an impact on us that is not just moral—since these are evils done purposely by some human beings to others—they touch us more and more in an almost physical sense as well, as something that directly threatens us. Yes, we live in a remarkable time. It is not just that we now learn, almost instantaneously, about all the deeply shocking atrocities that take place in the world; now is also a time when every local conflict has the potential to divide the international community and become the catalyst for a far wider conflict, one that in many cases is even global. Who among us, for instance, can tell where the present war in Bosnia and Herzegovina may lead, to what tragic confrontation of three spheres of civilization, if the democratic world remains as indifferent to that conflict as it has been so far?

This alarming state of affairs has not come home to a large part of humanity, particularly to those who do not yet feel directly threatened by any of the contemporary ills of civilization. Nevertheless, it is precisely this state of affairs, when human malice ceases to be merely an assault on our feelings and becomes a direct threat to us, that can lead to a reawakening in people of a sense of responsibility for the world. But how can that change in awareness be brought about? How can people be made to understand that every act of violence against individuals has ceased to be a reason just to feel compassion, and become a real act of violence against us all? How can it be explained to politicians and the public that a shortsighted focusing on purely personal or group interests, on immediate interests, is only paving the road to hell?

I think that, in these matters, writers and intellectuals can and must play a unique role. They are people whose profession—indeed, whose very vocation—is to perceive far more profoundly than others the general context of things, to feel a general sense of responsibility for the world, and to articulate publicly this inner experience.

To achieve this, they have essentially two instruments available to them.

The first is the very substance of their work—that is, literature, or simply writing. A deep analysis of the tangled roots of intolerance in our individual and collective unconscious and consciousness, a merciless examination of all the frustrations of loneliness, personal inadequacy, and the loss of metaphysical certainties that is one of the sources of human aggression—quite simply, a sharp light thrown on the misery of the contemporary human soul—this is, I think, the most important thing writers can provide. In any case, there is nothing new in this: they have always done it, and there is no reason why they should not go on doing so.

But there is another instrument, an instrument that intellectuals sometimes avail themselves of here and there, though in my opinion not nearly often enough. This other instrument is the public activity of intellectuals as citizens, when they engage in politics in the broadest sense of the word. Let us admit that most of us writers feel an essential aversion to politics. We see going into politics as a betrayal of our independence, and we reject it on the grounds that the job of the writer is simply to write. By taking such a position, however, we accept the perverted principle of specialization, according to which some are paid to write about the horrors of the world and about human responsibility, and others to deal with those horrors and bear the responsibility for them. It is the principle of a rather doubtful division of labor: some are here to understand the world and morality, without having to intervene in that world and turn morality into action; others are here to intervene in the world and behave morally, without being bound in any way to understand any of it. It reminds me of the kind of specialization that happens among scientists: some invent chlorofluorocarbons; others investigate the consequences of the holes in the ozone layer that the chlorofluorocarbons cause. A writer with an aversion to politics is like a scientist studying the holes in the ozone, while ignoring the fact that his boss is inventing chlorofluorocarbons.

I once asked a friend of mine, a wonderful man and a wonderful writer, to fill a certain political post. He refused, arguing that someone had to remain independent. I replied that, if everyone said that, it could happen that, in the end, no one would be independent, because there wouldn't be anyone around to make that independence possible and stand behind it.

In short, I am convinced that the world of today, with so many threats to its civilization and so little capacity to deal with them, is crying out for those who have understood something of that world, and know what to do about it, to play a far more vigorous role in politics. I felt this when I was an independent writer, and my time in politics has only confirmed that feeling. It has shown me how little there is in world politics of the mindset that makes it possible to look farther than the borders of one's own electoral district and its momentary moods, or beyond the next election.

I am not suggesting, dear colleagues, that you all become presidents in your own countries, or that each of you go out and start a political party. It would, however, be wonderful if you were to do something else, something less conspicuous but perhaps more important: that is, if you would gradually begin to create something like a worldwide lobby, a special brotherhood or, if I may use the word, a somewhat conspiratorial mafia whose aim is not just to write marvelous books or occasional manifestos, but to have an impact on politics and its human perceptions in a spirit of solidarity and, in a coordinated, deliberate way—if necessary with the kind of personal commitment Susan Sontag showed in Sarajevo—and in many visible and invisible ways, to help open our eyes.

Politicians, at least the wiser ones, will not reject such activity but, on the contrary, will welcome it. I, for instance, would welcome hearing, in this country, a really strong and eloquent voice coming from my colleagues, one that could not be ignored no matter how critical it might be, a voice that did more than merely grumble or engage in esoteric reflection, but became a clear public and political fact.

If it seems to you that I have used, and perhaps abused, this platform to deliver a small sermon, I ask you to forgive me. And if I have asked something of you that you have already been engaged in over the years, I apologize all the more.

Let me conclude with one final plea: do not fail to raise your common voice in defense of our colleague and friend Salman Rushdie, who is still the target of a lethal arrow, and in defense of Nobel Laureate Wole Soyinka, who is unable to join us here because his government prevented him from coming. I also beg you to express our common solidarity with all Bosnian intellectuals who have been waging a courageous and unequal struggle on the cultural front with the criminal fanaticism of ethnic cleansers, those living examples of the lengths to which human intolerance can eventually go.

The 1995 Geuzenpenning

VLAARDINGEN, THE NETHERLANDS,
MARCH 13, 1995

Throughout my life I have held in high regard all those who joined internal resistance movements during the Second World War and defied Nazi power. I have always asked myself: were I confronted with the same situation, would I be able to do what they did—to risk my life every day for the values I believe in. To me, resistance fighters have always personified the highest standards of moral strength, courage, and fidelity to oneself, standards that have offered to me a permanent challenge. Thus, I hardly need stress how greatly honored I am by the decoration I have received today. This medal commemorates the Geuzen, the first group of brave Dutch citizens who resisted evil, many paying for it with their lives. The Geuzen—like other Dutch resistance fighters and members of the resistance in my country and in all the other countries that were occupied by the Nazis, as well as German resistance fighters—were not just accidental victims of despotism. They were well aware what they were risking, but chose to go into battle, all the same, being deeply convinced that evil had to be combated from the very beginning, regardless of the odds against immediate success. It does not take much effort to arrive at the philosophic conviction that resistance to evil is never pointless. But it is not so easy to risk one's own life for that conviction and not to back down even in the face of death; in most cases, only a minority are able to take that course.

Thus, the significance of internal resistance lay not only in the tangible results of their efforts to thwart the pernicious work of the Nazis. More important, the resistance was a phenomenon that time and again restored standards, pointed out values that are worth fighting for under any circumstances, maintained the continuity of respect for those values, and carried the torch of good through the dark night, so that those who lived to see the dawn would have something to turn to, something on which they could build a new life in freedom. Resistance fighters were first and foremost bearers of light, founding fathers and mothers of a better future. To me personally, their endeavor serves as proof that the roots of a free, democratic, and equitable society lie deep in the sphere of morality—that such a society would in fact be unthinkable without a moral anchor. I would even go so far as to say that, if someone is prepared to risk his or her life in a fight whose outcome cannot be foreseen, to risk it not for his or her own sake but for the benefit that such an action may possibly bring to posterity, to humankind and human values as such, this decision emanates not from morality as mere human decency, but from morality as a metaphysical phenomenon.

Resistance against Nazism had another dimension as well. It would not have been possible without a sense of solidarity among those who took part. These were people who frequently risked or sacrificed their own lives rather than expose their associates to detection, whose silence, even during cruel interrogations, often saved lives, who helped one another in countless, immeasurably risky ways. The resistance was an authentic human community, growing out of the individual moral will of free human beings and based on the best human qualities. Man is a sociable animal, but there are different way of associating. The most valuable type of human togetherness is an association based on a free decision by each of its members to work for certain universal human values, on their conscious sharing of commitment to those values and their determination to vouch for them existentially and to vouch for each other. Such an attitude arises from openness toward others, love for one's fellow humans, mutual respect and trust, solidarity. A solidarity of free human beings.

Nazism, too, had its conceptual roots in a certain kind of togetherness. That, however, was a tribal togetherness of people who were prepared to relinquish their own individual responsibility for a collectivist notion of blood brotherhood and who let themselves be hypnotized by fanatic leaders preaching the perverted idea that collective responsibility for the prosperity of their own tribe and for the expansion of its state justified any betrayal of the basic moral feeling of the individual. People who are weak, who have no faith in themselves, and therefore crave some sort of collective self-confirmation; those who prefer dissolving in the anonymity of a crowd, where a leader does all the thinking for them, to carrying the burden of personal responsibility, who accept the identity of a pack rather than engage in the difficult process of seeking, building, and defending their identity as individuals—such people made possible the emergence of Nazism in Europe. Communist collectivism had a similar background. Both inevitably produced totalitarian systems that trampled the very foundations of humanity.

We can therefore say that the confrontation of the resistance with Nazism was the confrontation of an authentic human togetherness with a perverted, degenerate, false one—a confrontation of the solidarity of responsible, moral beings capable of managing their own affairs with a terrible conspiracy of people willing to abandon their individuality and exchange their own responsibility for obedience to a fanatic leader seeking to appeal principally to the one feature in them over which they had no control, that is, to their national affiliation.

We shall soon commemorate the fiftieth anniversary of the end of the Second World War. This occasion will undoubtedly cause us to debate and reflect on all aspects of that war as we try to determine what message it holds for us fifty years later.

I believe that the victory over Nazism meant, among other things—at least for the Western part of Europe—a victory for the individual human being, for his or her individual rights and freedoms as well as his or her individual responsibility. Thus, it was also a victory of the concept of authentic human togetherness over the destructive horror of another type of association, the collectivist togetherness of unfree humans who have given up their individual responsibility. It so happens that we shall observe the fiftieth anniversary of this victory at a time when the sinister historical role of communist collectivism has been played out as well.

What the resistance fighters, including the Geuzen, stood for became the starting point for the construction of a democratic Europe and its unification on a civic basis. In large part, we owe the values that have become the cornerstones of a new Europe and the new European institutions to the sacrifices made by the resistance, because they are the same values that the resistance fighters were dying for. In this context, it is of particular significance that today's democratic Germany, as an important partner in the process of European unification, is founded on these values as well.

Whereas fifty years ago the Allies gained a victory over Germany, today we can fairly say that Germany has gained a victory over Germany—that is, the democratic and liberal Germany has triumphed over both the nationalist and the communist Germanys.

We are entering an era when we shall all have to join forces in building a democratic Europe. In this era we—as nations—can no longer divide ourselves according to who were the victors and who the vanquished in the past. Now the same path lies before us all. Only two dangers stand in our way. One is the activity of those who would raise again the banner of national collectivism and thus go against the course of history again as well as against the interests of the individual. The other is weakness and indifference on the part of democrats and their reluctance to check the new nationalism, or symptoms of it, in a timely and resolute fashion. The irresolution of the democratic community vis-à-vis developments in the former Yugoslavia is the most visible example of the latter today.

I am confident that these obstacles, too, will be gradually overcome. I believe that the moral strength, solidarity, profound responsibility for the fate of humankind, and ability to resist evil from the very beginning, in the name of the fundamental values of humanity, manifested by all those who worked for domestic resistance movements in different European countries during the war, will stand as a source of inspiration and strength as we continue the struggle for a democratic Europe.

National Press Club

Let me begin with a brief personal remark: for virtually my whole life, with the exception of a short period in the late sixties, I was barred from leaving my country. As the long decades went by, I got so used to this absurd situation that I simply assumed I would never get to see any other parts of the world. Needless to say, visiting a continent as distant as Australia was, I thought, absolutely impossible. In my mind, Australia was one of those fabulous worlds beyond reach, worlds one cannot enter, just as one cannot land on a faraway star or step into another century.

A few years ago, everything changed. The world opened up to us all, and I—as head of state—began to travel all over the globe. The most important thing I learned from this sudden freedom was how small our planet really is, and how much closer together places are than I once believed. For this reason, I found it all the more astonishing that the people living on this small planet are incapable of living together, that they constantly wage war and concoct innumerable conflicts. Sometimes it takes only a few minutes to fly over a territory that has been the object of strife for centuries. Though on my official trips I travel by ordinary plane and not by spacecraft, I still feel that I am beginning to understand the experience of astronauts to whom all earthly conflicts appear to be no more than trifles—incomprehensible, petty, and nonsensical—when they look down on our planet from outer space.

Having said that, I should like—in my Czech accent, which, I'm afraid, is a far cry from the Australian one—to share with you certain thoughts that come to mind when I wonder about why people behave so badly, and where to look for the hope that they might behave better in the future.

For thousands of years, humans lived and evolved in different parts of the earth in fairly autonomous entities. Cultures and whole civilizations appeared and disappeared, cultures that—seen from a modern perspective—remained largely confined within their own territories, isolated from one another. If they knew about one another at all, their contacts were minimal. In those times, few if any events in the human world could have had a substantial and immediate impact on the world as a whole.

Nowadays, things are very different. Within a fairly brief period of time—no more than a fraction of human history—a global civilization has come into being and spread around the planet, linking the various parts of it together, absorbing cultures or spheres of civilization that had for so long developed as autonomous units, and forcing them to adapt and adjust. A great many of the problems in our world today, it seems to me, can be attributed to this new reality. They can be explained as struggles of different cultural identities, not against this global civilization, but within themselves, for the survival or enhancement of what they are and the ways in which they differ from one another—struggles for what they appear to be losing. Some say we are living at a time in which every valley wants to be independent. Sometimes this really does seem to be the case. This desire for independence is an understandable reaction to the pressure to integrate and unify exerted by our civilization. Cultural entities shaped by thousands of years of history are resisting this, for fear that within a few years they might dissolve altogether in some global cultural neutrality. If we mix all the colors together we get gray. Cultures of different colors are apparently wrestling with the danger of turning gray in the monstrous palette of a single civilization.

How can we overcome this contradiction? Where can we turn for hope?

The solution certainly does not lie in blindly putting our faith in the essentially atheistic technological civilization of today. We should not rely on the assumption that this civilization, supposedly more progressive than all the cultures and civilizations of the past, is more worthy than they are, or that it is justifiable to suppress and annihilate traditions in its name simply because they are believed to slow the victorious progress of history. Man is also man's own past; suppressing the past would mean declaring war on humanity itself. On the other hand, rejecting the present civilization, abandoning all the good things it has brought, and attempting to return to some bygone tribal life is not a solution, either.

The only wise course is the most demanding one: we must start systematically transforming our civilization into a truly multicultural civilization, one that will allow all to be themselves while denying none the opportunities it offers, one that strives for the tolerant coexistence of different cultural identities, one that clearly articulates the things that unite us and that could develop into a set of shared values and standards enabling us to lead a creative life together. I am happy to be able to reiterate this profound conviction here in Australia—a country that could serve to many others as an example of a working multicultural democracy that is trying to plot a course out of the maze of pitfalls humanity currently finds itself lost in.

The main question is this: where should we look for sources of a shared minimum that could serve as a framework for the tolerant coexistence of different cultures within a single civilization? It is not enough to take the set of imperatives, principles, or rules produced by the Euro-American world and mechanically declare them binding for all. If people are to accept these principles, identify with them, and follow them, the principles will have to appeal to something that has been present in them before, to some of their inherent qualities. Different cultures or spheres of civilization can share only what they perceive as genuine common ground, not something that a few merely offer to or even force upon others. The tenets of human coexistence on this earth can hold up only if they grow out of the deepest experience of everyone, not just some of us. They must be formulated so as to be in harmony with what man—as a human being, not as a member of a particular group—has learned, experienced, endured.

No unbiased person will have any trouble knowing where to look. If we examine the oldest moral canons, the commandments that prescribe proper human conduct and the rules of human coexistence, we find numerous essential similarities among them. It is often surprising to discover that virtually identical moral norms appear in different places and at different times, largely independently of one another. Another important point is that the moral foundations upon which different civilizations or cultures are built have always had transcendental, or metaphysical, underpinnings. It is scarcely possible to find a culture that does not derive from the conviction that a higher, mysterious order of the world exists beyond our reach, a higher intention that is the source of all things, a higher memory recording everything, a higher authority to which we are all accountable in one way or another. That order has had a thousand faces; human history has known a vast array of gods and deities, religious and spiritual beliefs, rituals and liturgies. Nevertheless, from time immemorial, the key to the existence of the human race, of nature, and of the universe, as well as the key to what is required of human responsibility, has always been found in what transcends humanity, in what stands above it. Humanity must respect this if the world is to survive. To this day, this point of departure has been present in all our archetypal notions and in our long-held instinctive knowledge, despite the obvious estrangement from these values that has come with modern civilization. Yet, even as our respect for the mysteries of the world wanes, we can see for ourselves again and again that a lack of such respect leads to ruin. All of this clearly suggests where we should look for what unites us: in an awareness of the transcendental.

I possess no specific advice on how to revive this awareness which was once common to the whole human race, how to retrieve it from the depths to which it has sunk, or how to do this in a way that is appropriate for this era and at the same time universal, acceptable to all. Yet, whenever I think about it, regardless of the context, I'm always forced to conclude that this is precisely where we should begin the search for a means of coexistence on this planet, and for saving the human race from the many dangers to its survival that our civilization generates. We should seek new ways to restore the capacity to be sensitive to what transcends humanity, to what gives a meaning to the world surrounding it, as well as to human life itself.

Dostoyevsky wrote that if there were no God everything would be permitted. Simply put, it seems to me that our present civilization, having lost the awareness that the world has a spirit, believes that anything is permitted. The only spirit we recognize is our own.

However different the paths followed by different civilizations, we can find at the core of most religions and cultures throughout history the same basic message: people should revere God as a phenomenon that transcends them; they should revere one another; and they should not harm their fellow humans.

To my mind, reflecting on this message is the only way out of the crisis the world finds itself in today. Of course, such a reflection must be free of prejudice and it must be critical, no matter who may turn out to be a target of that criticism.

Allow me to offer you a specific illustration of this general idea.

The Euro-American world of modern times has developed a fairly consistent system of values for human coexistence, which is now accepted as the basis of international coexistence as well. These values include the concept of human rights and liberties that grow out of respect for the individual human being and for his or her dignity. They include democracy, which rests on separation of the legislative, executive, and judicial powers, on political pluralism, and on free elections. And they include respect for private ownership of property and for the rules of the market economy. I unreservedly subscribe to this system of values, and so does the Czech Republic.

And yet, from different parts of the world, including the Pacific region, we hear voices calling these values into question, arguing that they are the creation of a single culture and cannot simply be transferred wholesale to other cultures. Naturally, such voices find much at fault in the West, to make their case that these values are flawed or inadequate. One typical argument is that Western democracy is marked by a profound crisis of authority, and that, without respect for authority as a means of ensuring law and order, society is bound to fall apart.

The odd thing is that those who say this are right and wrong at the same time.

They are certainly right in saying that the Western world is suffering from a crisis of authority. As someone who has arrived fairly recently in the world of high politics, and who has suddenly seen it from the inside, I have frequently experienced the odd fact that the public, other politicians, and the media most of all are far more interested in casting doubt on the authority of a particular politician than they are in determining whether it is desirable that he or she should wield authority in the first place. I don't take this personally—for one thing, nobody can possibly have as many doubts about myself as I do. But I am concerned about this phenomenon as a political reality. If politicians have no authority at all, the state and its various constituent parts can have no authority, either. This, in turn, has an adverse effect on society.

But is this crisis of authority a direct product of democracy? And if so, does it not follow that an authoritarian regime, a dictatorship or a totalitarian system is preferable to democracy after all?

That is certainly not the case.

The present crisis of authority is only one of a thousand consequences of the general crisis of spirituality in the world today. Humankind, having lost its respect for a higher, superterrestrial authority, necessarily loses respect for all earthly authority, too. Consequently, people also lose respect for their fellow humans, and eventually even for themselves. Such a loss of transcendental perspective, to which everything on this earth relates, inevitably leads to a collapse of earthly value systems as well. Humanity has lost sight of what I once called the absolute horizon; as a result, everything in life has become relative. All sense of responsibility disintegrates, including responsibility for the human community and its authorities. This is a philosophical, not a political problem. However, even a decaying or diminishing democratic authority is a thousand times better than the thoroughly artificial authority of a dictator imposed through violence or brainwashing.

Democracy is an open system, and thus it is capable of improvement. Among other things, freedom provides room for responsibility. If that room is not sufficiently used, the fault does not lie with democracy, but it does present democracy with a challenge. Dictatorship offers no room for responsibility, and thus it can generate no genuine authority. Instead, it fills all the available space with the pseudo-authority of a dictator.

Potential dictators are well aware of the crisis of authority in democracy. The less the atheistic man of today heeds the challenge that democracy presents him, and the less he succeeds in filling the room it offers by taking genuine and unquestioned responsibility, the faster a dictator, posing as the bearer of universal responsibility, will proceed to occupy that room until finally he will occupy it entirely. Hitler, Lenin, and Mao were typical examples of this species. Filling all the available room with a completely false authority, they closed it off, demolished it, and eventually destroyed democracy itself. We all know where this leads: to hecatombs of the dead, the tortured, and the humiliated. In short: whereas democracy paves the way to the creation of real authority, an authoritarian regime blocks that path with the caricature of authority.

The chances for a successful existential revolution—as I once metaphorically described the awakening of a deeper human responsibility—are far better under freedom and democracy than under a dictatorship, where the only room offered to anyone who wishes to take responsibility is a prison cell.

The Western world cannot be faulted for sticking to democracy. Though democracy may surely take different forms, it is, today, the only way open to us all. What the West can be faulted for is its failure to understand properly and safeguard this fantastic accomplishment. Paralyzed by a general moral crisis, it has been unable to realize all the potential of this great invention, or to give a meaningful content to the space it has opened up. It is because of these deficiencies that madmen have, again and again, managed to devastate democracy and unleash a variety of global horrors.

What conclusion should we draw from this? That there is no reason to fear democracy, or to perceive it as a system that necessarily destroys authority and tears everything apart. Another option is available to those who wish to prevent this destruction: they can rise to the challenge to demonstrate their own responsibility and to introduce—or, rather, restore—the spirit and substance democracy had when it first came into being. This is a superhuman task; yet, in the open system which democracy is, it can be accomplished.

In cultures where the roots of democracy are still shallow, or where democracy has not taken root at all so far, and where a free individual means virtually nothing and the leader is omnipotent, leaders often appeal to the centuries-old traditions of authority in their sphere, and seek to legitimize their dictatorial rule by claiming to continue these traditions.

Again, they are both right and wrong. They are wrong in that what they present as the continuity of ancient traditions is in fact their negation. Though recalling the natural authority that leaders may possess in their cultural systems, they replace it with an unnatural authority. Instead of an authority emanating from charisma, authority as an inwardly perceived and widely accepted higher vocation, authority marked by a high degree of responsibility toward their self-imposed task—instead of this, they establish the utterly secularized authority of the whip.

Thus—to put it in simplified terms—if the East can borrow democracy and its inherent values from the West as a space in which a reawakening sense of the transcendental can restore authority, then the West can learn from the East what true authority is, what it grows from, and how it conducts itself. It can then be spread throughout the zone of human freedom which it has created. I think in this context of Confucius, who so aptly described what it means to wield genuine authority. His standards have very little in common with the ideas of today's men of the whip. To him, authority—be it in the father of a family or the ruler of a state—is a metaphysically anchored gift whose strength derives from the holder's heightened responsibility, not from the might of the instruments of power he or she may wield. Moreover, charisma is lost when a person betrays that responsibility.

Though many see them as opposites, both East and West are in a sense enmeshed in the same problem: both are betraying their own deepest spiritual roots. If they were to look back and draw from these roots more of their life-giving sap, each might not only do better for itself, but might immediately begin to understand the other better than it does now.

This small example of what the West can give the East, and vice versa, may perhaps illustrate that a search for common principles and objectives can be useful for everyone, and that it may be pursued without anyone's losing his identity in the process. It also shows that such a search would be unimaginable if we did not make contact with the original, long-forgotten transcendental roots of our cultures. In the moral world of antiquity, Judaism, and Christianity, without which the West would hardly have come to modern democracy, we can find more points of agreement with Confucius than we would think, and more than is realized by those who invoke the Confucian tradition to condemn Western democracy.

.   .   .

I hope that you have understood what I meant to say, despite my Czech accent and the simplified way I have attempted to condense, in a few sentences, some of my thoughts about the present-day world. I see the only chance for today's civilization in a clear awareness of its multicultural character, in a radical enhancement of its inner spirit, and in a concerted effort to find the shared spiritual roots of all cultures, for they are what unites all people. It is on this basis that we should articulate anew the standards and practices that will enable us to live together in peace without having to forfeit our identities. We have an opportunity now to open up an entirely new era of mutual inspiration. The preconditions for this are genuine openness, the will to understand one another, and the ability to step beyond the confines of our own habits and prejudices. Identity is not a prison; it is an appeal for dialogue with others.

I invite you all most cordially to come to visit the Czech Republic, a small country situated in the very center of Europe. It is my hope that you will not have to pass through any battlefields on the way, and that you will feel what I feel whenever I travel: that our planet is small, and a rather nice place to live, and that it would be the greatest absurdity of all if those destined to live together on it were to fail to do so even though love for one's fellow humans is the central commandment of all our contending cultures.

Victoria University of Wellington

Some time ago a wise old man came to see me in Prague and I listened to him with admiration. Shortly afterward I heard that this man had died. His name was Karl Popper. He was a world traveler who observed the biggest war ever waged by human-kind—the war unleashed by the tribal fury of Nazi ideology—from this country, from New Zealand. It was here that he thought about the state of the world, and it was here that he wrote his most important books. Undoubtedly influenced by the harmonious coexistence of people of different cultures on these islands, he posed the question of why it was so difficult for the idea of an open society to prevail against wave after wave of tribalism, and inquired into the spiritual background of all ene-mies of open society and into the patterns of their thinking.

Addressing you on this ceremonial occasion, I should like to offer a few remarks on Sir Karl Popper's thoughts and thus pay tribute to the recently deceased thinker.

One of the targets of Popper's profound criticism—which he supported by ample evidence—was a phenomenon he called "holistic social engineering." He used this term to describe human attempts to change the world for the better completely and globally, on the basis of some preconceived ideology that purported to understand all the laws of historical development and to describe inclusively, comprehensively, and holistically a state of affairs that would be the ultimate realization of these laws. Popper clearly demonstrated that this pattern of human thinking and behavior can only lead to a totalitarian system.

I come from a country that lived under a communist regime for several decades. From my own experience, I can confirm that Sir Karl Popper was right. In the beginning was an allegedly scientific theory of historical laws; that Marxist theory subsequently gave rise to the communist utopia, the vision of a paradise on earth that eventually produced the gulags, the endless suffering of many nations, the endless violation of the human being. Anything that in any way countered the vision of the world offered by communism, thus calling that vision into question or actually proving it wrong, was mercilessly crushed. Needless to say, life, with its unfathomable diversity and unpredictability, never allowed itself to be squeezed into the crude Marxist cage. All the guardians of the cage could do was to suppress and destroy whatever would not fit into it. Ultimately, war had to be declared on life itself and on its innermost essence. I could give you thousands of concrete examples of how all the natural manifestations of life were stifled in the name of an abstract, theoretical vision of a better world. It was not just that there were what we call "human-rights abuses." This enforced vision led to the moral, political, and economic devastation of all of society.

Instead of such holistic engineering, Popper argued for a gradual approach, an effort to improve incrementally the institutions, mechanisms, and techniques of human coexistence, to improve them by remaining constantly in touch with life and by constantly enriching our experience. Improvements and changes must be made according to whatever has proven to be good, practical, desirable, and meaningful, without the arrogant presumption that we have understood everything about this world, and thus already know everything there is to know about how to ameliorate it.

In my country, one of the understandable reactions to the tragic experience of communism is the opinion we sometimes encounter that man should, if possible, refrain altogether from changing or ameliorating the world, from devising long-range concepts, strategic plans, or visions. All this is seen as part of the armory of holistic social engineering. This opinion, of course, is a grave error. Paradoxically, it has much in common with the fatalism Popper finds in those who believe they have grasped the laws of history and that they must simply serve those laws. This fatalism takes the form of the peculiar idea that society is nothing more than a machine that, once properly set in motion, can run on its own, automatically and permanently.

I am opposed to holistic social engineering. I refuse, however, to throw out the baby with the bathwater, and I am a long way from thinking that people should give up altogether on the constant search for ways of improving the world in which they must live together. It must be done, even though they may never achieve more than partial improvements in particular areas, will always have to wait to see whether the change was the right thing to do, and must always be prepared to rectify whatever life has shown to be wrong.

Recently I expressed this opinion in the presence of a philosopher friend of mine. He looked somewhat puzzled at first, and then began trying to persuade me of something I have never denied, that the world, in its very essence, is a holistic entity; that everything in it is interconnected; that whatever we do in any one place has an unfathomable impact everywhere, though we may not see the whole of it; that even the postmodern science of these days supplies evidence of that.

With this remark, my friend has compelled me to supplement what I said, and perhaps even what Popper wrote. Yes, it is true that society, the world, the universe—Being itself—is a deeply mysterious phenomenon, held together by billions of mysterious interconnections. Knowing all this and humbly accepting it are one thing; but the arrogant belief that humanity, or the human spirit or human reason, can grasp and describe the world in its entirety and derive from this description a formula for its improvement is something else. To be aware of the interconnectedness of all events is completely different from believing that we have fully understood this.

In other words: I believe, as Popper does, that neither politicians, nor scientists, nor entrepreneurs, nor anyone else should fall for the vain belief that they can grasp the world as a whole and change it as a whole by one single action. Seeking to improve it, people should proceed with utmost caution and sensitivity, on a step-by-step basis, always paying attention to what each change actually brings about. At the same time, however, I believe—possibly differing from Popper's views to some extent—that as they do so they should constantly bear in mind all the global interrelations that they are aware of, and should realize that beyond their knowledge exists an infinitely wider range of interrelations. My relatively brief sojourn in the realm of so-called high politics has convinced me time and again of the need to take this very approach: most of the threats hanging over the world now, as well as many of the problems confronting it, could be handled much more effectively if we were able to see past the ends of our noses and take into consideration, to some extent at least, the broader interconnections that go beyond the scope of our immediate or group interests. This awareness, of course, should never become an arrogant utopian conviction that we alone possess the whole truth about these interconnections. On the contrary, it should emanate from a deep and humble respect for them and for their mysterious order.

My country is now witnessing a debate about the role of intellectuals: about how important or how dangerous they are, about the degree to which they can be independent, about how much or in what ways they should become engaged in politics. At times, the debate has been confused, partly because the word "intellectual" means different things to different people. This is closely related to what I have just said here.

Let me try—just for the moment—to define an intellectual. To me, an intellectual is a person who has devoted his or her life to thinking in more general terms about the affairs of this world and the broader context of things. Of course, it is not only intellectuals who do this. But intellectuals do it—if I may use the word—professionally. That is, their principal occupation is studying, reading, teaching, writing, publishing, addressing the public. Often—though certainly not always!—this makes them more receptive toward general issues; often—though by far not always!—it leads them to embrace a broader sense of responsibility for the state of the world and its future.

If we accept this definition of an intellectual, it will come as no surprise that many an intellectual has done a great deal of harm to the world. Taking an interest in the world as a whole and feeling an increased sense of responsibility for it, intellectuals are often tempted to try to grasp the world as a whole, to explain it entirely, and to offer universal solutions to its problems. An impatience of mind and a propensity toward mental shortcuts are the usual reasons why intellectuals tend to devise holistic ideologies and succumb to the seductive power of holistic social engineering. For that matter, were not the forerunners of Nazi ideology, the founders of Marxism, and the first communist leaders intellectuals par excellence? Did not a number of dictators, and even some terrorists—from the leaders of the former German Red Brigades to Pol Pot—start off as intellectuals? Not to mention the many intellectuals who, though they neither created nor introduced dictatorships, time and again failed to stand up to them because they more than others were prone to accept the delusion that there was a universal key to eliminating human woes. It was to describe this phenomenon that the expression *"trahison des clercs"*—the treason of the intellectuals—was coined. The many different anti-intellectual campaigns in my country have always supported their case with reference to this type of intellectual. And it is from there that they derive their belief that the intellectual is a species dangerous to humankind.

Those who make this claim are committing an error very similar to the one committed by those whose utter rejection of socialist planning leads them to reject any conceptual thinking whatsoever.

It would be nonsense to believe that all intellectuals have succumbed to utopianism or holistic engineering. A great many intellectuals both past and present have done precisely what I think should be done: they have perceived the broader context, seen things in more global terms, recognized the mysterious nature of globality and humbly deferred to it. Their increased sense of responsibility for this world has not made such intellectuals identify with an ideology; it has made them identify with humanity, with its dignity and its prospects. These intellectuals build people-to-people solidarity. They foster tolerance, struggle against evil and violence, promote human rights, and argue for their indivisibility. In short, they represent what has been called "the conscience of society." They are not indifferent when people in an unknown country on the other side of the planet are annihilated, or when children starve there, nor are they unconcerned about global warming and whether future generations will be able to lead an endurable life. They care about the fate of virgin forests in faraway places, about whether humankind will soon destroy all its nonrenewable resources, or whether a global dictatorship of advertising, consumerism, and blood-and-thunder stories on TV will ultimately lead the human race to a state of complete idiocy.

And where do intellectuals stand in relation to politics? There have been many misunderstandings about that, too.

My opinion is simple: when meeting with utopian intellectuals, we should make every effort not to give in to their siren calls. If they enter politics, we should believe them even less. The other type of intellectual—who knows about the interconnections between everything in this world together, who approaches the world with humility but also with an increased sense of responsibility, who wages a struggle for every good thing—should be listened to with the greatest attention, regardless of whether they work as independent critics, holding up a much-needed mirror to politics and power, or are directly involved in politics. These two roles are very different from each other. My friend Timothy Garton Ash, with whom I have been discussing this subject for years, is certainly right about that. But though this is clearly so, it does not follow that we should bar such intellectuals from the realm of politics on the pretext that they belong only at universities or in the media. On the contrary: I am deeply convinced that, the more such people engage directly in practical politics, the better our world will fare. By its very essence, politics induces those who work in it to focus their attention on short-term issues that have a direct bearing on the next election instead of on what will happen a hundred years from now. It compels them to pursue group interests rather than the interests of the human community as a whole, to say things that please everyone and not those that people are not so happy to hear, to treat even truth itself with caution. But this is not a sign that intellectuals have no place in politics. It is instead a challenge to draw into it as many of them as possible. After all, who is better equipped to decide about the fate of this globally interconnected civilization than someone who is most keenly aware of those interconnections, who pays the greatest regard to them, who takes the most responsible attitude toward the world as a whole?

It is magnificent that a man can think about the problems of our world and read works by an outstanding philosopher in the Czech Republic, tens of thousands of kilometers away from here, and then, just a few hours later, share his thoughts with a receptive audience here in New Zealand, where that philosopher once wrote his books. I am grateful to you for offering me this opportunity, and I am grateful to Victoria University for allowing me to consider myself, as of this day, a New Zealand doctor.

Catalonia International Prize

The fiftieth anniversary of the end of the Second World War has once again led me to contemplate the eventful modern history of my country. Once again I have come to the realization that the central theme of this period is a constant theme, in which I have always taken a special interest—namely, the relationship between morality and politics. Thus, when Mr. Pujol asked me to say a few words about this particular subject, I immediately thought of taking the opportunity to examine it in the light of the modern history of my country.

In that period of time there have been several crucial moments that put before the representatives of our state the same agonizing dilemma: whether to harm the nation by yielding to somebody's dictate or by not yielding. They always opted for the former, and I have always considered that choice a fatal error. I still think so, but, compared with the times when I was only an independent observer of history, with no experience of how difficult decision-making is for a person saddled with political office and thus bearing a direct responsibility for the fate of his or her fellow citizens and their descendants, I now understand much better what kind of a burden lay on the shoulders of those who were required to make such historic decisions. I will admit that many times lately I have tried to look back at their situation as they must have seen it, and to imagine what I would have done in their place. Would I have been able to make the decision, I thought, before I myself tasted the responsibilities of a political office?

The first of such ominous dilemmas was faced by Czechoslovak President Edvard Beneš at the time of the Munich *diktát*. He knew he was facing aggression by a madman, sanctioned by our then allies, who thus betrayed not only the treaties they had signed but also the values they professed. He was aware that, to preserve national honor and the moral integrity of our national community, the right thing to do was to refuse to give in to the *diktát* and proceed to defend the country. On the other hand, he knew what that could have meant: thousands of lost lives, the devastation of the country, and the probability of early military defeat by a far stronger adversary. He realized that such a decision could well have met with misunderstanding and even rejection on the part of the democratic world, and that he himself might well have been branded a peace-breaker and provocateur foolishly attempting to draw other nations into a totally unnecessary war. He decided to capitulate without fighting, because that course seemed more responsible than risking an eventual capitulation after heavy losses.

The same man found himself in a similar situation in February 1948. Then he could have resisted the communist putschists supported not only by the powerful Soviet Union but also by a part of his nation. He could have risked bloodshed that might have ended with a victory of the communists anyway. The other option was to succumb, and thus pave the way for many years of communist totalitarian rule. At that time, too—old, ailing, and disappointed—he once more chose capitulation.

For a third time, Czechoslovak representatives capitulated after the Soviet occupation of our country in 1968. Having been abducted to the Soviet Union and exposed for several days to humiliation and threats, all—with one laudable exception—signed the so-called Moscow Protocols, thus legalizing the occupation *de facto* and taking the first, and essential, step in the ensuing course of events that was called, rather perversely, "normalization."

Any parallels between different historical situations may of course be misleading. This is true of the cases I mention here as well: different people, equipped with different experience and acting in different circumstances, both international and domestic, decided considerably different matters. Whole libraries of testimonies, memoirs, and historical analyses now exist on each of the three dilemmas, and to delve into them is to realize all too quickly how facile it would be simply to equate those three dark moments of our modern history.

Nevertheless, we should not overlook certain general similarities among them:

1) Those making the decisions did not have the benefit of hindsight. They had only their own judgment to draw on, their own understanding of the given situation, and their own idea of what the consequences of their choice would be. They all knew that they were deciding between two evils, and they all tried responsibly to determine which of them was the lesser.

2) All three dilemmas had one thing in common: those who were thrown into them had to choose between a course of action that was more moral yet carried with it the risk of incalculable loss of life and suffering, and one that was more realistic and promised fewer direct losses. Actually, they were torn between two dimensions of political responsibility—on the one hand, responsibility for the moral integrity of society; on the other, responsibility for human lives. This must be a dreadful dilemma, and someone who has never been faced with it personally can hardly stand in judgment over someone who has.

3) None of us knows, nor shall we ever know, what would have happened had those who made the decisions in the three cases decided otherwise. History is characterized by what physicists call singularity—it always takes one course only, with no alternatives we could compare it with and no plausible ifs, ands, or buts. Therefore, we should be very careful when passing judgment on past decisions, and avoid jumping to conclusions.

4) Each of these decisions brought about a similar consequence: a deep traumatization and a long-term demoralization of the society. This, perhaps, is where we can find a thread of causality between them, thin though it may be. The postwar situation in my country would probably not have been as favorable to the communist offensive, nor the democrats so pliant, had it not been for the trauma of Munich; and the reform-

minded communists would hardly have given up so easily in 1968 had it not been for the easy victory of the communists in 1948. I do not think that the Czechs, or Czechs and Slovaks, are worse than any other nation from the moral point of view. I only believe that in the decades following the Munich *diktát* of 1938 my country suffered a specific type of moral frustration, and that the three political decisions I am discussing here were to a substantial extent instrumental in its emergence and subsequent deepening. Three times, our democracy, or our longing for it, was surrendered without a fight, and this has left deep scars upon the soul of our society and has adversely affected its development. I could give you hundreds of specific examples bearing this out, but that is not the purpose of this speech.

Its purpose is to demonstrate how problematic it is to set politics and morality against one another. Didn't the "less moral" decisions have deeply adverse effects in the political sense as well? Didn't the moral traumas resulting from these decisions have a profound and long-lasting political impact? We do not know what the consequences would have been of decisions to the contrary—the "more moral" ones. But we can well imagine that in the latter case the effects might not have been so deep, so long-lasting, or so fatal. There would most likely have been heavier immediate losses of both human life and property, and greater immediate physical suffering. But wouldn't we have been spared other losses, the less visible yet deeper and more permanent ones—the losses caused by the damage done to the moral integrity of our national community? It is difficult to weigh different kinds of loss against one another. How many lost human lives would still be a justifiable price for the long-term sanity of the society and its long-term immunity against new evils? Is there a point at which the price becomes too high? One thing, however, is certain: both morality and immorality have direct political consequences, just as political decisions have a direct bearing on morality. That is why I think it is nonsense to separate politics from morality, or to say the two are totally unrelated. To put such thoughts into practice, or even just to speak them, is—paradoxically—not only deeply immoral, but very wrong politically as well.

Morality is omnipresent, and so is politics, and politics that dissociates itself from morality is simply bad politics.

But I have not yet answered the question of what I would have done had I been in the place of my predecessors and had I faced the dilemmas they faced.

I will admit that I don't know. I can only say I think I would probably have acted differently, but I cannot rule out the possibility that I think this because I know, as they did not, the consequences of their decisions.

Thus, it appears more to the point to ask myself another question: what would I do if I found myself today faced with a dilemma similar to theirs, not knowing or able to know—as they didn't—what the ultimate impact of my decision would be?

I believe I would try to judge objectively all the relevant factors, consult with many people who have my full confidence, analyze the whole situation, and attempt to make a rational estimate of the different consequences that my actions could possibly have. And when, having done all that, I still did not know what to do, I would probably turn to an authority that, though it may not be wholly reliable in a strict sense of the word, has more than once proved to be the most reliable source to me: my conscience, my moral instincts, the part of me that—as I see it—transcends me.

We all know what qualms of conscience are, the strange and dejected feeling that we have betrayed something in ourselves, or something above us, that we have sunk into a mire, or soiled ourselves; the feeling of having done something we must constantly justify before someone near us, something in us or someone above us, while suspecting that the more we seek such justification the less convinced we shall be in our own minds that what we did was truly right. This is a state of deep existential distress, because it touches what some philosophers call nothingness. On the other hand, we all know the uplifting state of mind that comes from having decided to do something that does not bring us any visible benefits, but which we can be certain satisfies the requirements we are called upon to meet, through our conscience, by what is called the moral order of the world.

I do not know whether these thoughts will win the applause of politicians. But I can't help it: nothing has convinced me so far that doing what our hearts tell us to do is not the best politics of all.

Harvard University

CAMBRIDGE, JUNE 8, 1995

One evening not long ago I was sitting in an outdoor restaurant by the water. My chair was almost identical to the chairs they have in restaurants by the Vltava River in Prague. They were playing the same rock music they play in most Czech restaurants. I saw advertisements I'm familiar with back home. Above all, I was surrounded by young people who were similarly dressed, who drank familiar-looking drinks, and who behaved as casually as their contemporaries in Prague. Only their complexion and their facial features were different—for I was in Singapore.

I sat there thinking about this, and again—for the umpteenth time—I realized an almost banal truth: that we now live in a single global civilization. The identity of this civilization does not lie merely in similar forms of dress, or in similar drinks, or in the constant buzz of the same pop music all around the world, or even in international advertising. It lies in something deeper: thanks to the modern idea of constant progress, with its inherent expansionism, and to the rapid evolution of science that follows directly from it, our planet has, for the first time in the long history of the human race, been blanketed in the space of a very few decades by a single civilization—one that is essentially technological. The world is now enmeshed in webs of telecommunication networks consisting of millions of tiny threads or capillaries that not only transmit information of all kinds at lightning speed, but also convey integrated models of social, political, and economic behavior. They are conduits for legal norms, as well as for billions of dollars crisscrossing the world while remaining invisible even to those who deal directly with them. The life of the human race is completely interconnected, not only in the informational sense, but in the casual sense as well.

Anecdotally, I could illustrate this by reminding you—since I've already mentioned Singapore—that today all it takes is a single shady transaction initiated by a single devious bank clerk in Singapore to bring down a bank on the other side of the world. Thanks to the accomplishments of this civilization, practically all of us know what checks, bonds, bills of exchange, and stocks are. We are familiar with CNN and Chernobyl, and we recognize the Rolling Stones, Nelson Mandela, and Salman Rushdie. More than that, the capillaries that have so radically integrated this civilization also convey information about certain modes of human coexistence that have proved their worth—like democracy, respect for human rights, the rule of law, the laws of the marketplace. Such information flows around the world and, in varying degrees, takes root in different places.

In modern times, this global civilization emerged in the territory occupied by European and ultimately by Euro-American culture. Historically, it evolved from a combination of traditions—classical, Judaic, and Christian. In theory, at least, it gives people not only the capacity for worldwide communication, but also a coordinated means of defending themselves against many common dangers. And it can, in an unprecedented way, make our life on this earth easier and open up to us hitherto unexplored horizons in our knowledge of ourselves and the world we live in.

And yet there is something not quite right about it.

Allow me to use this ceremonial gathering for a brief meditation on a subject which I have dwelt upon a great deal, and which I often bring up on occasions resembling this one. I want to focus today on the source of the dangers that threaten humanity in spite of this global civilization, and often directly because of it. Above all, I would like to speak about the ways in which these dangers can be confronted.

Many of the great problems we face today, as I understand them, have their origin in the fact that this global civilization, though in evidence everywhere, is no more than a thin veneer over the sum of human awareness. This civilization is immensely fresh, young, new, and fragile, and the human spirit has accepted it with dizzying alacrity, without itself changing in any essential way. Humanity has evolved over long millennia and in all manner of civilizations and cultures that have gradually, and in very diverse ways, shaped our habits of mind, our relationships to the world, our models of behavior, and the values we accept and recognize. In essence, this new epidermis of the single world civilization merely conceals an immense variety of cultures, of peoples, of religious worlds, of historical traditions and historically formed attitudes—all of which in a sense lie "beneath" it. At the same time, even as the veneer of world civilization expands, this "underside" of humanity, this hidden dimension of it, demands more and more avidly to be heard and to be granted a right to life.

Thus, while the world as a whole increasingly accepts the new habits of global civilization, another, contradictory process is taking place: ancient traditions are reviving, different religions and cultures are awakening to new ways of being, seeking new room to exist, and struggling with growing fervor to realize what is unique to them and makes them different from others. Ultimately they seek to give their individuality a political expression.

It is often said that in our time every valley cries out for its own independence and will even fight for it. Many nations, or parts of them at least, are struggling against modern civilization or its main proponents for the right to worship their ancient gods and obey ancient divine injunctions. They carry on their struggle with weapons provided by the very civilization they oppose. They employ radar, computers, lasers, nerve gases, and perhaps, in the future, even nuclear weapons—all products of the world they challenge—to help defend their ancient heritage against the erosions of modern civilization. In contrast with these technological inventions, other products of this civilization—like democracy and the idea of human rights—are not accepted in many places, because they are deemed hostile to local traditions.

In other words: the Euro-American world has equipped other parts of the globe with instruments that not only could effectively destroy the enlightened values that, among other things, made possible the invention of precisely these instruments, but could well cripple the capacity of people to live together on this earth.

What follows from all of this?

It is my belief that this state of affairs contains a clear challenge, not only to the Euro-American world but to our present-day civilization as a whole. It is a challenge to this civilization to start understanding itself as a multicultural and multipolar civilization, whose purpose lies not in undermining the individuality of different spheres of culture and civilization but in allowing them to be themselves more completely. This will be possible, even conceivable, only if we all accept a basic code of mutual coexistence, a kind of common minimum we can all respect, one that will enable us to go on living side by side. Yet such a code won't stand a chance if it is the product of merely a few who then proceed to force it on the rest. It must be an expression of the authentic will of everyone, growing out of the genuine spiritual roots hidden beneath the skin of our common, global civilization. If it is merely disseminated through the capillaries of this skin, the way Coca-Cola ads are—as a commodity offered by some to others, and at a price—such a code can hardly be expected to take hold in any profound or universal way.

But is humanity capable of such an undertaking? Is this not a hopelessly utopian idea? Haven't we so lost control of our destiny that we are condemned to gradual extinction in ever-harsher high-tech clashes between cultures, because of our fatal inability to cooperate in the face of impending catastrophes, be they ecological, social, demographic, or generated by the state of our civilization as such?

I don't know.

But I have not lost hope.

I have not lost hope because I am persuaded again and again

that dwelling in the deepest roots of most, if not all, cultures is an essential similarity—something that could be made (if the will to do so existed) a genuinely unifying starting point for a new code of human coexistence that would be firmly anchored in the great diversity of human traditions.

Don't we find somewhere in the foundations of most religions and cultures, though they may take a thousand and one distinct forms, such common elements as respect for what transcends us, whether we mean the mystery of Being or a moral order that stands above us; certain imperatives that come to us from heaven, or from nature, or from our own hearts; a belief that our deeds will live after us; respect for our neighbors, for our families, for certain natural authorities; respect for human dignity in general and for nature; and a sense of solidarity and benevolence toward guests who come with good intentions?

Isn't the common, ancient origin of our multiple spiritualities, each of which is merely another kind of human understanding of the same reality, the thing that can genuinely bring people of different cultures together?

And aren't the basic commandments of this archetypal spirituality in harmony with what even an unreligious person—without knowing exactly why—may consider proper and meaningful?

Naturally, I am not suggesting that modern people be compelled to worship ancient deities and accept rituals they have long since abandoned. I am suggesting something quite different. We must come to understand the deep mutual connection or kinship between the various forms of human spirituality. We must recollect our original spiritual and moral substance, which grew out of the same essential experience of humanity. I believe that this is the only way to achieve a genuine renewal of our sense of responsibility for ourselves and for the world. And at the same time, it is the only way to achieve among cultures a deeper understanding that will enable them to work together in a truly ecumenical way to create a new order for the world.

.   .   .

The unitary civilization that envelops the modern world and the human consciousness has, as we all know, a dual nature that calls into question, every step of the way, the very values it is based upon and propagates. The thousands of marvelous achievements of this civilization that work so well for us and enrich us so much can equally impoverish, diminish, and destroy our lives, and frequently do. Instead of serving people, many of these creations enslave them. Instead of helping people to develop their identities, they snatch them away. Almost every invention or discovery—from the splitting of the atom and the discovery of DNA to television and the computer—can be turned against us and used to our detriment. How much easier it is today than it was during the First World War to destroy an entire metropolis in a single air-raid! And how much easier it would be today, in the era of television, for a madman like Hitler or Stalin to pervert the spirit of a whole nation. Terrorists have so much more destructive potential at their disposal today than at the beginning of this century. And when have people ever had the power we now possess to alter the climate of the planet and deplete its mineral resources or the wealth of its fauna and flora in the space of a few short decades?

In our era, it would seem that one part of the human brain—the rational part, which has made all these morally neutral discoveries—has undergone exceptional development, while the other part, which should be alert to ensure that these discoveries really have served humanity and will not destroy it, has lagged behind catastrophically.

Yes, regardless of where I begin my thinking about the problems facing this generation, I always return to the theme of human responsibility, which seems incapable of keeping pace with civilization and preventing it from turning against the human race. It's as though the world has simply become too much for us to handle.

There is no way back. Only a dreamer can believe that the solution lies in curtailing the progress of civilization in some way or other. The main task in the coming era is something else: a radical renewal of our sense of responsibility. Our conscience must catch up to our reason—otherwise we are lost.

It is my profound conviction that there is only one way to achieve this: we must divest ourselves of our egotistical anthropocentrism, our habit of seeing ourselves as masters of the universe who can do whatever occurs to us. We must acknowledge what transcends us: the universe, the earth, nature, life, and reality. Our respect for other people, for other nations, and for other cultures can grow only from a humble respect for the cosmic order and from an awareness that we are a part of it, that we share in it, and that nothing that we do is lost, but, rather, that what we do becomes part of the eternal memory of Being, where it is judged.

A better alternative for the future of humanity, therefore, would be to imbue our civilization with a spiritual dimension. This is not a matter just of understanding its multicultural nature and finding inspiration for a new world order in the common roots of all cultures. It is also essential that the Euro-American cultural sphere—the one that created this civilization and taught humanity its destructive pride—now return to its own spiritual roots and become an example to the rest of the world in the search for a new humility.

General observations of this type are certainly not difficult to make, nor are they new or revolutionary. Modern people are brilliant at describing the crises and the miseries of the world for which we are responsible. We are much less adept at putting things right.

So what specifically can be done?

I do not believe in some universal key or panacea. I am not an advocate of what Karl Popper called "holistic social engineering," particularly because I had to live most of my adult life in circumstances that resulted from an attempt to create a holistic Marxist utopia. I know more than enough, therefore, about such efforts.

This does not relieve me, however, of the responsibility to think of ways to make the world better.

It will certainly not be easy to awaken in people a new sense of responsibility for the world, or to convince them to conduct themselves as if they were to live on this earth forever and be held answerable for its condition one day. Who knows how many horrific cataclysms humanity may have to experience before such a sense of responsibility is generally accepted? But this does not mean that those who wish to work for it cannot begin at once. It is a great task for educators, intellectuals, the clergy, artists, entrepreneurs, journalists, people active in all forms of public life.

Above all, it is a task for politicians.

Even in the most democratic of conditions, politicians have immense influence, perhaps more than they themselves realize. This influence does not reside in their actual mandates, which in any case are considerably limited. It resides elsewhere: in the spontaneous impact their charisma has on the public.

The main task of the present generation of politicians is not, I think, to ingratiate themselves with the public through their decisions or their smiles on television. It is not to go on winning elections and ensuring themselves a place in the sun till the end of their days. Their role is something quite different: to assume their share of responsibility for the long-range prospects of our world and thus to set an example for the public in whose sight they work. Their responsibility is to think ahead boldly, not to fear the disfavor of the crowd; to imbue their actions with a spiritual dimension (which of course is not the same thing as ostentatious attendance at religious services); to explain again and again—both to the public and to their colleagues—that politics must do far more than reflect the interests of particular groups or lobbies. After all, politics is a matter of serving the community, which means that it is morality in practice. And how better to serve the community and practice morality than by seeking in the midst of the global (and globally threatened) civilization their own global political responsibility:

that is, their responsibility for the very survival of the human race?

I don't believe that a politician who sets out on this risky path will inevitably jeopardize his or her political survival. This is a wrongheaded notion which assumes that the citizen is a fool and that political success depends on playing to this folly. That is not the way it is. A conscience slumbers in every human being, something divine. And that is what we have to put our trust in.

I find myself at perhaps the most famous university in the most powerful country in the world. With your permission, I will say a few words on the subject of the politics of a great power.

It is obvious that those who have the greatest power and influence also bear the greatest responsibility. Like it or not, the United States of America now bears the greatest responsibility for the direction our world will take. The United States, therefore, should reflect most deeply on this responsibility.

Isolationism has never paid off for the United States. Had it entered the First World War earlier, perhaps it would not have had to pay with anything like the number of casualties it actually incurred. The same is true of the Second World War: when Hitler was getting ready to invade Czechoslovakia, and in so doing finally expose the lack of courage on the part of the Western democracies, your president wrote a letter to the Czechoslovak president imploring him to come to some agreement with Hitler. Had he not deceived himself and the whole world into believing that an agreement could be made with this madman, had he instead shown a few teeth, perhaps the Second World War need not have happened, and tens of thousands of young Americans need not have died fighting in it.

Likewise, just before the end of that war, had your president, who was otherwise an outstanding man, delivered a clear "no" to Stalin's decision to divide the world, perhaps the Cold War, which cost the United Sates hundreds of billions of dollars, need not have happened either.

I beg you: do not repeat these mistakes! You yourselves have always paid a heavy price for them. There is simply no escaping the responsibility you have as the most powerful country in the world. And there is far more to accomplish here than simply to stand up to those who would like once again to divide the world into spheres of interest, or subjugate others who are different from themselves, and weaker. What is now at stake is the survival of the human race. In other words, it's a question of what I've already discussed: of understanding modern civilization as a multicultural and multipolar civilization, of turning our attention to the original spiritual sources of human culture and, above all, of our own culture, and of drawing from these sources the strength for a courageous and magnanimous creation of a new order for the world.

Not long ago I was at a gala dinner to mark an important anniversary. There were fifty heads of state present, perhaps more, who came to honor the heroes and victims of the greatest war in human history. This was not a political conference, but the kind of social event that is principally intended to show hospitality and respect to the invited guests. When the seating plan was given out, I discovered to my surprise that those sitting at the table next to mine were not identified simply as representatives of a particular state, as was the case with all the other tables; they were referred to as "permanent members of the UN Security Council and the G7." I had mixed feelings about this. On the one hand, I thought, How marvelous that the richest and most powerful of this world can see one another often and, even at this dinner, can talk informally and get to know one another better. On the other hand, a slight chill ran down my spine, for I could not help observing that one table had been singled out as special and particularly important. It was a table for the super powers. Somewhat perversely, I began to imagine that the people sitting at it were dividing the rest of us up among themselves, along with their Russian caviar, without asking our opinion. Perhaps all this is merely the whimsy of a former and perhaps future playwright. But I wanted to express it here for one simple reason: to emphasize the terrible gap that exists between the responsibility of the great powers and their hubris. The architect of that seating arrangement—I should think it was none of the attending presidents—was guided not by a sense of responsibility for the world, but by the banal pride of the powerful.

Pride, however, is precisely what will lead the world to hell. I am suggesting an alternative: humbly accepting our responsibility for the world.

In the matter of coexistence between nations and spheres of civilization, cultures, and religions there is one great opportunity that should be grasped and exploited to the limit. This is the appearance of supranational, regional communities. By now, there are many such communities in the world, with diverse characteristics and differing degrees of integration. I believe in this approach. I believe in the importance of organisms that lie somewhere between nation-states and a world community, organisms that can be an important medium of global communication and cooperation. I believe that this trend toward integration in a world where—as I've said—every valley longs for independence, must be given the greatest possible support. These organisms, however, must not be an expression of integration merely for the sake of integration. They must be one of the many instruments enabling each region, each nation, to be both itself and capable of cooperation with others. That is, they must be one of the instruments enabling countries and peoples who are close to one another geographically, ethnically, culturally, and economically, and who have common security interests, to form associations and better communicate with one another and with the rest of the world. At the same time, all such regional communities must rid themselves of fear that other, similar communities are directed against them. Regional groupings in areas that have common traditions and a common political culture ought to be a natural part of the complex political architecture of the world. Cooperation between such regions ought to be a natural component of cooperation on a worldwide scale. As long as the broadening of NATO member-ship to include countries who feel culturally and politically a part of the region the alliance was created to defend is seen by Russia, for example, as an anti-Russian undertaking, it will be a sign that Russia has not yet understood the challenge of this era.

The most important world organization is the United Na-tions. I think that the fiftieth anniversary of its birth could be an occasion to reflect on how to infuse it with a new ethos, a new strength, and a new meaning, and make it truly the most impor-tant arena of good cooperation among all the cultures that make up our planetary civilization.

But neither the strengthening of regional structures nor the strengthening of the UN will save the world if both processes are not informed by that renewed spiritual charge which I see as the only hope that the human race will survive another millennium.

So I have touched on what I think politicians should do.

There is, however, one more force that has at least as much influence on the general state of mind as politicians do, if not more.

That force is the mass media.

Only when fate sent me into the realm of high politics did I become fully aware of the media's double-edged power. Their dual impact is not unique to the media. It is merely a factor in, or an expression of, the dual nature of today's civilization, of which I have already spoken.

Thanks to television, the whole world discovered, in the course of an evening, that there is a country called Rwanda where people are suffering beyond belief. Thanks to television, the whole world, in the course of a few seconds, was shocked and horrified by what happened in Oklahoma City and, at the same time, understood it as a great warning for all. Thanks to television, the whole world knows that there exists a country called Bosnia and Herzegovina and that, from the moment it recognized this country, the international community has tried unsuccessfully to divide it into grotesque ministates according to the wishes of warlords who have never been recognized as anyone's legitimate representatives.

That is the wonderful side of today's mass media, or, rather, of those who gather the news. Humanity's thanks belong to all those courageous reporters who voluntarily risk their lives wherever something evil is happening, in order to arouse the conscience of the world.

There is, however, another, less wonderful aspect of television, one that merely revels in the horrors of the world or, unforgivably, makes them commonplace, or compels politicians to become first of all television stars. But where is it written that someone who is good on television is necessarily also a good politician? I never fail to be astonished at how much I am at the mercy of television directors and editors, at how much more my public image depends on them than it does on myself, at how important it is to smile appropriately on television, or to choose the right tie, at how television forces me to express my thoughts as sparely as possible, in witticisms, slogans, or sound bites, at how easily my television image can be made to seem different from the real me. I am astonished by this, and at the same time I fear it serves no good purpose. I know politicians who have learned to see themselves only as the television camera does. Television has thus expropriated their personalities, and made them into something like television shadows of their former selves. I sometimes wonder whether they even sleep in a way that will look good on television.

I am not outraged at television or the press for distorting what I say, or ignoring it, or editing me to appear like some strange monster. I am not angry with the media when I see that a politician's rise or fall often depends more on them than on the politician concerned. What interests me is something else: the responsibility of those who hold the mass media in their hands. They, too, bear responsibility for the world, and for the future of humanity. Just as the splitting of the atom can immensely enrich humanity in a thousand and one ways and yet can also threaten it with destruction, so television can have both good and evil consequences. Quickly, suggestively, and to an unprecedented degree, it can disseminate the spirit of understanding, humanity, solidarity, and spirituality—or it can stupefy whole nations and continents. And just as our proper use of atomic energy depends solely on our sense of responsibility, so the proper use of television's power to enter practically every household and every human mind depends on our sense of responsibility as well.

Whether our world is to be saved from everything that threatens it today depends above all on whether human beings can come to their senses, whether they can understand the degree of their responsibility and can discover a new relationship to the very miracle of Being. The world is in the hands of us all. But some have a greater influence on its fate than others. The more influence a person has—be he politician or television announcer—the greater the demands placed on his sense of responsibility, and the less he should think merely about personal interests.

In conclusion, allow me a brief personal remark. I was born in Prague and I lived there for decades without being allowed to study properly or visit other countries. Nevertheless, my mother never abandoned one of her secret and quite extravagant dreams: that one day I would study at Harvard. Fate did not permit me to fulfill her dream. But something else happened, something that would never have occurred even to my mother: I have received a doctoral degree at Harvard without even having to study here.

More than that, it has been given to me to see Singapore, and countless other exotic places. It has been given to me to understand how small this world is and how it torments itself with countless things it need not torment itself with, if only people could find within themselves a little more courage, a little more hope, a little more responsibility, a little more mutual understanding and love.

I don't know whether my mother is looking down at me

from heaven, but if she is I can guess what she's probably thinking: she's thinking that I'm sticking my nose into matters that only people who have properly studied political science at Harvard have the right to stick their noses into.

I hope that you don't think so.

Conclusion of the Month of Bosnia and Herzegovina in the Czech Republic

PRAGUE, OCTOBER 13, 1995

In this Month of Bosnia and Herzegovina we have had an opportunity to contemplate works by Bosnian artists and listen to the voices of Bosnian intellectuals. In response, we feel again the need to ask ourselves what is actually going on in that severely troubled country, who is fighting whom, and for what reason, and how these events concern us all.

I shall try—not for the first time—to give my own answer to these questions.

At first glance, it seems that this is a battle among peoples with old scores to settle, peoples who hate one another and fight to gain for themselves as much territory as possible so as to rule it on their own, preferably without being disturbed by the presence of others. To a degree, this highly superficial assessment was long accepted by the international community and its various negotiators: In their attempts to work out a peaceful settlement, the central term used to describe the different peoples and their troops was "warring parties." The international community thus endorsed, *de facto,* a purely ethnic interpretation of the conflict, putting all the parties on the same level. This created, or strengthened, the completely false impression that it was no more than a local conflict among a number of quarreling factions who could become reconciled if someone proposed an enlightened compromise. It was clear what compromise this was supposed to be: a new map to delimit sovereign territories for the "warring parties," thus cleverly eliminating the reason for the fighting.

It was not because the negotiators were inept at drawing maps or devising compromises, however, that their tireless and well-meaning efforts remained so long unsuccessful. Nor was their failure caused by the fact that, in the former Yugoslavia, ethnic frontiers run through every town, every village, every house, and every family, dooming any attempt to re-draw maps. No, the reason they did not succeed is that, in accepting an ethnic interpretation of the conflict and attempting to reach an eth-nic settlement by seeking a fair ethnic division of territory, the negotiators unwittingly played into the monstrous ideology of the instigators of the conflict, and in doing so, forsook the very values of the civilization they were called upon to defend. In other words, they remained blind to what the conflict was all about.

What, then, is the conflict all about?

To my mind, what appears to be a conflict between peoples is in its very essence a conflict between two different notions of society, of the state, and of the world in general. On the one side is the modern concept of an open civil society in which people of different nationalities, ethnic backgrounds, religions, tradi-tions, and convictions can live together and cooperate creatively. On the other side is the archaic notion of a tribal state as a com-munity of people of the same blood. That is, on the one side stands a concept that has been one of the cornerstones of the European integration process, one that represents the only hope for the survival of today's global civilization; on the other side is a concept that for centuries—or, rather, millennia—has stained human history with blood, the most horrifying instance to date being the Second World War. On the one side, an emphasis on equality and equal dignity for all human beings; on the other side a commitment to the exclusive status of some group who belong to a certain tribe only through a chance of birth. On the one side an emphasis on bringing all people together, on respect for differences, and on solidarity with others; on the opposing side an emphasis on what makes them different and what divides them. On the one side a respect for the unique individual with his or her own sense of responsibility; on the other a cult of collectivism under which affiliation with the group is more important than a person's own qualities. One side holds out hope for an auspicious future for the human race; the other side represents a relapse into its darkest past.

It is my profound conviction that the conflict in Bosnia and Herzegovina has never been a conflict between the Serbian people and the rest of the population. It is a conflict of principles, not of nationalities.

Isn't it obvious that the fundamental and crucial dividing line in the former Yugoslavia actually separates the ethnic fanatics, adherents of authoritarian government based on national collectivism, and those who wish to live in peace, in an environment of democracy and civic cooperation? And aren't the geographical boundaries between ethnic groups of far less importance than the mental and moral boundaries between the initiators of ethnic cleansing, of organized rape, of genocidal killings and terrorist attacks against civilians, and those who simply want to live like human beings?

To my mind, this is a clash between the ideal of civilized coexistence of civic-minded people (one that has a specific tradition in Bosnia and Herzegovina) and an onslaught of inhumanity, violence, and the evil of ethnic fanaticism. I consider it an offense against the Serbian people and a betrayal of the civic notion of society when evil is identified with Serbian nationality. But I find it equally misguided when evil is not defined at all, for fear of hurting Serbian feelings. All peoples have their Karadzics and Mladics, either real or potential. If such men—as the result of a mix of historical, social, and cultural circumstances—gain greater influence than they have in other parts of the world, it does not mean that they come from a criminal people. Such individuals harm everyone, including their own people, whom they usually violate first when launching their pernicious work.

In other words, let us beware of attempts to lay the blame for evil on whole peoples. That would be tantamount to adopting the ideology of the ethnic fanatics. Let us instead consistently oppose the evil perpetrated by ethnic fanatics, regardless of in whose name they claim to act.

This dangerous notion of "warring parties" has not only a philosophical, or moral, dimension, which consists in the unwitting acceptance of the ethnic principle as the highest value, while ignoring the difference between aggressor and victim. It also has a political dimension: it is clearly impossible to equate the lawful army of a state recognized within its present borders by the entire international community with clandestinely armed units terrorizing a civilian population in the name of a political entity that has never been recognized by anyone. And it is most absurd indeed when a person who is supposed to answer to an international tribunal as a war criminal is at the same time accepted as a party to negotiations about the division of an internationally recognized state.

I trust that what I am saying here, which has always seemed clear enough to me, is beginning now, though rather belatedly—after a delay that has cost immeasurable human suffering—to be understood by many other politicians as well. The international community is, I believe, awakening to its responsibility.

The hatred purposefully fomented among the peoples of Bosnia and Herzegovina, as well as in the larger territory of the former Yugoslavia, appears to grow with every new day. The evil committed in the name of a certain people provokes hatred for that people as a whole. Moreover, evil, as we very well know, is contagious. Hatred breeds hatred; atrocities perpetrated by one person prompt another to commit atrocities. The concepts of the tribal state and blood vengeance draw peoples into a vicious circle of revenge with no end. The solution is not to join one side against another. The solution is to oppose most forcefully all those who implant and nurture hatred in human minds, and to support most forcefully those who want to break out of this vicious circle and restore mutual respect and commitment to coexistence and cooperation.

I believe that all the Bosnian artists, scientists, church officials, and other public figures of different nationalities who have come to the Czech Republic to take part in the Month of Bosnia and Herzegovina support the latter approach and therefore deserve our esteem and support.

They are not fighting for themselves alone. They are fighting for us all, for the values of the civilization we share. We must not betray that civilization by remaining indifferent to their fight. We know from our own history what the consequences of indifference turned into betrayal are. It took a heavy toll then, not only from our nation but from the entire democratic world that had to pay dearly for the restoration of its freedom.

Let us not allow such fatal events to be repeated. Let us not allow concessions to evil in one part of Europe again to pave the way for evil on a global scale. What is happening and threatening to happen in the former Yugoslavia is a test for the whole of Europe, a test of the sincerity of its commitment to the principles it has declared and on which it wants to build its better future.

If the concept of civic coexistence loses in Bosnia and Herzegovina, it has lost all over Europe.

That must not happen.

The Future of Hope
Conference

HIROSHIMA, DECEMBER 5, 1995

The theme of this conference is hope. It is taking place in Hiroshima, a city where we cannot help thinking about death. Allow me therefore a few observations on the subject of "hope and death."

Let me begin on a personal note.

Many times in my life—and not just when I was in prison—I found myself in a situation in which everything seemed to conspire against me, when nothing I had wished for or worked for seemed likely to succeed, when I had no visible evidence that anything I was doing had any meaning whatsoever. This is a situation we all know well, a situation that appears to promise nothing good, either for ourselves or for the world. It is a situation we describe as hopeless.

Whenever I found myself immersed in such melancholy thoughts, I would ask a very simple question over and over again: why don't you just give up on everything? Or, more radically, why do you endure, when your life is so clearly pointless? What use is a life in which you must look at the suffering of others as well as your own, helpless to prevent either?

Each time, I would eventually realize that hope, in the deepest sense of the word, does not come from the outside, that hope is not something to be found in external indications simply when a course of action may turn out well, nor is it something I have no reason to feel when it is obvious that nothing will turn out well. Again and again, I would realize that hope is above all a state of mind, and that as such either we have it or we don't, quite independently of the state of affairs immediately around us. Hope is simply an existential phenomenon which has nothing to do with predicting the future. Everything may appear to us in its darkest colors, and yet—for some mysterious reason—we do not lose hope. On the other hand, everything may be turning out just as we would like, and yet—for no less mysterious a reason— hope may suddenly desert us. Clearly, this type of hope is related to the very feeling that life has meaning, and as long as we feel that it does, we have a reason to live. If we lose this feeling, we have only two alternatives: either we take our own life, or we choose the more usual way, that of merely surviving, vegetating, remaining in this world only because we happen to be there already.

True, hope is usually hope *in* something or *for* something. Thus, it is linked with something specific: as a prisoner, for example, I may hope that one day someone will see the meaning of my imprisonment, and that all the deprivations I underwent in prison can eventually be turned into some good, perhaps as a reinforcement of certain values. Or, as president, I can hope that a complicated set of political negotiations will succeed and that I shall be able to look back with gratification at a job well done. Yet the fact that hope may be hope for something specific does nothing to alter what I said earlier: that hope in its deepest essence does not come from the world around us. Its real source is not the object that has apparently inspired it, just as the loss of hope is not ultimately caused by the external circumstance that appears to be withdrawing it irrevocably from us. This may be the case somewhere on the surface, at the level of psychological disposition: when things go well, we feel satisfied; when they go wrong, our mood worsens. Yet, in the existential sense of the word, hope does not draw its life-giving sap from its specific object. It works the other way around: hope enlivens its object, infuses it with life, illuminates it.

If, however, hope is not merely a derivative of the outside world, where do we get it from?

I have thought about this and examined myself a thousand

times, and eventually—to the delight of some and the astonishment of others—I have always come to the conclusion that the primary origin of hope is, to put it simply, metaphysical. By that I mean to say that hope is more, and goes deeper, than a mere optimistic inclination or disposition of the human mind, determined genetically, biologically, chemically, culturally, or otherwise. Of course, all of these factors—from our education and cultural background to the presence of certain compounds in our body—do influence our attitude toward the world and our behavior. But they do not explain them entirely. Somewhere behind all that, acknowledged or unacknowledged, and articulated in different ways, but always most profound, is humanity's experience with its own Being and with the Being of the world.

This brings me to the subject of death.

Man appears to be the only known creature about whom we can say with certainty that he knows he will die. Death is to us not merely some strange occurrence we see in television reports on war or terrorism or road accidents. On the contrary, it is with us every step of our way. Our loved ones die; we are reminded of death with every illness we go through, every airplane flight and fast car ride we take. Death is present in our everyday behavior: even when we wait for a green light to cross the road, we do so to avoid death. It is true that all living creatures share the instinct for self-preservation. But human beings are probably the only ones who are fully aware of that instinct. And only a human being knows that all his maneuvering and scrupulous waiting for the green light will be to no avail in the end, because he will die anyway.

If we know that we shall die and that any effort to prevent death is doomed, why, then, do we go on living? Why do we try to achieve anything? Or, more important, why do nearly all the essential things we strive for, through which we give our life meaning, so clearly transcend the horizon of our own lives? The feeling of well-being I enjoy because I am in good health at the moment, or because I am looking forward to meeting some

interesting people, or because you take an interest in my observations, can be explained in part because I do not see death as an
immediate prospect, because I have forgotten about it, or have
simply put it out of my mind. But hope in the radical and
profound sense I'm talking about here cannot be understood
against this background. This profound hope, in its very essence,
reaches beyond our death. Even more, this hope would be quite
incomprehensible and absurd in the context of our knowledge
that we shall die. We cannot believe in the meaning of our own
lives and cherish hope as a permanent state of mind if we are certain that our death means the end of everything.

The only thing that can explain the existence of genuine hope
is humanity's profound and essentially archetypal certainty—
though denied or unrecognized a hundred times over—that our
life on this earth is not just a random event among billions of
other random cosmic events that will pass away without a trace,
but that it is an integral component or link, however minuscule,
in the great and mysterious order of Being, an order in which
everything has a place of its own, in which nothing that has once
been done can be undone, in which everything is recorded
in some unfathomable way and given its proper and permanent value. Indeed, only the infinite and the eternal, recognized
or surmised, can explain the no less mysterious phenomenon
of hope.

Some may find these thoughts rather far-fetched. But I cannot
help believing them. I do not know of a single case in which
there is genuine acceptance of some bitter, personal fate, or in
which an act of courage is undertaken without regard for any
immediate possibility of success, that can be explained by anything other than humankind's sense of something that transcends
earthly gratification—a belief that such a fate, or such an apparently hopeless act of courage, whose significance is not easily
understood, is recorded in some way and adds to the memory
of Being.

With a little exaggeration we might say that death, or the

awareness of death—this most extraordinary dimension of man's stay on this earth, inspiring dread, fear, and awe—is at the same time a key to the fulfillment of human life in the best sense of the word. It is an obstacle put in the way of the human mind to test it, to challenge it to be truly the miracle of creation it considers itself to be. Death gives us a chance to overcome it—not by refusing to recognize its existence, but through our ability to look beyond it, or to defy it by purposeful action.

Without the experience of the transcendental, neither hope nor human responsibility has any meaning.

We live on a planet that is now—for the first time in its history—embraced by a single human civilization. Within this global civilization, the destinies of billions of people and hundreds of nations are so interknit that they merge together in a single destiny. This has a thousand advantages and a thousand disadvantages. The main disadvantage is that any threat facing the world today becomes a global threat. There is certainly no need for me to remind you, in particular, of the multitude of threats confronting today's civilization, threats that the world has so far been rather inept at handling. I shall therefore mention just one such threat, which used to be called "the conflict of civilizations."

Convinced that we now live in a single civilization, I call this, rather, a conflict between different spheres of civilization, culture, or religion. Undeniably, there is a danger that such a conflict might actually break out in the future. The more closely we are all linked together within a single civilization, and the more we have to accept its accomplishments—whether joyfully or out of necessity, regardless of how much they homogenize our lives—the more noticeably our varied cultural and religious traditions come to life again, and the more energetically the different spheres of civilization defend their individuality. Thus, the growing uniformity within this single civilization is accompanied by its opposite—an increasingly vigorous self-defense of diverse cultural identities.

How should we counter this threat? What kind of world order, what system of global cooperation should we build to avert the danger that our grandchildren may experience horrors far more dreadful than the Second World War, whose end we are now commemorating after fifty years? How can we avoid new Hiroshimas?

Without belittling everything currently being done to this end by many wise people, and all the projects and visions aimed at eliminating this and other threats looming over humankind, I should like to stress one element that I consider especially important. This element is directly related to what I have said here on the subject of hope and death.

When we examine man's archetypal experiences with himself and with the world he is thrown into—the experiences that allow him to know he will die and yet allow him as well to act as though he never will—we find that, in one way or another, such experiences are present in the primeval foundations of all religions. For aren't all religions marked by a belief in a higher authority than human authority, in the existence of a higher order than the one that we have created on this earth? Don't they all embrace the notion of a justice higher than earthly justice? Aren't they all based, expressly or by implication, on hope, in that metaphysical meaning of the word I have reflected on here? Don't they all, in some form or another, take the infinite and the eternal as the ultimate measures of human affairs? Don't they all turn our attention to what is beyond our death? And do they not also remain humble before that which transcends us, and from that, derive moral imperatives which they offer us as guidelines to living meaningful lives?

It is my firm belief that, if there is a bond uniting the diverse religious and cultural worlds that make up our civilization today, it can only be their unwavering certainty that the key to solid human coexistence, and to a life that does not become a hell on earth, lies in respect for what infinitely transcends us, for what I call the miracle of Being. True goodness, true responsibility, true justice, a true sense of things—all these grow from roots that go much deeper than the world of our transitory earthly schemes. This is a message that speaks to us from the very heart of human religiosity.

Why, then, should different forms of religiosity so fatefully divide humanity? Are not the spiritual roots of the different religions, emanating from certain archetypal experiences of the human species as a conscious one, precisely what is common to humankind, and therefore what could unite it?

I do not believe in any global religion. I am not even sure whether the salvation of humanity and the restoration of its sense of responsibility for itself and for the world lies solely in a renaissance of religiosity or even of piety. I am speaking of something slightly different: the need to grasp and articulate anew humanity's essential, fundamental spiritual experience and to infuse the spirit of this experience into the creation of a new world order, one that would allow us all to live and work together in peace without forcing anyone to give up his cultural autonomy. I am speaking of the necessity to proceed much more forcefully than before to reveal and identify that which unites us rather than that which divides us. It is in this that I see the principal challenge for the coming century and the coming millennium.

Not only is this probably the best way to avert the threat of a "conflict of civilizations." It is also perhaps the only way of awakening or reviving a sense of responsibility that transcends the personal, the kind of responsibility that could avert as well the other threats humanity will have to deal with in the future, such as the impact of the population explosion, environmental degradation, and the deepening gulf between the rich and the poor.

To sum up: if humanity has any hope of a decent future, it lies in the awakening of a universal sense of responsibility, the kind of responsibility unrepresented in the world of transient and temporary earthly interests.

. . .

As you can see, I, too, have pinned my hope on something specific—the undeniable, and undeniably universal, roots of humanity's awareness of itself. I do not know whether or not the world will take the path which that reality offers.

But I will not lose hope.

Trinity College

DUBLIN, JUNE 28, 1996

When I contemplate the links between my homeland and this beautiful and glorious country, which fate has allowed me to see today for the first time in my life, three fundamental thoughts come to my mind.

First, there is our Celtic past. The Czech lands were part of the territory on the continent that was the original home of the Celts; it was from there that the Celts went to Ireland. And though the Celtic population in our country—unlike Ireland's—was later subjugated and eventually assimilated by other tribes, many perceptive people in my homeland still feel a trace of the Celtic legacy in our shared spiritual consciousness. This feeling has manifested itself in many ways, for instance, through a strong interest in Celtic culture and through Celtic inspirations in our music and visual arts. Moreover, some of my kinsmen who are philosophically minded refuse to explain our national penchant for self-reflection entirely in terms of our Slavic roots, and search our Celtic past for another dimension of our contemporary spirituality and general outlook on the world.

The second bond between us is the historical reality, over many centuries, of small nations compelled repeatedly to assert their identity and fight for their place in the sun in regions dominated by larger neighbors.

The third feature that we obviously share is the important role culture plays in the history of our countries.

These three things are interrelated: the Celtic character has embraced both a singular spirituality and an extraordinary attachment to culture and art, and the increased role of art has a special relevance to the fate of a small nation constantly defending its identity, for it is precisely in culture and language that a national character proves its authenticity. And where but to the spiritual sphere can—indeed must—a small nation turn when looking for its identity and summoning energy to claim the rights belonging to that identity?

Such a commitment to culture does not merely presuppose more writers and readers, or more musicians with greater audiences. It also bespeaks a keen sensitivity to the general affairs of our world and a heightened perception of the dangers that threaten it; it suggests foresight or at least a deeper awareness of interconnections. Isn't it true that our two countries produced two of the greatest twentieth-century authors, who gave us profound and fundamental reflections on the existential situation of modern humanity? I refer, of course, to Samuel Beckett and Franz Kafka.

This kinship between the Czechs and the Irish gives me, I believe, a valid reason for using this opportunity to discuss the Europe of today from a viewpoint that we may share—that is, from the perspective of a small nation which, partly due to its size, has a sharper sense of the spiritual or cultural dimension of things, and has derived from bitter experience a heightened perception of the historical hopes as well as the historical dangers of the continent with which it lives.

The people who more than five thousand years ago erected one of the most renowned Irish structures, the fascinating passage tombs at Newgrange, made an opening in the roof above the entrance through which a ray of sunlight could penetrate to the tomb for a brief moment during the winter solstice. That ray symbolizes, to me, a link connecting humanity with the eternal, the infinite, and the absolute, which stands behind all transitory things. It is a reminder that, once done, nothing can ever be undone, that every human life and every deed is recorded forever in the history of Being and has forever changed that history in some way or other. In this manner, every human existence can be considered eternal. This is a great source of hope and meaning, but it is also a tremendous commitment and an appeal to our sense of responsibility. Knowing this, we must act so as to be able to justify ourselves not only in the imperfect sight of our fellow mortals but also in the perfect sight of eternity or, if you prefer, of Him who is omniscient.

We are witnessing today an admirable undertaking aimed at uniting Europe on the principles of peaceful cooperation and justice—that is, of the equality of large and small alike. This is also a construction of a great and complex edifice, no less ingenious than the Newgrange tombs. But are at least some of the thousands of designers and builders of this edifice thinking of the opening that would connect it with the great beyond—that would infinitely transcend the project, and yet alone could give it true meaning? I am thinking of the Czech poet Vladimír Holan, who once wrote that "without genuine transcendence, no construction shall ever reach completion." In other words, has this admirable European construction found its transcendental idea?

I am not quite sure.

Yes, we are all familiar with the essential values which unite so many different European countries and constitute the foundation of their current integration. We could name them even in our sleep: democracy, the rule of law, respect for human rights, the civil society, the market economy.

But why, in fact, are we committed to these values, and why should we remain so? Is it only because we have agreed on them because they are to everyone's advantage? My feeling is that there has to be more to it than a mere contract. And yet, increasingly, it looks as if that were all there is.

No contract can be effective, nor can it stand a chance of being universally respected, unless the parties have something in common that has been there before. This something may remain unarticulated, or it may be an obvious thing which everyone takes for granted; without it, however, no contract can ever work, because this unspoken common ground allows the parties to understand what their contract is all about, and what it binds them to do. In other words: a legal relationship or legal order must be preceded by a connection to or an order from the realm of morality, because only a moral commitment imbues the legal arrangements with meaning and makes them truly valid. Nor can the moral order be narrowed to a mere "moral contract": in the end, its roots are always found to be metaphysical.

Indeed, underlying every contractual arrangement there must be something called conscience or responsibility. And what is conscience or responsibility, if not a certain attitude of man toward that which reaches beyond him—that is, toward infinity and eternity, the transcendental, the mystery of the world, the order of Being or the Omniscient?

It is my impression that Europeans are increasingly reluctant to admit this, as if such thoughts were to them largely a matter of a private whim or personal hobbyhorse that does not belong on the public scene of politics.

But shrinking from the transcendental aspect of one's own endeavors is a very dangerous attitude. It is as if the builders of a Gothic cathedral had forgotten they were building a cathedral and had begun to think of it as no more than a high and solid building with space for many people. With such a state of mind, their creation would inevitably cease to be a cathedral and would gradually turn—as in a fairy tale—into a mere mass of stone.

You certainly know what I am talking about. I find that as Europe goes ahead with its unification it has to rediscover, consciously embrace, and in some way articulate its soul or its spirit, its underlying idea, its purpose, and its inner ethos. It has to look itself in the face, appreciate anew the strength of all its good traditions, and realize the dangers of all the bad ones; it has to perform a true self-reflection and, finally, ascertain what its mission is.

I truly believe that Europe has a mission. In my opinion, it is called upon to become, through the pattern of its own being, the embodiment of the kind of responsibility for the world that is essential to its salvation. I am not implying that Europe alone will save the world. I am simply saying that we should start with ourselves. This does not require that we devise any new ideologies. All it takes is to rededicate ourselves to the authentic meaning and content of the spiritual wealth that Europe has created in the course of its history.

This is a time when the European Union is conducting negotiations about complex institutional, bureaucratic, economic, financial, technical, and other aspects of its future. It is also a time when doubts are beginning to spread among its population about the purpose of the whole integrationist cause. And now your country is taking over the presidency of the Union. Let me, at this particular time, make one appeal: that Europeans should give deeper thought to the historical significance of their magnificent unification effort, that they should look for the true and innermost reason behind it and for its broader mission, that they should reflect upon their relationship to the world as a whole, to its future, to nature, and to the grave dangers looming over humankind today.

In keeping with the spirit of its own universalism, Europe should realize that the European question is a human and global question as well. It is in the answer to this question that Europe should look for its soul. The way in which we apprehend the task we face as inhabitants of this planet will tell us who we are and what makes, or what could make, the soul of Europe.

I am simply pleading that we not forget about the opening above the entrance, which links our edifice with the universe.

Academy of Performing Arts

PRAGUE, OCTOBER 4, 1996

Some time ago I read a newspaper article headlined "Politics as Theater." It was a persuasive and rather devastating criticism of everything I have tried to do in politics. Its basic premise was that in the serious realm of politics there is no place for frivolities from a realm as superfluous as theater. The author may have been right on some points; I am well aware that in the early months of my presidency, some of my ideas had more theatrical flair than political foresight. I believe that he was quite wrong about one fundamental issue, however, and that he utterly misunderstood both the primeval origin and meaning of theater and a crucial aspect of politics.

You will certainly understand why—as I was thrust virtually overnight from the world of theater into the world of high politics—I might wish, on this august occasion, to offer a few observations on the theatrical dimension of politics.

It seems—and current research into the most ancient history of the human race corroborates this—that one of the principal sources of human self-awareness was the new image of the world that appeared to our forebears when they stood up and began to walk on two feet. From a hitherto unstructured environment, the world as we know it gradually emerged. It now had an "above" and a "below," a "left" and a "right," a "near" and a "far." People began to realize that the sun rises and sets in different places; they recognized a regularity and a logic in its movement across the sky, and in the ensuing patterns of darkness and light. This coming into being of a structured world marked the beginning of our awareness of space and time—or of space-time, as we would now say—as something that obeys a certain order. It was also then that humanity was becoming aware of its own being and of the world as world: that we first began thinking in a religious sense. This is understandable. Where else could our ancestors have found an explanation for the fact that the world was more than just a terrain through which they moved and in which they found nourishment, but was also governed by a mysterious order? And so they surmised a place from which this order emanated, and a being who had shaped it. An order, not completely understood but dimly perceived as an intelligent creation, could not have come about by accident: it had to be the product of a will. And if there were indeed one or more mysterious partners in the cosmos, how could we not have sought for ways to communicate with them?

The awareness of a structure in space and time, of composition, of order—and thus of deviations from that order, or disturbances to it—has been an integral part of our being in the world since the dawn of humanity, and, indeed, must have played an essential role in the first place, for a self-conscious human being lacking this awareness is almost impossible to imagine.

It now appears that this awareness, the source of human spirituality and religiosity, has been a part of our history for longer than we used to assume. And I venture to claim that in this same awareness lie the primeval origins of drama and theater as well. I believe that a sense of the dramatic—or the theatrical, if I may put it this way—has also been a part of human life ever since we became human, and long before drama and theater became autonomous cultural phenomena or artistic genres. In other words, what we perceive as drama or theater today is merely one of the many late cultural manifestations of our fundamental experience of the world and our place in it. As soon as we began to realize that one thing may follow another, that some things may be repeated, that different occurrences may be connected, that space-time, and thus the world, are structured, we began to experience a sense of the dramatic. And as soon as we began to use ritual to communicate with the forces we believed responsible for the order of the world, we were doing theater. Because what else is theater but an attempt to grasp the world in a focused way by grasping its spatiotemporal logic? Do not the basic phases of drama—from exposition to catharsis—derive from the primordial rhythm of the seasons? And what else is theater but a successor to magic—an attempt to communicate, through the language of ritual, with the hidden forces that run the world? Aristotle once wrote that every drama or tragedy had to have a beginning, a middle, and an end, with antecedent following precedent. This is a precise expression of what I mean when I say that theater is a particular attempt to comprehend the logic of space and time, and thus the logic of Being itself.

In short, the world as the experience of a structured environment has an inherent dramatic dimension, and theater is actually an expression of our desire for a concise way of seizing this dramatic element. A play of no more than two hours always presents, or is meant to present, a picture of the whole world and attempts to say something about it.

And what, in fact, is politics?

The traditional definition has it that politics is the conduct of public affairs, the concern for them, and their administration. Obviously, concern for public affairs means concern for humanity and the world we live in. And that, in turn, requires an understanding of humanity and a recognition of all aspects of our self-awareness in the world. I do not see how a politician can achieve that without recognizing the dramatic element as inherent in the world as seen by human beings and thus as a fundamental tool of human communication. Politics without a beginning, a middle, and an end, without exposition and catharsis, without gradation and suggestiveness; politics lacking in the kind of transcendence that develops a real drama, using real people, into a testimony about the world as a whole, that politics is, in my opinion, a castrated, one-legged, toothless politics. In other words, it is bad politics. I am not saying that I am always successful in practicing what I preach—witness the criticism in the article I mentioned at the beginning—but I have worked toward a politics that knows that it matters what comes first and what follows, a politics that acknowledges that all things must have their proper sequence and order, a politics that realizes that citizens, without necessarily theorizing as I am doing now, know perfectly well whether political actions have a direction, a structure, a logic in time and space, a gradation, and a suggestiveness, or whether they lack all these qualities and are merely a haphazard response to circumstances.

Theater is a phenomenon of space and time. In the limited space of a stage, in a limited amount of time, with a limited set of figures and props, theater says something about the world as a whole, about its history, about human existence. As a descendant of ancient rituals, it explores the world in order to influence it. Theater is always in the nature of a symbol, and also of abbreviation. In theater, the immeasurable wealth and unfathomable complexity of Being are compressed into a concise code which, while a simplification, attempts to extract what is most essential from the substance of the universe and to convey this to its audience. This, in fact, is what thinking creatures do every day when they speak, study, write, or meditate. Theater is simply one of the many ways of expressing the basic human ability to generalize and comprehend the invisible order of things. Anything we say, including my present remarks, is a combination of hopeless simplification and an attempt to draw from the tangled web of things and events something essential that may, at first sight, have remained hidden.

Theater has other features as well. It possesses a special ability to allude to, and to convey, multiple meanings. A specific action shown on stage always radiates a broader message, without necessarily being expressed in words. The collective nature of a theatrical experience is no less important: theater always presupposes the presence of a community—actors and audience— who go through it together, and this sharing is an important part of the experience.

All these things, banal and obvious though they may seem to theater people such as yourselves, have their counterparts in politics as well. A friend of mine once said that politics is "the sum of all things concentrated." It encompasses law, economy, philosophy, and psychology. Inevitably, politics is theater as well—theater as a system of symbols addressing us as individuals and as members of a community; testifying, through the specific event in which it is embodied, to the great happening of life and the world; and enhancing our imagination and sensibilities.

I cannot imagine a politics aiming at long-term success without an awareness of these things.

Let me give you a few examples.

The national and historic symbols which politics employs are akin to theatrical symbols. National anthems, flags, decorations, national holidays, and so forth do not mean much in and of themselves as visual phenomena, but the meanings and associations that they evoke are important instruments of a society's understanding of itself, an important means of creating an awareness of social identity and continuity. More than that, these symbols of statehood are linked with such sentiments as national pride, readiness to defend one's country, and society's gratitude to those who have rendered it distinguished service.

Beyond that, politics is charged with symbols in many other less visible respects as well. When the German president came to Prague shortly after our Velvet Revolution—on March 15, 1990, the anniversary of the Nazi occupation of the Czech lands—he did not have to say much because the mere fact of his visit on such a day spoke volumes. It was equally auspicious when the French president and the British prime minister arrived at the time of the anniversary of the Munich Agreement. And when—for perhaps the first time—the highest representatives of all Central European countries began to meet regularly in small towns throughout the region, this fact alone would have been an important political sign, even if these meetings had produced no results at all.

I admit that I, too, engage in symbolic politics; often I meet different people during my working day—fellow citizens or foreign delegations—not because I have something urgent to discuss with them, but simply that we might meet, for the very fact that we have met conveys a message. I do not hide the fact that sometimes I find this somewhat of an imposition. On the other hand, I am well aware that this kind of encounter is an integral part of politics and that it would be foolish to avoid certain meetings simply because I had no particular agenda to discuss at the time.

I could give you a much longer list of examples, but in many respects, all these and other symbolic political acts resemble theater more than anything else. They too involve allusion, multiplicity of meaning, and suggestiveness; they too portray an abridged reality, making an essential connection without being explicit; they too have a universally accepted ritual framework that has stood the test of time.

Of course a political action cannot serve as a symbol or play an important role unless it is known about. Today, in the era of mass media, it is often true that if a deed lacks adequate coverage, particularly on television, it might just as well have remained undone. Even those who doubt the political importance of spatiotemporal architecture or the meaning of political symbols and rituals cannot deny one aspect of theatricality in politics: the dependence of politics on the media. We live in a time when someone who is not media-friendly cannot become, for instance, the president of the United States. Politicians now employ consultants to enhance their media image, and many would be helpless without coaching in the techniques of performing and delivering speeches in front of the cameras. Some politicians become virtual slaves of the media, so much so that they smile at cameras instead of at people; even when they pat children on the head, they wait for the media to record the occasion from the best angle. Other spend a great part of their lives talking to influential journalists, knowing that the tone conveyed by opinion-makers carries more weight than the merits of the issues being discussed. Thus all politicians, including those who sneer at theater as something superfluous, as an embellishment of life that has no place in politics, unwittingly become actors, dramatists, directors, and entertainers.

Whatever we may think about it, we have to acknowledge that in this respect, at least, the theatrical art is present in politics after all.

The significant role that a sense of the theatrical plays in politics is—and let us admit this—double-edged and ambivalent. Those possessing this quality can arouse society to great and meritorious deeds and can nurture in the public a democratic political culture, civic courage, and a sense of responsibility. But such people can also mobilize the worst human instincts and passions, can make the masses fanatic and lead them into hell. Let me remind you of one of many examples: the Nazis' aptitude for impressive shows. Let us remember the gigantic congresses of the NSDAP, the torchlight processions and other ceremonies that went along with them, the inflammatory speeches by Hitler and Goebbels, the Nazi cult of German mythology, and Göring's uniforms. We could hardly find a more monstrous abuse of the theatrical aspects of politics. How many people were swayed at that time! But this is not something confined to Nazism or communism. Today as well—even in Europe—we can point to many rulers who use the whole panoply of theatrical tools to arouse the kind of blind, callous nationalism that eventually leads to wars, ethnic cleansings, and the atrocities of concentration camps and genocide.

Theater is clearly an integral part of politics. But it is also true that it can be turned into a highly effective instrument of abuse.

Where is the borderline? Where is the boundary between a legitimate respect for national identity, history, and the symbols of statehood, and the devilish music of the pied pipers, the dark magicians, and the mesmerizers? Where does the remarkable art of passionate public speaking end, and outright demagogy and hoax begin? How can we recognize the point beyond which the expression of an understanding of the dramatic structure of human existence and of people's natural need for the collective experience of certain integrating rituals becomes evil manipulation and an assault of human freedom? When does it become the first step down the road to universal disaster?

Modern science, I'm afraid, does not offer us an exact method of determining this dividing line. We must therefore rely on such unscientific factors as common sense, moderation, responsibility, good taste, feeling, instinct, and conscience.

This is where we see a huge difference between theater as art and the theatrical dimension of politics. A mad theatrical performance by a group of fanatical actors is part of cultural pluralism, and as such, helps to expand the realm of freedom without posing any serious threat to anyone. A mad performance by a fanatical politician can plunge millions into endless calamity.

This brings me to a subject I often deal with—the theme of the special demands politics places on conscience and responsibility. But I have already said much about these things, and will not dwell on them today.

Notes

PRAGUE, JANUARY 1, 1990

It was traditional for the president of Czechoslovakia to address the nation each January 1—though under the communist regime such speeches were generally ignored. Two days before giving this address, Havel had been elected president of Czechoslovakia by a parliament still dominated by communist representatives. The speech was translated and widely reproduced. The present version has been slightly edited. *Translator unknown.*

WASHINGTON, D.C., FEBRUARY 21, 1990

On his first official working visit to the United States, Havel spoke to a joint session of the House of Representatives and the Senate. It was not his first address to a foreign parliament, but it was his first major speech in the English-speaking world. *Translated by Paul Wilson.*

PRAGUE, MARCH 15, 1990

President von Weizsäcker's visit to Prague was timed, with typical dramatic flair, to coincide with the fifty-first anniversary of the Nazi occupation of Czechoslovakia. *Translated by the Office of the President.*

JERUSALEM, APRIL 26, 1990

During his first official visit to Israel, a country that had long been unrecognized by the former Czechoslovak regime, Havel was awarded an honorary doctorate in literature by the Hebrew University in Jerusalem. *Translated by Paul Wilson.*

STRASBOURG, MAY 10, 1990

The Council of Europe is the oldest intergovernmental organization of democratic states on that continent. This occasion afforded Havel the opportunity to reflect on the future shape of Europe after the fall of communism. *Translator unknown.*

SALZBURG, JULY 26, 1990

Havel was invited to open the seventieth annual music festival in Salzburg in the fall of 1989, when he was still persona non grata in his own country. Later, as president, he was urged not to attend because of the controversy surrounding Austrian president Kurt Waldheim's attempt to hide the truth about his Nazi past. Havel insisted on keeping his word, and used the occasion to speak directly to Waldheim, who was in the audience, about the phenomenon of falsifying history. *Translated by Káča Poláčková-Henley.*

OSLO, AUGUST 28, 1990

The "Anatomy of Hate" conference was sponsored by the Elie Wiesel Foundation for Humanity and the Norwegian Nobel Committee. It was attended by seventy politicians and intellectuals from thirty countries, including François Mitterrand, President Jimmy Carter, and the speaker of the Lithuanian parliament, Vytautas Landsbergis. *Translated by Paul Wilson.*

NEW YORK CITY, SEPTEMBER 30, 1990

Representatives from seventy-one countries attended this first United Nations World Summit for Children. Havel delivered his speech on the opening day. *Translated by Paul Wilson.*

COPENHAGEN, MAY 28, 1991

During a state visit to Denmark Havel accepted the Sonning Prize for his contribution to European civilization. The biennial prize has been awarded by the University of Copenhagen since 1950 and numbers among its laureates Winston Churchill, Sir Laurence Olivier, Simone de Beauvoir, and Ingmar Bergman. *Translated by Paul Wilson.*

PRAGUE, OCTOBER 19, 1991

Havel delivered this tribute at the end of an official visit to Czechoslovakia by the Israeli president Chaim Herzog, who also spoke on this occasion. The concert was held in Prague's Smetana Hall. *Translated by Alexandra Brabcová.*

LOS ANGELES, OCTOBER 25, 1991

Havel was awarded a medal during an official visit to the United States, which included a meeting with President Bush in Washington, where he was presented with the original Czechoslovak Declaration of Independence, signed by the first Czechoslovak president, Tomáš Masaryk. *Translated by Michael Henry Heim.*

NEW YORK CITY, OCTOBER 27, 1991

This speech was delivered during the same official visit as his Los Angeles address. He was awarded an honorary doctorate. The long quotation on pages 83–85 is from Havel's own book *Summer Meditations. Translated by Paul Wilson.*

DAVOS, SWITZERLAND, FEBRUARY 4, 1992

Along with Prince Charles of Great Britain, Havel spoke at the closing ceremonies of the annual World Economic Forum, attended by two thousand economists and twenty-five heads of state from around the world. *Translated by Paul Wilson.*

TOKYO, APRIL 23, 1992

Havel delivered this address to a gathering of Japanese intellectuals during his official state visit of April 22–26, 1992. The speech was reprinted, to great public response, in many Japanese newspapers. *Translated by Paul Wilson.*

PARIS, OCTOBER 27, 1992

This and the following speech in Wrocław are the only two in this book delivered by Havel after he resigned as president of Czechoslovakia in July 1992 and before he was elected the first president of the Czech Republic in January 1993. It was given on the occasion of his being admitted to the Academy of Humanities and Political Sciences as an associate member. *Translated by Paul Wilson.*

WROCŁAW, POLAND, DECEMBER 21, 1992

On this occasion, Havel was awarded an honorary doctorate for literature and for his political activities. *Translated by Paul Wilson.*

Havel received the President's Medal from the president of George Washington University. The medal is given to important international figures. After the speech was published in *The New York Review of Books*, it provoked an exchange of letters between Havel and the poet Joseph Brodsky. *Translated by Paul Wilson.*

ATHENS, MAY 24, 1993

This prize, for "merit in the struggle for human rights and dignity, and for contributions to the renewal of democracy and respect for human rights in one's homeland and in the world," was awarded to Havel in January 1993, before he became president of the Czech Republic. It was presented to him by President Konstantinos Karamanlis. *Translated by Alexandra Brabcová.*

VIENNA, OCTOBER 8, 1993

This address was delivered to an assembly of heads of state and government officials from the member states of the Council of Europe. *Translator unknown.*

DECEMBER 22, 1993

This was an article commissioned by the quarterly *Foreign Affairs*. It appeared in the March-April 1994 issue, and has been edited slightly. *Translated by Paul Wilson.*

PRAGUE, JANUARY 1, 1994

Translated by Paul Wilson.

NEW DELHI, FEBRUARY 8, 1994

The Indira Gandhi Prize is awarded for "consistent work on behalf of friendship, democracy, peace, and understanding among nations." Along with the prize goes an award of $80,000, which Havel gave to the mission of Mother Teresa, the Ramakrishna Mission, and the Dalai Lama for the support of Tibetan refugees. *Translated by Paul Wilson.*

Havel wrote a message for International Theater Day to be read simultaneously in theaters around the world. The purpose of International Theater Day is to call attention to theater and its role in society. *Translated by Paul Wilson.*

The Philadelphia Liberty Medal honors those who have "demonstrated leadership and vision in the pursuit of liberty of conscience or freedom from oppression, ignorance, or deprivation." Havel delivered his speech in English outside Independence Hall, where Tomáš Masaryk had declared independence for Czechoslovakia seventy-six years earlier. Previous medalists have been Lech Wałesa, Jimmy Carter, Oscar Arias Sánchez, Thurgood Marshall, Frederik de Klerk, and Nelson Mandela. *Translated by Paul Wilson.*

The Jackson H. Ralston Prize and Professorship in International Law is awarded by the Law Faculty of Stanford University for a significant contribution to the development of law in international relations. Former winners include Jimmy Carter, Olof Palme (former Swedish premier), and Pierre Trudeau. *Translated by Paul Wilson.*

Havel delivered the opening address to The World Congress of the International PEN Club. It was the second time the World Congress was held in Prague, the first having been in 1938, when Karel Čapek was president of the PEN Czech center. The theme of the congress was literature and tolerance. *Translated by Paul Wilson.*

The Geuzenpenning is a medal awarded each year in the Netherlands to honor the memory of the Geuzen, a Dutch underground movement that was the first to initiate resistance against the German occupiers in 1940. The medal was awarded in the Grote Kerk in Vlaardingen by the Netherlands' premier

Wim Kok, in the presence of Queen Beatrix. *Translated by Alexandra Brabcová and Roger Falcon.*

CANBERRA, AUSTRALIA, MARCH 29, 1995

Havel gave this speech the title "Authority and Democracy in the Contemporary World." It was delivered in English during an official state visit to Australia, and was carried by many television networks in the Asian Pacific region. *Translated by Alexandra Brabcová and Paul Wilson.*

WELLINGTON, NEW ZEALAND, MARCH 31, 1995

Havel was given an honorary doctorate in literature. He delivered the speech in English. *Translated by Alexandra Brabcová and Paul Wilson.*

BARCELONA, MAY 11, 1995

The Catalonia International Prize is given for creative contributions to the development of cultural, scientific, and humane values in the world. It was presented to Havel and to former German president Richard von Weizsäcker by Queen Sophia of Spain. *Translated by Alexandra Brabcová and Roger Falcon.*

CAMBRIDGE, JUNE 8, 1995

Havel was awarded an honorary doctorate of law and spoke to the graduating class and faculty of Harvard. He delivered the acceptance speech in English. *Translated by Paul Wilson.*

PRAGUE, OCTOBER 13, 1995

This address was delivered in the Spanish Hall at a concert concluding the Month of Bosnia and Herzegovina in the Czech Republic, in the presence of Bosnia-Herzegovina's president, Alija Izetbegović, and the general secretary of the Council of Europe, Daniel Tarschys. *Translated by Alexandra Brabcová and Alistair Barclay.*

HIROSHIMA, DECEMBER 5, 1995

The Future of Hope Conference marked the fiftieth anniversary of the end of the Second World War in the Pacific. Havel was awarded the Future of Hope Medal for his political and ethical stance on the fundamental problems of the present. He delivered this speech in English. *Translated by Alexandra Brabcová and Paul Wilson.*

DUBLIN, JUNE 28, 1996

Havel was granted an honorary degree by Trinity College. *Translated by Alexandra Brabcová and Lise Stone.*

PRAGUE, OCTOBER 4, 1996

Havel's honorary doctorate from the Academy of Performing Arts in Prague—the occasion of this speech—was the first such doctorate offered by his alma mater, where he had studied dramaturgy from 1962 to 1966. *Translated by Alexandra Brabcová and Paul Wilson.*

Index

civilization
  general threat to, 90–1, 99, 121
  traditional concept of, 175–6
  see also global civilization
civil service purge of former
    communists, 85–6
civil service reform, 145–6
civil society, 144–5
  civil service and, 145–6
  democracy and, 145, 147–8
  nonprofit organizations and,
    146–7
  politics and, 150–1
  "standard" civil society, 148
  uniting of peoples through,
    148–50
coexistence of cultures, 121–2, 162
  authority and, 198–201
  framework for, 158, 195–7, 220
  global civilization and, 157–9,
    168–9, 195, 219–20
  "Helsinki" security system and, 41
  mass media and, 227–9
  moral minimum and, 160
  supranational, regional
    communities and, 226–7
  transcendence and, 196–7
  see also Bosnian conflict
Cold War, 12, 138, 224
collective hatred, 59–65, 189–90
collective responsibility, 26–7, 85–6
colonialism, 156
  decolonization, 153–4, 168
Comenius, John Amos, 7
communism, 190
  as false savior, 107
  as holistic social engineering, 204
  lessons learned while living under
    communism, 137
  objectivity, cult of, 89
  politics and, 95

  as totalitarian system, 117
  uniformity, enforcement of, 118
  see also fall of communism
communist government of
    Czechoslovakia, 3–4, 8, 17
  "après nous le déluge" principle, 80
Conference on Security and
    Cooperation in Europe, 38
confession, 53
conflicts of 1990s, 156–7, 162, 176–7
  see also Bosnian conflict
Confucius, 201
conscience, politics and, 19, 214–15
conscience of society, 208
Consciousness, 18
Council of Europe, 32
  European integration and, 42–3,
    132–3
Czechoslovakia
  anti-Semitism in, 76
  challenges of newly won freedom,
    6, 34–5
  civil service purge of former
    communists, 85–6
  communist takeover in 1948, 211,
    212–13
  creation following First World
    War, 11
  division into two countries, 111
  elections, 8, 10, 34, 48
  environmental degradation, 3, 78
  German Czechs, expulsion of, 23
  Germany, relations with, 22–3
  Havel's dream for, 9
  Havel's election as president
    (1989), 10
  Havel's election as president
    (1990), 48
  intellectuals as politicians, 96
  military of, 16
  moral contamination, 4–5

Nazi rule, 23, 25–6
revolution of 1989, 5–6, 34, 67,
    152–3
self-confidence of, 7
social problems, 3
Soviet occupation in 1968, 211,
    212–13
Soviet withdrawal, 14, 15–16
strategic significance in Europe,
    13–14
U.S. assistance, 17
see also communist government of
    Czechoslovakia; Munich
    Agreement
Czech Republic
  Celtic legacy, 244
  civil service reform, 145–6
  civil society, creation of, 144–51
  constitution of, 143
  economic transformation, 143–4
  first year of existence, 142
  nonprofit sector, 146–7
  postcommunism and, 117–18
  recognition from international
      community, 143

death, 238–40, 241
Declaration of Independence, 20,
    172
decolonization, 153–4, 168
democracy
  authority and, 198–201
  civil society and, 145, 147–8
  depersonalization of, 124–7
  global civilization and, 169,
      177–82
  of Greek civilization, 124, 126–7
  journey toward, 17
  limited ability to address humanity
      in genuinely universal ways, 179

non-Westerners' distrust of, 178
transcendence and, 179–82
universal resonance, restoration
    of, 179–82
the West's failure to safeguard,
    200
dictatorship, 199
Dienstbier, Jiří, 33
disarmament, 16, 37, 40
dissident experience in practical
    politics, 110–12, 114
dissidents
  backlash against dissidents
      following fall of communism,
      109
  children of, 67
  intellectuals as, 95–6
  patience of, 104
  spirituality of, 110
Dostoyevsky, Fyodor, 197
Dreaming of Europe (Dienstbier), 33

Eastern Europe, see Central and
    Eastern Europe
elections, 8, 10, 34, 48
environmental degradation, 3,
    78–81, 141
ethnically pure state, 131
European Civic Assembly, proposed,
    44
European Economic Community,
    43
European integration, 15
  civic structures, 43–4
  civil society and, 149–50
  conflict resolution and, 131–2
  Council of Europe and, 42–3,
      132–3
  economic integration, 43
  German unification and, 44

Göring, Hermann, 255
Gottwald, Klement, 66
great powers, responsibilities of,
    11–12, 224–6
Greece, ancient, 124, 126–7

hatred, 55
    Bherunda bird myth, 65
    in Central and Eastern Europe,
        62–5
    characteristics of haters, 55–9
    collective hatred, 59–65, 189–90
    humor and, 57
    love-hate relationship, 55–6
    objects of, 57
    states of mind that create
        antecedents for hatred, 60–2
    transcendence and, 56–7
Havel, Václav
    depression of, 48–9
    dream for Czechoslovakia, 9
    election as president (1989), 10
    election as president (1990), 48
    friends' avoidance of, 115
    honorary degrees, attitude toward,
        29
    hopelessness of, 236
    political service, motives for, 70–1
    politics, concept of, 82
    presidential experiences, 83–6
    self-concept, 29–31
    writing of his own speeches,
        xv–xvi, xix
"Helsinki" security system, 15
    bipolar division of world and,
        41
    coexistence of cultures and, 41
    Cold War alliances and, 36–8
    European political integration
        and, 41–2

European Security Commission,
    proposed, 38, 39
    nuclear weapons and, 40–1
    Soviet Union and, 45
    summit meeting on, proposed,
        38–9
    treaties on cooperation and
        assistance, 39
history
    accelerated course of, 11, 20, 32,
        33
    postcommunism and, 118–19,
        135
    singularity in, 212
    transitional periods of, 165–6
Hitler, Adolf, 21, 66, 199, 255
Holan, Vladimír, 246
holistic social engineering, 203–5,
    207–8, 222
Holocaust, 75–7, 122–3
hope, 5, 236
    Being and, 239
    death and, 238–40, 241
    hopelessness as source of, 54
    metaphysical origin, 237–8
    as state of mind, 236–7
    waiting and, 103–4, 107
humor, 57
Hungary, 6, 96
Hussein, Saddam, 66

independence, desire for, 194
India, 152, 159–61
Initiative Four, 42
intellectuals
    characteristics of, 206–7
    as dissidents, 95–6
    holistic social engineering and,
        207–8
    intolerance, analysis of, 185

intellectuals *(continued)*
   as politicians, 19–20, 96–102,
      185–7, 208–9
   responsibility for world, sense of,
      185, 208
   role in society, 206–8
interconnectedness of all events,
      205–6, 209
intolerance, 157, 183–5
Ireland, 244–5
isolationism, 224

Japan, 95
Jefferson, Thomas, 20
Jews
   as Chosen People, 75–6, 123
   Holocaust, 75–7, 122–3
justice, 27

Kafka, Franz, 29–31, 245
Kierkegaard, Søren, 74
Kocáb, Michael, 10

Lenin, V. I., 199
lies, 52–3
Lincoln, Abraham, 13
literature, 185
Lithuania, 96
love-hate relationship, 55–6

Mao Zedong, 199
Masaryk, Tomáš Garrigue, 7, 11
mass media
   coexistence of cultures and,
      227–9
   politics and, 228, 254–5

Mazowiecki, Tadeusz, 42
Memory of Being, 175
metaculture, 122
minority rights, 132
Mitterrand, François, 42
moral canons, 196
morality
   contaminated moral environment
      of Czechoslovakia, 4–5
   politics and, 7–8, 85–6, 112,
      210–15
   responsibility and, 18–20
moral minimum, 160
Moscow Protocols, 211
multicultural coexistence, *see*
      coexistence of cultures
multipolarity, 13
   fall of communism and, 153–4
   global civilization and, 155–9
Munich Agreement, 21, 123, 224
   Beneš's reaction, 210–11
   long-term impact on
      Czechoslovakia, 212–13

national identity, 244–5
nationalism, 141
Nazism, 21–2, 130
   Czechoslovakia under Nazi rule,
      23, 25–6
   Holocaust, 75–7, 122–3
   theatricality of, 255
   tribal togetherness of, 189–90
Newgrange passage tombs, 245
nihilism, 26, 80
nonprofit organizations, 146–7
North Atlantic Treaty Organization
      (NATO), 36, 37–8
   expansion of, 140, 227
nothingness, 214
nuclear weapons, 40–1

objectivity, cult of, 89, 105, 106–7
Oklahoma City bombing, 227
order in universe, 249–50
"otherness" of different
  communities, 61–2, 63–4

Papi, Giuseppe Ugo, 103
"Partnership for Peace" project,
  139–40
patience, 104–8
Patočka, Jan, 137
perestroika, 12
Petržalka housing estate, 3
Poland, 6, 24, 96
  border issues, 44
political power, temptations of,
  69–74
political scientists, 11
politics
  as art of the impossible, 8
  Being and, 92, 93–4, 101
  civil society and, 150–1
  communism and, 95
  conscience and, 19, 214–15
  decision-making in, 210–15
  dissident experience in practical
    politics, 110–12, 114
  emotional commitment in, 100
  global civilization and, 223–4
  good taste and, 84
  great powers, responsibilities of,
    11–12, 224–6
  Havel's concept of, 82
  indifference to public affairs,
    32–3
  intellectuals as politicians, 19–20,
    96–102, 185–7, 208–9
  mass media and, 228, 254–5
  model politician, characteristics
    of, 74, 84–5

morality and, 7–8, 85–6, 112,
  210–15
as never-ending process, 105
patience and, 105–8
postmodern approach to, 91–3,
  98–101, 106
public's attitude toward
  politicians, 125
spirituality and, 98–101, 110–14
symbols used in, 253–4
theater and, 249, 251–6
see also democracy
Pol Pot, 207
Popper, Karl, 203–6, 222
postcommunism, 115–16
  as challenge to think and act, 116,
    121–2
  characteristics of, 116
  global implications, 120
  history and, 118–19, 135
  individuality and, 118
  problems of postcommunist
    countries, 116–20
  terminology issue, 135
  West's responsibility toward
    postcommunist countries,
    136–41
postmodern politics, 91–3, 98–101,
  106
postmodern state of mind, 166, 167
prenatal experiences, 173
prescientific knowledge, 174
prison life, 157
protectionism, 138

racism, 26, 61
Red Brigades, 207
religiosity, see spirituality;
  transcendence
resistance fighters, 188–92

transitional periods, 165–6
tribal togetherness, 189–90

United Nations, 227
United States
  Cold War victory, attitude
    toward, 138
  Constitution of, 20
  Czechoslovakia, assistance to, 17
  "great power" responsibilities,
    11–12, 224–6
  military presence in Europe, 13,
    14–15
  Soviet Union, assistance to, 14

waiting, 103
  patience, 104–8

waiting for Godot (universal
    salvation), 103–4, 107,
    108
Wałesa, Lech, 44
Warsaw Pact, 36, 37, 38, 135
West, the
  democracy, failure to safeguard,
    200
  fall of communism: impact of,
    87–8; regrets about, 134–6
  global civilization,
    co-responsibility for creation
    of, 136–41
  sacrifice issue, 137–8
Wilson, Woodrow, 11
world order, *see* global civilization

Yugoslavia, *see* former Yugoslavia

A   NOTE   ABOUT   THE   AUTHOR
AND   THE   TRANSLATOR

Václav Havel was born in Czechoslovakia in 1936. Among his plays are *The Garden Party*, *The Memorandum*, *Largo Desolato*, *Temptation*, and three one-acts, *Audience*, *Private View*, and *Protest*. He is a founding spokesman of Charter 77 and the author of many influential essays on totalitarianism and dissent. In 1979, he was sentenced to four and a half years in prison for his involvement in the Czech human-rights movement; out of this came his book of letters to his wife, *Letters to Olga* (1988). In November 1989, he helped found the Civic Forum, his country's first legal opposition movement in forty years, and the following month he became president of Czechoslovakia. Since January 1993, he has been president of the Czech Republic.

Paul Wilson lived in Czechoslovakia from 1967 to 1977. Since his return to Canada in 1978, he has translated into English work by many Czech writers, including Josef Škvorecký, Bohumil Hrabal, and Ivan Klíma, and has translated and edited most of Václav Havel's prose writings that have appeared in English. He lives in Toronto.

A NOTE ON THE TYPE

The text of this book was set in Bembo, a facsimile of a typeface cut by Francesco Griffo for Aldus Manutius, the celebrated Venetian printer, in 1495. The face was named for Pietro Cardinal Bembo, the author of the small treatise entitled *De Aetna* in which it first appeared. Through the research of Stanley Morison, it is now generally acknowledged that all old-style type designs up to the time of William Caslon can be traced to the Bembo cut.

The present-day version of Bembo was introduced by the Monotype Corporation of London in 1929. Sturdy, well balanced, and finely proportioned, Bembo is a face of rare beauty and great legibility in all of its sizes.